OVID
Amores
Metamorphoses

Selections
Third Edition

ANNOTATED COLLECTION

Ovid: *Amores, Metamorphoses* Selections, Third Edition (2013)
Writing Passion: A Catullus Reader, Second Edition (2013)
Writing Passion Plus: A Catullus Reader Supplement (2013)

Forthcoming
Horace: Selected *Odes* and *Satire* 1.9, Third Edition
Cicero: *Pro Archia Poeta Oratio*, Third Edition
Cicero: *De Amicitia*, Second Edition
Cicero: *Pro Caelio*, Fourth Edition

OVID
Amores
Metamorphoses

Selections
Third Edition

Charbra Adams Jestin
&
Phyllis B. Katz

Bolchazy-Carducci Publishers, Inc.
Mundelein, Illinois USA

Editor: Bridget Dean
Contributing Editors: Laurie Haight Keenan and Laurel Draper
Maps: Charlene M. Hernandez and Benjamin J. Jansky
Design and Layout: Adam Phillip Velez
Cover Graphic: Aphrodite & Eros, Terracotta from Tanara, IVc BC
 Seattle Museum of Art, Photo: R. Schoder, S.J.

© 2013 Bolchazy-Carducci Publishers, Inc.
All rights reserved.

Bolchazy-Carducci Publishers, Inc.
1570 Baskin Road
Mundelein, Illinois 60060
www.bolchazy.com

Printed in the United States of America
2013
by United Graphics

ISBN 978-0-86516-784-1

Library of Congress Cataloging-in-Publication Data

Ovid, 43 B.C.-17 or 18 A.D.
 [Selections]
 Amores, Metamorphoses : selections / Ovid. -- Third edition / Charbra Adams Jestin & Phyllis B. Katz.
   pages. cm. -- (Annotated collection)
 Includes bibliographical references.
 ISBN 978-0-86516-784-1 (pbk. : alk. paper)
 I. Jestin, Charbra Adams, 1951- II. Katz, Phyllis B., 1936- III. Ovid, 43 B.C.-17 or 18 A.D. Amores. Selections. 2013. IV. Ovid, 43 B.C.-17 or 18 A.D. Metamorphoses. Selections. 2013. V. Title. VI. Series: Annotated collection.
 PA6519.A3 2013
 871'.01--dc23

2013001898

To Loftus and Arnie,
maritis optimis quibuscum
"concordes egimus annos"

ACKNOWLEDGMENTS

Without the help of many classicists, colleagues, friends, and other keen-eyed readers, this textbook could not have reached its present form. Initially a thesis written by C. A. Jestin for an MA degree in Classics granted by Wesleyan University, it first fell under the watchful eyes of Professors James O'Hara, advisor, and Michael Roberts, second reader, each of whom contributed pages of commentary and criticism. Their careful and ever-encouraging editing helped to shape the work in its earliest stages.

Margaret Graver of the Classics Department, Dartmouth College, read nearly every page of this manuscript. Her background in the teaching of Latin to high school, college, and university students gave her an ideal perspective for this textbook. Her careful and thoughtful editing of the Latin text and glossaries helped us to clarify and refine material, and her insightful comments on the introductions to the passages were always helpful.

Claire Loiselle, Latin teacher at Avon High School, Avon, Connecticut, also read much of the text in manuscript. She contributed many important suggestions based on her knowledge as a classicist and as a highly reagarded teacher of long experience.

Laurie Haight Keenan of Bolchazy-Carducci Publishers has shepherded this work throughout its preparation. She has encouraged us at every turn and willingly answered all of our questions, profound or tedious. Bridget Dean, also of Bolchazy-Carducci Publishers and shepherd of this third edition, has worked patiently and wisely with us to produce this revised and supplemented text.

We wish to thank those reviewers of the first edition whose identifications of errors and suggestions for further explications have helped to improve the second edition of this textbook.

We wish to thank Lou Bolchazy, whose unstinting dedication to publishing accessible and affordable texts by Greek and Roman authors has accomplished so very much to support the continued study of the Classics.

To all of these people we express our thanks for guiding us to the completion of this textbook. Their suggestions and advice have been indispensable to us. Whatever weaknesses remain are entirely our own.

CONTENTS

Acknowledgements vii

List of Maps xi

A Note to the Student xiii

Ovid's Life and Works. xv

Topical Bibliography for Ovid xix

Introduction to the *Amores* 3
   Amores I. 1 5
   Amores I. 3 11
   Amores I. 9 17
   Amores I. 11 23
   Amores I. 12 29
   Amores II. 19 35
   Amores III. 12 43
   Amores III. 15 51

Introduction to the *Metamorphoses* 57
   Creation I. 1–88 61
   Apollo and Daphne I. 452–567 75
   Pyramus and Thisbe IV. 55–166 97
   Daedalus and Icarus VIII. 183–235 .115
   Philemon and Baucis VIII. 616–724 125
   Orpheus and Eurydice X. 1–85 143
   Pygmalion X. 238–97 155

Appendices
>   Metrical Terms 165
>   Figures of Speech 167
>   High-Frequency Word List. 171
>   Glossary 177

LIST OF MAPS

Ovid's World..xvi

Map of Places in *Amores* I. 1 2

Map of Places in the *Amores* (except I. 1) 16

Map of Places in Apollo and Daphne...........................76

Map of Places in Pyramus and Thisbe, Philemon
 and Baucis, and Pygmalion...............................98

Map of Places in Daedalus and Icarus and in
 Orpheus and Eurydice..................................116

A NOTE TO THE STUDENT

What is the appeal of Ovid's *Amores* and *Metamorphoses*? His collection of love poems, the *Amores*, is written with the wit and humor, and sometimes the regret, of one who has seen love at first hand. His epic story of transformations from creation to the reign of Augustus, the *Metamorphoses*, is the work of a consummate storyteller. Ovid speaks to us today through a voice as clear at the beginning of the third millennium as it was to his contemporaries on the eve of the first.

This book is organized to help you to read, comprehend, and enjoy the poetry of Ovid. The textbook begins with eight of the *Amores*, each with an introduction that highlights the main theme of the poem and places it within the context of love elegy in general. Seven selections from the *Metamorphoses* follow, each illustrating a different type of metamorphosis or change. The introductions to the selections place the characters and their metamorphoses in the larger context of the work.

Each page provides help with vocabulary, grammatical structures, and a variety of poetic devices. We hope that by the end of the text you will have developed an eye and ear for picking up the more obvious ones on your own. A full vocabulary is provided at the back of the book as well as a list of all words occurring five or more times in the Latin text. Appendices include explanations of metrical terms and figures of speech that also occur in the on-page glosses in small capital letters.

Ovid's language and style are not difficult. You should note, however, the following points as you begin to read his poetry:

- Latin poetry was written to be heard as well as to be read. You should practice reading each poem aloud and look for the ways by which the sound of words reinforces the meaning expressed.

- Your reading aloud will be enhanced by an understanding of the meters employed and the many possibilities the poet used to vary the metrical pattern so that a line moves faster or slower. Macrons are provided in the glossed vocabulary and in the full glossary at the end.

- Be aware of sound patterns such as alliteration, assonance, and onomatopoeia (see Appendix of Figures of Speech for definitions of these terms).
- Pay attention to nuances of word order; word order in poetry is often quite different from prose. Ovid is particularly fond of using chiastic and interlocked word order and uses the Golden Line with great effect (again see the Appendix of Figures of Speech for definitions of these terms).
- Some features of Ovid's language may be unfamiliar to you. For example, you will often find:
  - the first person plural (we) in place of I
  - the alternate form of the third person plural perfect active indicative (-*ere* in place of -*erunt*)
  - a plural noun substituted for a singular such as *amores* for *amor*
  - the perfect passive participle as an adjective
  - the ablative alone without a preposition in phrases telling where or when
  - many poetic lines enjambed—the syntactical meaning carried over from one line to the next (therefore you need to look for a full stop, i.e., a period, colon, or semi-colon, when you are translating to be sure that you are reading for a complete thought)
  - the dative case used with compound verbs
  - an abrupt shift from the past to the present tense (the historical present) for vividness
  - an adjective in the third foot of the line paired with the noun at line end and
  - the alternate -*is* accusative plural third declension ending

OVID'S LIFE AND WORKS

Publius Ovidius Naso was born in Sulmo, in the North of Italy, in 43 B.C., just a year after the assassination of Julius Caesar. The Battle of Actium, which would strengthen the power of Octavian, Caesar's grandnephew and avenger, occurred twelve years after Ovid's birth, and Ovid approached adulthood while Octavian consolidated his authority.

Through skillful manipulation, Octavian secured complete loyalty and favor from the Senate. When in 27 B.C. he voluntarily "relinquished" all military power, he was rewarded with the responsibility of administering Gaul, Spain, Syria, and Egypt, and was granted the honorary title Augustus, by which he was known thereafter. Augustus maintained the allegiance of the Roman citizenry through his persuasive influence and great wealth: his authority became absolute, although he fostered the illusion that Rome was governed by the *Senatus Populusque Romanus*.

Augustus brought peace to Rome after years of civil strife. He instituted many public works projects and restored traditional gods and religious practices. To counteract the ostentation of the new and wealthy Rome, he tried to inculcate a simple lifestyle, offering his own as an example. He also established laws with very severe penalties against adultery and with rewards for those who married and produced children. Augustus banished his own daughter, Julia, in 2 B.C., for her repeated scandalous affairs.

At the same time, Augustus did much to encourage the arts. He drew young and promising poets, among them Vergil and Horace, into his sphere of influence, encouraging them to write works that would glorify Rome. Although Vergil and Horace maintained their independent voices and their integrity as poets, they did serve Augustus's political and cultural ambitions. Ovid felt no such compelling allegiance, writing with an independence, even an irreverence, which his older colleagues did not dare to display openly; it was these independent and iconoclastic works which were, in part, responsible for Ovid's permanent banishment from Rome.

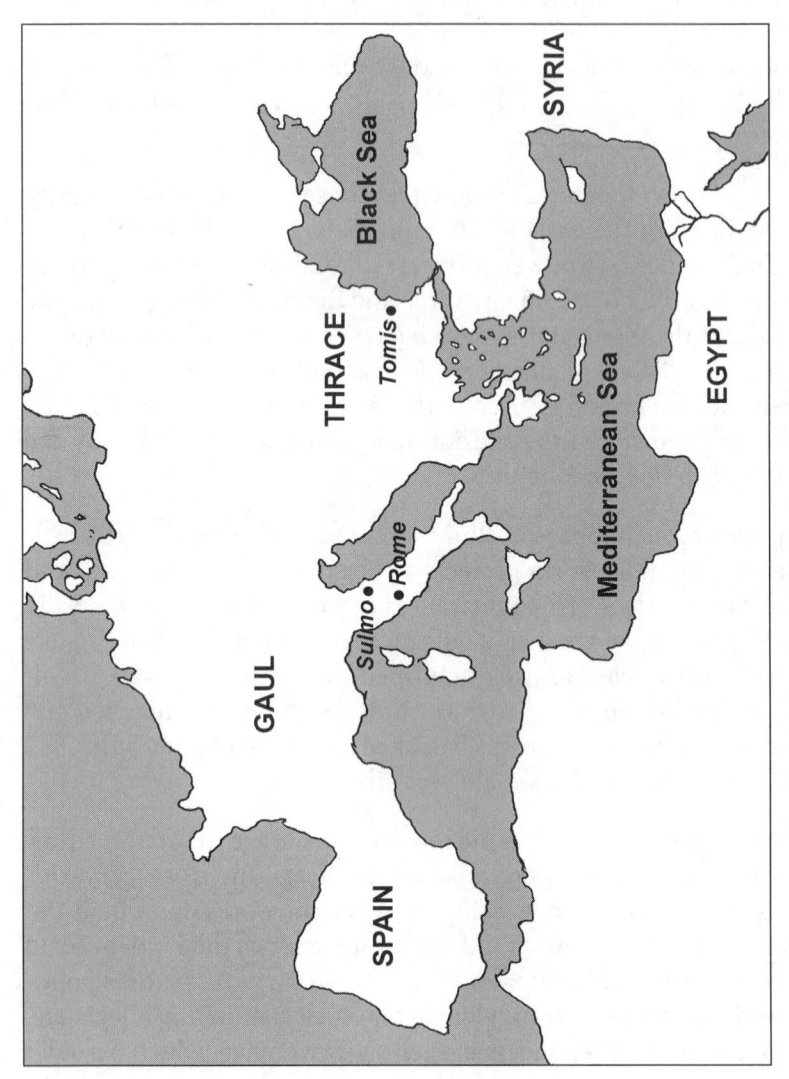

Ovid's World, 43 B.C.–17 A.D.

Born into an equestrian family, Ovid received a traditional upper class education that readied him for an active political life. He was sent to Rome to study rhetoric with the great orators of his day. Nevertheless, Ovid preferred poetry to speechmaking. He traveled and began a political career, but abandoned it in 24 B.C. against the advice of his father; in an autobiographical poem written in exile, the poet confesses that everything he wrote turned to poetry.

Ovid wrote his first major collection of poems, the *Amores*, at the age of twenty. In choosing to write love elegy, he was working within a long tradition; his predecessors included Tibullus and Propertius, Gallus, whose poetry has been lost, and, to some extent, Catullus. While still working on the *Amores*, Ovid began the *Heroides*, a series of elegiac love letters written by great female characters from mythology. Ovid blends here for the first time the genres of elegy, epic, and tragedy, a mingling that anticipates his rhetorical strategy in the *Metamorphoses*. From elegy, Ovid turned to tragedy and produced a version of the *Medea*, which has not survived.

In his mid-thirties, Ovid returned to his former theme of love in a series of didactic or instructional works devoted exclusively to this motif. The *Medicamina Faciei* is a treatise on the use of cosmetics. The *Ars Amatoria* is a manual of three books of instructions for male and female lovers; two books advise men on how to attract and keep women; a third advises women on attracting men. This irreverent, provocative poem is a kind of satire of Augustus's official, legislated morality, and may have been one of the causes of Ovid's exile. At age forty-three he wrote the *Remedia Amoris*, a handbook that tells readers how to combat love and cure themselves of this passion.

During all this time, Ovid was also working on his *Metamorphoses*, and from the ages of forty-three to fifty he devoted himself almost exclusively to this work. His fifteen-book poem of nearly 12,000 lines switches smoothly from epic to elegy when the subject matter warrants. As he reached the end of this work, Ovid embarked on a new project, the *Fasti*, a poem in twelve books, each treating a calendar month and explaining contemporary indigenous religious practices by giving the historical precedents for them. This poem would certainly have appealed to Augustus; it was incomplete, however, when Ovid was banished in 8 A.D.

After banishment from Rome at the age of fifty, Ovid spent the remainder of his days cut off from family and friends in the remote Thracian city of Tomis on the west shore of the Black Sea. Here he was isolated from all the civilization that had nourished and sustained him. We do not know the exact cause of his banishment; the poet himself speaks of a *carmen* and an *error* in one of the poems in the *Tristia*, poems he wrote during his banishment, in the hope that they would move Augustus to recall him. The *carmen* is almost certainly the *Ars Amatoria*; the *error* may be connected with the banishment of Augustus's daughter, but there is no indisputable evidence for either cause. In addition to the *Tristia*, poems that chronicle the poet's grim life in Tomis, Ovid wrote four books of poems in elegiac couplets, the *Epistulae ex Ponto,* letters to his friends and relations back in Rome.

Ovid's final work was a poem called the *Ibis,* a six-hundred–line attack on a former acquaintance who had tried to profit from Ovid's banishment. Several other short works from this period are now lost; at the time of his death the poet had begun a major poem, the *Halieutica,* about fishing; we have some 130 lines of this poem. Ovid died in Tomis at the age of sixty.

TOPICAL BIBLIOGRAPHY FOR OVID

General

Boyd, Barbara Weiden. *Brill's Companion to Ovid* (Leiden: Brill, 2002).

Boyd, Barbara Weiden, and Cora Fox, eds. *Approaches to Teaching the Works of Ovid and the Ovidian Tradition* (New York: The Modern Language Association of America, 2010).

Knox, Peter, ed. *A Companion to Ovid* (Blackwell: Oxford, 2009).

Hardie, Philip R. *The Cambridge Companion to Ovid* (Cambridge, UK: Cambridge University Press, 2002).

Volk, Katharina. *Ovid* (Oxford: Wiley-Blackwell, 2010).

General: Amores

Boyd, Barbara Weiden. *Ovid's Literary Loves. Influence and Innovation in the "Amores"* (Ann Arbor: University of Michigan Press, 1997).

Buchan, M. "*Ovidius Imperamator*: Beginnings and Endings of Love Poems and Empire in the *Amores*." *Arethusa* 28 (1995) 53–85.

Cahoon, L. "The Bed as Battlefield: Erotic Conquest and Military Metaphor in Ovid's *Amores*." *Transactions and Proceedings of the American Philological Association* 118 (1988) 293–307.

Davis, John T. *Fictus Adulter Poet as Actor in the "Amores"* (Amsterdam: J. C. Gieben, 1989).

Davis, P. J. "Ovid's *Amores*: A Political Reading." *Classical Philology* 94.4 (1999) 431–99.

Gold, Barbara, ed. *A Companion to Latin Love Elegy.* (Oxford: Blackwell Publishing, 2012).

Greene, Ellen. *The Erotics of Domination: Male Desire and the Mistress in Latin Love Poetry* (Baltimore: The Johns Hopkins University Press, 1998).

James, Sharon L. "Slave-Rape and Female Silence in Ovid's Love Poetry." *Helios* 24.1 (1995) 60–76.

———. *Learned Girls and Male Persuasion: Gender and Reading in Roman Love Elegy* (Berkeley: University of California Press, 2003).

Katz, Phyllis. "Teaching the Elegiac Lover in Ovid's *Amores*." *Classical World* 102.2 (2009) 163–67.

Keith, A. M. "*Corpus Eroticum*: Elegiac Poetics and Elegiac *Puellae* in Ovid's *Amores*." *Classical World* 88 (1994) 27–40.

———. "Etymological Wordplay in Ovid's 'Pyramus and Thisbe' (Met. 4.55–166)." *The Classical Quarterly* 51.1 (2001) 309–12.

Kenney, E. J. "The Tradition of Ovid's *Amores*." *The Classical Review* 5.1 (1955) 13–14.

Lively, Genevieve, and Patricia B. Salzman-Mitchell. *Latin Elegy and Narratology: Fragments of Story* (Columbus: Ohio State University Press, 2008).

Luck, George. *The Latin Love Elegy* (New York: Barnes and Noble, 1960).

Martin, Christopher. *Policy in Love: Lyric and Public in Ovid, Petrarch, and Shakespeare* (Pittsburgh: Duquesne University Press, 1994).

McKie, D. S. "Ovid's *Amores*: The Prime Sources for the Text." *The Classical Quarterly* 36.1 (1986) 219–38.

O'Gorman, Ellen. "Love and the Family: Augustus and Ovidian Elegy." *Arethusa* 30 (1997) 103–24.

Paxson, J., and Cynthia Gravlee, eds. *Desiring Discourse: the Literature of Love, Ovid through Chaucer* (Selinsgrove: Susquehanna University Press, 1998).

Stapleton, M. L. *Harmful Eloquence: Ovid's* Amores *from Antiquity to Shakespeare* (Ann Arbor: University of Michigan Press, 1996).

Tracy, V. A. "Dramatic Elements in Ovid's *Amores*." *Latomus* 36 (1977) 496–500.

Veyne, P. *Roman Erotic Elegy: Love, Poetry and the West*. David Pellauer, trans. (Chicago: University of Chicago Press, 1988).

Volk, Katharina. "*Ille Ego*: (Mis)Reading Ovid's Elegiac Persona." *Antike und Abendland* 51 (2005) 83.

Commentaries: Amores

Barsby, John A. *Ovid's "Amores" Book* 1 (Oxford: Clarendon Press, 1973).

Booth, Joan. *The Second Book of the Amores* (Warminster: Aris & Phillips, 1991).

McKeown, J. C. *Ovid, Amores: Text, Prolegomena, and Commentary*, Volumes I–III (Liverpool, England: F. Cairns, 1987).

Ryan, Maureen B., and Caroline A. Perkins. *Ovid's Amores, Book One: A Commentary* (Norman: University of Oklahoma Press, 2011).

Translations: Amores

Green, P., trans. *Ovid. The Erotic Poems* (New York: Penguin, 1982).

Humphries, Rolfe. *The Loves, The Art of Beauty, The Remedies for Love, and The Art of Love* (Bloomington: Indiana University Press, 1957).

Lee, Guy. *Ovid's Amores* (New York: Viking Press, 1968).

Melville, A. D. *Ovid. The Love Poems* (Oxford, UK: Oxford University Press, 1990).

Showerman, Grant. *Ovid I: Heroides and Amores* (Cambridge: Harvard University Press, Loeb Edition, 1986).

Slavitt, David R., trans. *Love Poems, Letters, and Remedies of Ovid* (Cambridge: Harvard University Press, 2011).

Amores I. 1

Keith, Alison M. "*Amores* 1.1: Propertius and the Ovidian Programme." In *Studies in Latin Literature and Roman History,* ed. C. Deroux (Bruxelles: *Latomus*, 1992) 6.327–44.

Amores I. 3

Barsby, J. A. "*Desultor amoris* in *Amores* 1.3." *Classical Philology* 70 (1975) 44–45.

Olstein, K. "*Amores* 1.3 and Duplicity as a Way of Love." *Transactions and Proceedings of the American Philological Association* 105 (1975) 241–57.

Amores I. 9

Cahoon, Leslie. "The Bed as Battlefield: Erotic Conquest and Military Metaphor in Ovid's A*mores.*" *Transactions of the American Philological Association* (1988) 293–307.

McKeown, J. C. *"Militat omnis amans."* *Classical Journal* 90 (1995) 295–304.

Murgatroyd, P. *"Militia Amoris* and the Roman Elegists." *Latomus* 34 (1974) 57–59.

———. "The Argumentation in Ovid *Amores* 1.9." *Mnemosyne* 52.5 (1999) 569–71.

Olstein, K. *"Amores* 1.9 and the Structure of Book I." *Studies in Latin Literature and Roman History,* ed. C. Deroux. *Latomus* 164 (1979) 286–300.

Amores I. 11

McKie, D. S. " Love in the Margin: Ovid, *Amores* 1.11.22." *Proceedings of the Cambridge Studies in Classical Philology* 30 (1984) 79–83.

Amores I. 12

Baker, R. *"Duplices Tabellae*: Propertius 3.23 and Ovid *Amores* 1.12." *Classical Philology* 68 (1973) 109–13.

Amores II. 19

Buhner, Emily Dawn. "Rivalry and Desire: Male-Male Relations in Ovid's *Amores* and French Feminist Theory." Thesis. University of North Carolina, Chapel Hill, 2009.

Amores III. 12

Buhner, Emily Dawn. "Rivalry and Desire: Male-Male Relations in Ovid's *Amores* and French Feminist Theory." Thesis. University of North Carolina, Chapel Hill, 2009.

Greene, Ellen. "Sexual Politics in Ovid's *Amores*: 3.4, 3.8, and 3.12." *Classical Philology* 89 (1994) 344–50.

McKeown, J. C. "Ovid, *Amores* 3.12" In *Papers of the Liverpool Latin Seminar, Second Volume 1979*, ed. Francis Cairns (Liverpool, 1979) 163-77.

Amores III. 15

See general works on the *Amores*.

General: Metamorphoses

Ahl, Frederick. *Metaformations: Soundplay and Wordplay in Ovid and Other Classical Poets* (Ithaca: Cornell University Press, 1985).

Anderson, William S. "Multiple Changes in the *Metamorphoses*." Transactions and Proceedings of the American Philological Association 94 (1963) 1-27.

———. "Aspects of Love in Ovid's *Metamorphoses*." *Classical Journal* 90 (1995) 265-69.

Barchiesi, Alessandro. *The Poet and the Prince: Ovid and Augustan Discourse* (Berkeley: University of California Press, 1997).

Brown, Sarah Annes. *Ovid: Myth and Metamorphosis*. (London: Bristol Classical Press, 2005).

Cahoon, Leslie. "Let the Muse Sing On: Poetry, Criticism, Feminism and the Case of Ovid." *Helios* 17 (1990) 197-211.

Culham, Phyllis. "Decentering the Text: The Case of Ovid." *Helios* 17 (1990) 161-70.

Curran, L. C. "Rape and Rape Victims in the *Metamorphoses*." *Arethusa* 11 (1978) 213-41.

Due, Otto Steen. *Changing Forms: Studies in the Metamorphoses of Ovid* (Copenhagen: Gyldendal, 1974).

Fantham, Elaine. *Ovid's Metamorphoses* (Oxford, UK: Oxford University Press, 2004).

Fränkel, Hermann. *Ovid: A Poet Between Two Worlds* (Berkeley: University of California Press, 1945).

Feldherr, Andrew. *Playing Gods: Ovid's Metamorphoses and the Politics of Fiction* (Princeton: University Press, 2010).

Galinsky, G. Carl. *Ovid's Metamorphoses: An Introduction to the Basic Aspects* (Berkeley: University of California Press, 1975).

Ginsberg, Warren. "Ovid's 'Metamorphoses' and the Politics of Interpretation." *The Classical Journal* 84.3 (1989) 222–31.

Glen, Edgar M. *The Metamorphoses: Ovid's Roman Games* (Lanham, MD: University Press of America, 1986).

Hallett, Judith. "Contextualizing the Text: The Journey to Ovid." *Helios* 17 (1990) 187–95.

Hardie, Philip, Alessandro Barchiesi, and Stephen Hinds. *Ovidian Transformations: Essays on the Metamorphoses and its Reception.* (Cambridge: Cambridge Philological Society, 1999).

Hinds, Stephen. "Generalizing about Ovid." *Ramus* 16 (1987) 4–31.

Johnson, Patricia J. *Ovid before Exile: Art and Punishment in the Metamorphoses* (Madison: University of Wisconsin Press, 2008).

Kenney, E. J. "The Style of the *Metamorphoses*." In *Ovid*, ed. J. W. Bins (Boston: Routledge and Kegan Paul, 1973) 116–53.

Knox, Peter. *Ovid's* Metamorphoses *and the Traditions of Augustan Poetry* (Cambridge: Cambridge Philological Society, 1986).

Mack, Sara. *Ovid* (New Haven: Yale University Press, 1988).

Myers, K. Sara. "The Metamorphosis of a Poet: Recent Work on Ovid." *Journal of Roman Studies* 89 (1999) 190–204.

Nagle, Betty Rose. "*Amor, Ira,* and Sexual Identity in Ovid's Metamorphoses." *Classical Antiquity* 3 (1984) 236–55.

———. "Ovid: A Poet between Two Novelists." *Helios* 12:1 (1985) 65–73.

Otis, Brooks. *Ovid as an Epic Poet* (Cambridge: Cambridge University Press, 1966).

Richlin, Amy. "Reading Ovid's Rapes." *Pornography and Representation in Greece and Rome* (Oxford: Oxford University Press, 1994) 158–89.

Salzman-Mitchell, Patricia B. *A Web of Fantasies: Gaze, Image, and Gender in Ovid's* Metamorphoses. (Columbus: Ohio State University Press, 2005)

Segal, Charles. *Landscape in Ovid's* Metamorphoses: *A Study in the Transformation of a Literary Symbol* (Wiesbaden: Franz Steiner, 1969).

———. "Narrative Art in the Metamorphoses." *Classical Journal* 66 (1971) 331–37.

Solodow, Joseph. *The World of Ovid's* Metamorphoses (Chapel Hill: University of North Carolina Press, 1988).

Steiner, Grundy. "Ovid's *Carmen Perpetuum*." *Transactions and Proceedings of the American Philological Association* 89 (1958) 218–36.

Tissol, Garth. *The Faces of Nature: Wit, Narrative, and Cosmic Origins in Ovid's Metamorphoses* (Princeton: Princeton University Press, 1997).

———. "Ovid's Little *Aeneid* and the Thematic Integrity of the *Metamorphoses*." *Helios* 20.1 (1993) 69–79.

Wheeler, Stephen Michael. *A Discourse of Wonders: Audience and Performance in Ovid's* Metamorphoses (Philadelphia: University of Pennsylvania Press, 1999).

Commentaries: Metamorphoses

Anderson, William S. *Ovid's* Metamorphoses, *Books 1–5* (Norman: University of Oklahoma Press, 1997).

———. *Ovid's* Metamorphoses, *Books 6–10* (Norman: University of Oklahoma Press, 1972).

Bömer, Franz, and Ulrich Schmitzer. *P. Ovidius Naso, Metamorphosen: Kommentar Von Franz Bömer: Addenda, Corrigenda, Indices* (Heidelberg: C. Winter, 2006).

Hill, D. E. *Metamorphoses* (Warminster, Wiltshire: Aris & Phillips, I–IV; V–VIII; IX–XII; XIII–XV, 1985–1999).

Lee, A. G. *Ovid*: Metamorphoses *Book I* (Wauconda, IL: Bolchazy-Carducci Publishers, 1988).

Translations: Metamorphoses

Hughes, Ted. *Tales from Ovid* (New York: Farrar, Straus and Giroux, 1995).

Mandelbaum, A. *The* Metamorphoses *of Ovid* (New York: Harcourt Brace, 1993).

Melville, A. D. *Metamorphoses* (Oxford: Oxford University Press, 1986).

Miller, Frank J. *Metamorphoses* (Cambridge, MA: Harvard University Press, 1976).

Raeburn, D. A. Ovid. *Metamorphoses*. A new Verse Translation with an Introduction by D. Feeney (London: Penguin Books, 2004).

Simpson, Michael. *The* Metamorphoses *of Ovid* (Amherst: University of Massachusetts Press, 2001).

Slavitt, David R. *The* Metamorphoses *of Ovid* (Baltimore: Johns Hopkins University Press, 1994).

Creation

McKim, Richard. "Myth against Philosophy in Ovid's Account of Creation." *The Classical Journal* 80.2 (Dec. 1984–Jan. 1985) 97–108.

Myers, K. Sara. *Ovid's Causes: Cosmogony and Aetiology in the* Metamorphoses (Ann Arbor: University of Michigan Press, 1994).

O'Hara, James. "Some God... or His Own Heart: Two Kinds of Epic Motivation in the Proem to Ovid's *Metamorphoses*." *The Classical Journal*, 100.2 (Dec. 2004–Jan. 2005) 149–61.

Tarrant, Richard. "Chaos in Ovid's *Metamorphoses* and its Neronian Influence." *Arethusa* 35.3 (Fall 2002) 349–60.

Wheeler, Stephen. "*Imago Mundi*: Another View of the Creation in Ovid's *Metamorphoses*." *The American Journal of Philology* 116.1 (Spring 1995) 95–121.

Apollo and Daphne

Barnard, Mary E. *The Myth of Apollo and Daphne from Ovid to Quevedo: Love, Agon and the Grotesque* (Durham: Duke University Press, 1987).

Francese, C. "Daphne, Honor, and Aetiological Action in Ovid's *Metamorphoses*." *Classical World*, 97.2 (2004) 153–57.

Gross, N. P. "Rhetorical Wit and Amatory Persuasion in Ovid." *Classical Journal* 74 (1979) 305–18.

Hollis, A. S. "Ovid, *Metamorphoses* 1.455ff.: Apollo, Daphne, and the Pythian Crown." *Zeitschrift für Papyrologie und Epigraphik* 112 (1996) 69–73.

Knox, Peter E. "In Pursuit of Daphne." *Transactions and Proceedings of the American Philological Association* 120 (1990) 183–202.

Nethercut, W. R. "Daphne and Apollo. A Dynamic Encounter." *Classical Journal* 74 (1979) 333–47.

Nicoll, W. S. M. "Cupid, Apollo, and Daphne (Ovid, Met. 452ff.)." *Classical Quarterly* (1980) 174–82.

Pyramus and Thisbe

Crockett, Bryan. "The 'Wittiest Partition': Pyramus and Thisbe in Ovid and Shakespeare." *Classical and Modern Literature* 12 (1991) 49–58.

Duke, T. T. "Ovid's Pyramus and Thisbe." *Classical Journal* 66 (1971) 320–27.

Fowler, Don. "Pyramus, Thisbe, King Kong: Ovid and the Presence of Poetry." In *Roman Constructions*. (Oxford: Oxford University Press, 2000) 156–67.

Glendinning, Robert. "Pyramus and Thisbe in the Medieval Classroom." *Speculum* 61 (1986) 103–15.

Jacobson, Howard. "Etymological Wordplay in Ovid's 'Pyramus and Thisbe' (MET. 4.55–166)." *Classical Quarterly* 51 (2001) 309–14.

Jann, Micaela. "There Beneath the Roman Ruin Where the Purple Flowers Grow: Ovid's Minyeides and the Feminine Imagination." *The American Journal of Philology* 115.3 (1994) 427–48.

Knox, Peter. "Pyramus and Thisbe in Cyprus." *Harvard Studies in Classical Philology* 88 (1989) 315–28.

Newlands, Carole. "The Simile of the Fractured Pipe in Ovid's *Metamorphoses* 4." *Ramus* 15 (1986) 145–53.

Perraud, Louis A. "*Amatores Exclusi*: Apostrophe and Separation in the Pyramus and Thisbe Episode." *The Classical Journal* 79.2 (1983) 135–39.

Rhorer, Catharine. "Red and White in Ovid's *Metamorphoses*: The Mulberry Tree in the Tale of Pyramus and Thisbe." *Ramus* 9 (1980) 79–88.

Rudd, Niall. "Pyramus and Thisbe in Shakespeare and Ovid: *A Midsummer Night's Dream* and *Metamorphoses* 4:1–166." In *Creative Imitation and Latin Literature*, ed. David West and Tony Woodman (Cambridge: Cambridge University Press, 1979) 173–93.

Shorrock, Robert. "Ovidian Plumbing in *Metamorphoses* 4."*Classical Quarterly* 53.2 (2003) 624–27.

Daedalus and Icarus

Davisson, Mary H. T. "The Observers of Daedalus and Icarus in Ovid." *Classical World* 90 (1997) 263–78.

Hoefmans, Marjorie. "Myth into Reality: The Metamorphosis of Daedalus and Icarus (Ovid, *Metamorphoses*, VIII, 183–234)." *L'Antiquité Classique* 63 (1994) 137–60.

Pavlock, Barbara. "Daedalus in the Labyrinth of Ovid's *Metamorphoses*." *Classical World* 92.2 (1998) 141–57.

Rudd, Niall. "Daedalus and Icarus (i) From Rome to the End of the Middle Ages; (ii) From the Renaissance to the Present Day." In Martindale 1988: 21–53 (see full reference in section Ovid's Influence on Art and Literature).

Wise, V. M. "Flight Myths in Ovid's *Metamorphoses*." *Ramus* 6 (1977) 44–59.

Philemon and Baucis

Gamel, M. K. "Baucis and Philemon. Paradigm or Paradox?" *Helios* 11 (1984) 117–31.

Green, Steven J. "Collapsing Authority and 'Arachnean' Gods in Ovid's Baucis and Philemon (Met. 8.611–724)." *Ramus* 32.1 (2003) 39–56.

Griffin, Alan H. F. "Philemon and Baucis in Ovid's *Metamorphoses*." *Greece and Rome* 38 (1991) 62–74.

Jones, C. P. "A Geographical Setting for the Baucis and Philemon Legend (Ovid, *Metamorphoses* 8.611–724)." *Harvard Studies in Classical Philology* 96 (1997) 200–3.

Orpheus and Eurydice

Bowra, C. M. "Orpheus and Eurydice." *The Classical Quarterly* 2.2&3 (1952) 113–26.

Makowski, John F. "Bisexual Orpheus: Pederasty and Parody in Ovid." *The Classical Journal* 92.1 (1996) 25–38.

Young, Elizabeth Marie. "Inscribing Orpheus: Ovid and the Invention of a Greco-Roman Corpus." *Representations* 101.101 (2008) 1–31.

Pygmalion

Arkins, Brian. "Sexy Statues: Pygmalionism in Irish Literature." *Classical and Modern Literature* 18.3 (1998) 247–50.

Davis, Sally. "Bringing Ovid into the Latin Classroom: Pygmalion." *Classical Journal* 90 (1995) 273–78.

Griffin, A. H. F. "Ovid's *Metamorphoses*." *Greece and Rome* 24 (1977) 57–70. [On the Narcissus and Pygmalion episodes].

James, Paula. "She's All That: Ovid's Ivory Statue and the Legacy of Pygmalion on Film." *Classical Bulletin* 79.1 (2003) 63–91.

Knowles, Ronald. "A Kind of Alaska: Pinter and Pygmalion." *Classical and Modern Literature* 16.3 (1996) 231–40.

Miller, J. H. *Versions of Pygmalion* (Cambridge, MA: Harvard University Press, 1990).

Ovid's Influence on Art and Literature

Aghion, Irene, Claire Barbillon, and Francois Lissarague, eds. *Gods and Heroes of Classical Antiquity* (Flammarion: Paris, 1996). [Source for works of art on myth].

Barkan, Leonard. *The Gods Made Flesh: Metamorphosis and the Pursuit of Paganism* (New Haven: Yale University Press, 1986).

Boardman, John, et al., eds. *Lexicon Iconographicum Mythologiae Classicae* [LIMC] (Zurich: Artmeis Verlag, 1981–1997). [Eight volumes published (A–Z). Articles in German, English, French, or Italian. Each volume consists of: pt. 1: text; pt. 2: plates. Includes bibliographies. Focuses on ancient art to 1200 A.D.].

Hoffman, Michael, and James Lasdun. *After Ovid: New Metamorphoses* (New York: Farrar, Straus and Giroux, 1995). [Poems by contemporary poets modeled on the *Metamorphoses*].

Martindale, Charles, ed. *Ovid Renewed: Ovidian Influences on Literature and Art from the Middle Ages to the Twentieth Century* (Cambridge: Cambridge University Press, 1988).

Reid, Jane D. *The Oxford Guide to Classical Mythology in the Arts 1300–1990s*, 2 vols (Oxford: Oxford University Press, 1993).

Wilkinson, L. P. *Ovid Recalled* (Cambridge: Cambridge University Press, 1955). [General influence].

Web sites with Information on Ovid

http://ancienthistory.about.com/cs/people/a/ovid.htm

http://www.uvm.edu/~hag/ovid/baur1703/index.html

http://www.perseus.tufts.edu/

http://www.vroma.org/vromalinks.html

http://www.stoa.org/avclassics/

http://etext.virginia.edu/latin/ovid/

http://lilt.ilstu.edu/drjclassics/links.htm

http://larryavisbrown.homestead.com/files/xeno.ovid1.htm/

The Amores

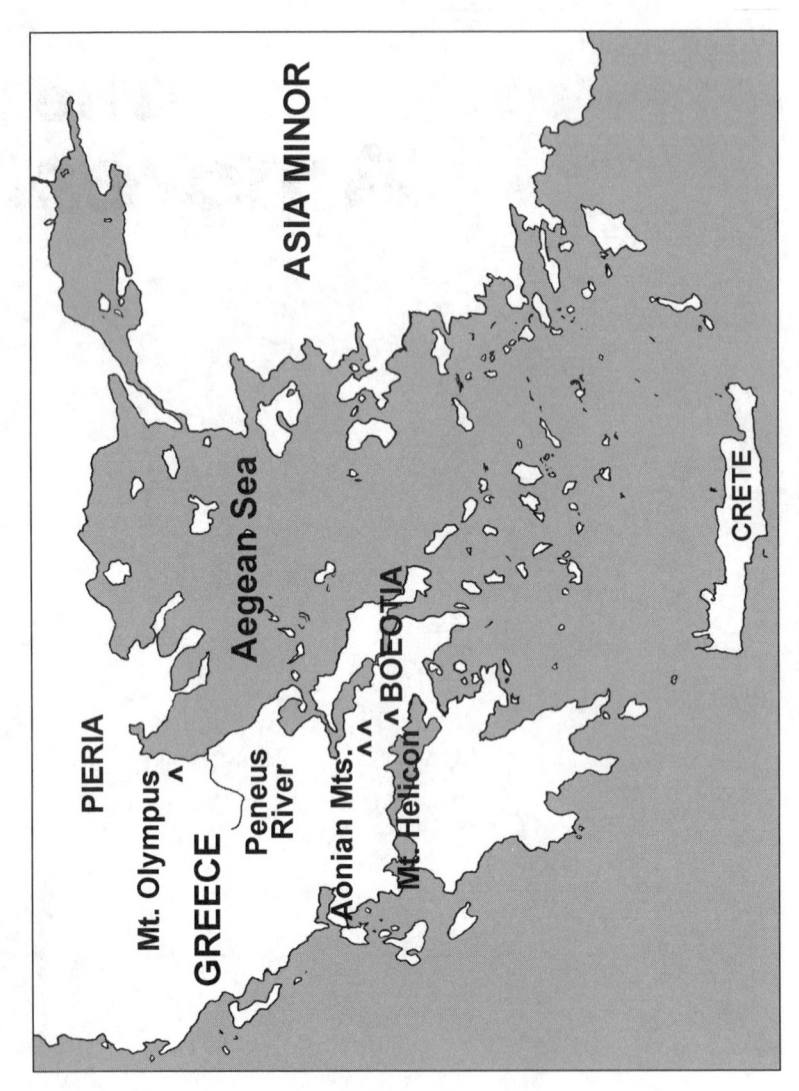

Map of Places in Amores I. 1

INTRODUCTION TO THE AMORES

Ovid's *Amores* is a collection in three books. In Ovid's epigram to the collection, the poems themselves declare that they were edited from five to three books in order to provide less work for their readers. This explanation sets the humorous tone employed by the poet throughout the *Amores*.

Ovid began his love elegies at the age of 18 in 26 B.C., wrote the bulk of the poems after 20 B.C., and published the second edition around 7 B.C. At the same time, the poet was also composing his other major works (see Ovid's Life and Works), most of which were completed before his exile in 8 A.D.

In choosing to write love elegy, Ovid placed himself squarely among Roman poets who developed a uniquely Roman genre. The topic of the trials and tribulations of the lover was already popular in fourth-century B.C. Greek New Comedy and in the Greek novels of the Hellenistic periods. The metrical form of the elegiac couplet (see Appendix of Metrical Terms) was used by some of the Greek poets; it was the Romans, however, who developed love elegy as a genre and who first composed collections of love poems addressed to one or more women.

By the time Ovid began his collection, Catullus (c. 88–55 B.C.) had already died, leaving behind his Lesbia poems, a group of poems that describe his tumultuous love affair with Clodia, a married woman from a very distinguished family. Some of Catullus's Lesbia poems were written in the elegiac meter. The popular works, now lost, of the poet Gallus (69–26 B.C.) seem to have been the first to take on the form and characteristic themes we associate with the genre of love elegy. Also important to Ovid were the works of his older contemporaries, Propertius and Tibullus. Their poems similarly described the vicissitudes of a love affair with a married woman and often explored serious issues of life, love, and art. Ovid's challenge in writing his poems was to continue this Roman tradition, but at the same time to achieve something new. He accomplished this by using the traditional themes of love elegy, but at the same time by redefining the characters of the lover and his mistress. His are not the poems of a lover who is deeply and emotionally involved with his beloved. Rather, he presents a *persona*, or character of a lover, who is witty, urbane, but emotionally detached. Ovid appears to be more concerned with demonstrating his poetic skill and versatility than he is with documenting a personal love affair. The degree to which these poems are or are not biographical is far less important than the clever artistry with which the poet develops his themes.

That Ovid wanted to reinvent the genre of love elegy is clear from the very first. Ovid's collection does not begin with a dedicatory poem to his mistress, but with a poem about Cupid's tricking him into writing love elegy (I. 1). The collection ends with a farewell to the poetic form itself (III. 15), not to his mistress, as one might expect. Nevertheless, the poet achieves unity by using the story of the love affair as a loosely chronological narrative that spans the three books. His first book documents the joyous beginnings of a love affair with the mysterious Corinna, a married woman whose true identity and even existence is in question. The second and third books continue with disillusionment and parting—both the girl and the love elegy itself are renounced. But throughout the work, the poet exploits the traditional topics of love poetry, continually overturning established patterns.

AMORES I. 1

This short poem introduces the entire *Amores*. Ovid begins by saying that, although he had attempted an epic poem, he soon discovered he could not write about wars and heroes in dactylic hexameter (the meter traditionally used for epic verses), because Cupid had stolen one metrical foot from the second line. This mischief turned his epic into elegy. (See the Appendix of Metrical Terms for examples of epic and elegiac meter.) The poet rebukes Cupid for meddling in a realm that does not belong to him. To give weight to his argument against such interference, the poet points out how inappropriate it would be for Venus and Minerva, or Ceres and Diana, to exchange roles, as Cupid has done with the poet. Ovid then adds that, as he has no lover, he has no subject for love elegy. This defiance of the god leads to a surprising consequence: Cupid fires an arrow into the poet that suddenly and dramatically transforms him into both a lover and a love poet. Ovid ends by bidding farewell to epic poetry.

This poem is a humorous and ironic justification of Ovid's decision to write elegy rather than epic. Ovid cleverly pretends that he has been forced into this choice and imagines the scene as a real event with a real conversation between apparent equals.

AMORES I. 1

Arma gravi numero violentaque bella parabam
    edere, materia conveniente modis.
par erat inferior versus; risisse Cupido
    dicitur atque unum surripuisse pedem.
5   "quis tibi, saeve puer, dedit hoc in carmina iuris?
    Pieridum vates, non tua, turba sumus.

✦ ✦ ✦

1   **arma ... numero:** recalls the opening line of the *Aeneid: Arma virumque cano*.
    gravi numero: refers to the DACTYLIC HEXAMETER traditionally used for epic poetry, most particularly by Vergil in the *Aeneid*.
2   **ēdō, -ere, -idī, -itum:** *to give out, put forth, produce*.
    materia: refers back to *arma* and *bella*, the material most suitable for epic tales.
    modis: a direct reference to the DACTYLIC HEXAMETER meter required for epic verse.
3   **inferior:** in DACTYLIC HEXAMETER all lines are of equal length, six metrical feet.
    risisse: from *rīdeō, rīdēre, rīsī, rīsum*.
    Cupido, -inis (m.): the eternally youthful son of Venus whose arrows could inflict either love or revulsion upon their victims.
5   **saeve puer:** Ovid here addresses Cupid directly. The scene is parallel to the Apollo/Daphne story in *Met*. I. 453 where Ovid describes Cupid's wrath as *saeva ira* and to 456 where Apollo refers to Cupid as a *lascive puer*. In that scene Apollo expresses his annoyance with the boy-god for using a weapon (the bow) that Apollo felt was more rightfully suitable to his own epic-scale deeds than to the amatory deeds of Cupid. Here, Ovid scolds the mischievous god for interfering with the writer's desire to compose epic verse.
    iuris: partitive genitive used after the neuter demonstrative pronoun *hoc*.
6   **Pīerides, -um (f. pl.):** the Muses from Pieria on the northern slope of Mt. Olympus.
    vātēs, -is (m.): *poet, prophet*. Ovid ironically chooses the ancient term for a poet, *vates*, which once carried the meaning of "prophet."
    turba, -ae (f.): *a crowd of followers, attendants, troop*.

quid si praeripiat flavae Venus arma Minervae,
    ventilet accensas flava Minerva faces?
quis probet in silvis Cererem regnare iugosis,
10   lege pharetratae virginis arva coli?
    crinibus insignem quis acuta cuspide Phoebum

✤ ✤ ✤

7   **praeripiō, -ere, -ripuī, -reptum:** *to take away, snatch, tear away.* A present subjunctive in the protasis of a future-less-vivid construction with the apodosis understood.
    flāvus, -a, -um: *yellow, having yellow hair.* The phrase *flavae . . . Minervae* is a kind of embracing word order.
    Venus, -eris (f.): goddess sacred to love and lovers.
    Minerva, -ae (f.): Ovid here chooses to contrast Love and War *(arma).*
8   **ventilō, -āre, -āvī, -ātum:** *to brandish in the air, fan.* A second protasis in the future-less-vivid construction.
    accensas . . . faces: CHIASMUS. The *faces* refers to the torch symbolizing love and always present at marriages, where Venus would be expected to reign.
9   **probō, -āre, -āvī, -ātum:** *to authorize, sanction.* Translated like a potential subjunctive but used to convey doubt.
    Cerēs, -eris (f.): the goddess of open fields and agriculture.
    iugōsus, -a, -um: *mountainous.*
10 **pharetrātus, -a, -um:** *furnished with or wearing a quiver, quivered.*
    pharetratae virginis refers to the goddess of the hunt and of the woodlands, Diana. Just as Ovid has contrasted Love and War in lines 7–8, here there is a contrast between Ceres whose appropriate territory is the open fields and Diana who frequents wooded areas.
    arvum, -ī (n.): *ploughed or cultivated land, a field.*
11 **crīnis, crīnis (m.):** *hair, tresses.*
    insignis, -e: *distinguished, outstanding, memorable.*
    acūtus, -a, -um: *sharp, pointed.*
    cuspis, -idis (f.): *spear, javelin, lance.*
    Phoebus, -ī (m.): an epithet for Apollo as the god of light.

8 ✦ OVID

[margin note: Abl. absolute]
instruat, Aoniam Marte movente lyram?
 sunt tibi magna, puer, nimiumque potentia regna: [margin note: Dat. of poss]
  cur opus affectas ambitiose novum?
15 an, quod ubique, tuum est? tua sunt Heliconia tempe?
  vix etiam Phoebo iam lyra tuta sua est?
 cum bene surrexit versu nova pagina primo,
  attenuat nervos proximus ille meos.

✦ ✦ ✦

12 **instruō, -ere, -xī, -ctum:** *to instruct, equip, furnish.* Translate like a potential subjunctive, here used to express doubt, as does *probet*, I. 9.
 Aoniam: refers to Boeotia, a region in Greece, which includes the Aonian mountains and Mt. Helicon. Often an epithet for the Muses.
 lyra, -ae (f.): *lute, lyre.* The four-word phrase *Aoniam Marte movente lyram* is in CHIASTIC word order. The lyre is the standard emblem for Apollo and so suggests poetry. Ovid sets up a third contrast here between Poetry (Apollo) and War (Mars).
13 **tibi:** dative of possession with *sunt*.
 nimium (adv.): *extremely, very much, too much.*
 potens, -tis: *powerful, mighty, influential.*
14 **affectō, -āre, -āvī, -ātum:** *to strive after a thing, to pursue.*
 ambitiōsus, -a, -um: *ambitious, vain, vainglorious, conceited.*
15 **quod ubique:** supply a missing *est* to complete the clause. It is a common occurrence in Ovid for the verb *sum* to be omitted from phrases.
 Helicōnius, -a, -um: *of or pertaining to Mt. Helicon, the mountain sacred to the Muses.*
 tempe (n. pl.): (indecl.) *valley*; in particular the beautiful valley at the foot of Mt. Olympus through which ran the Peneus river.
16 **Phoebo:** dative of reference with *tuta*.
17 **pāgina, -ae (f.):** *page.*
18 **attenuō, -āre, -āvī, -ātum:** *to weaken, enfeeble, lessen, diminish.*
 nervus, -ī (m.): *string of a musical instrument or bow.*

>   nec mihi materia est numeris levioribus apta,
> 20   aut puer aut longas compta puella comas."
>   questus eram, pharetra cum protinus ille soluta
>   legit in exitium spicula facta meum
>   lunavitque genu sinuosum fortiter arcum
>   "quod" que "canas, vates, accipe" dixit "opus."
> 25 me miserum! certas habuit puer ille sagittas.
>   uror, et in vacuo pectore regnat Amor.

✦ ✦ ✦

19 **mihi:** dative of possession with *est*.
    materia ... apta: the material most suitable to the light meter (i.e., ELEGIAC COUPLETS) is Love. But as the next line reveals, Ovid is not in love.
    aptus, -a, -um: (+ dat.) *fitted, suitable, appropriate*.
20 **longas ... comas:** CHIASTIC word order. The *longas comas* surround the *compta puella* just as her hair would fall about her body. The accusative here is a Greek accusative used of the part of the body affected.
    comptus, -a, -um: *adorned*.
    coma, -ae (f.): *hair*.
21 **pharetra, -ae (f.):** *quiver*.
22 **exitium, -ī (n.):** *destruction, ruin, hurt*. The expression *exitium ... meum* is in CHIASTIC word order.
    spīculum, -ī (n.): *arrow*. Although technically this word refers to a pointed end, here it stands for the whole weapon, the arrow or dart itself. The figure of speech that uses the part for the whole is called SYNECDOCHE.
23 **lūnō, -āre, -āvī, -ātum:** *to bend like a half-moon or crescent*.
    genu, -ūs (n.): *the knee*.
    sinuōsus, -a, -um: *bent, winding, sinuous, pliant*.
    arcus, -ūs (m.): *a bow*.
24 **canas:** subjunctive in a relative clause of characteristic.
25 **me miserum:** accusative used in an exclamation. This is a standard phrase by which elegiac poets describe themselves as lovers.
26 **ūrō, -ere, ussī, ustum:** *to burn, inflame, consume with passion*. The use of this word here is parallel to the language and situation of *Met*. I. 495–96 when Apollo is struck by Cupid's golden-tipped arrow.

> [Jussive subjunctive] sex mihi surgat opus numeris, in quinque residat;
>   ferrea cum vestris bella valete modis.
>   cingere litorea flaventia tempora myrto,
> 30   Musa per undenos emodulanda pedes. [Fut. pass. part.]

✦ ✦ ✦

27 **surgat:** a jussive subjunctive.
    residō, -ere, -sēdī, -sessum: *to sink or settle down, subside, grow calm.* Here, a jussive subjunctive.
28 **ferreus, -a, -um:** *hard, unfeeling, made of iron.*
    modis: this is the last reference to DACTYLIC HEXAMETER, the meter of epic poetry and war. It echoes lines 1 and 2 of the poem.
29 **lītoreus, -a, -um:** *of the seashore.*
    litorea . . . myrto: CHIASTIC word order.
    flāvens, -entis: *golden-yellow.*
    tempus, -oris (n.): *the temple of the head.*
    myrtus, -ī (f.): *a myrtle tree.*
30 **undēnī, -ae, -a:** *eleven each, eleven at a time.*
    ēmodulor, -ārī, -ātum: *to sing, celebrate in rhythm.* Ovid ends with a reference to the meter of Love, the defined theme of all three books of the *Amores*.

AMORES I. 3

In this poem the poet swears eternal love for a girl *(puella)* who is as yet unnamed. He prays that the girl will love him in return and that there will be eternal fidelity between them. Neither rich nor of an aristocratic lineage, he admits that his credentials may not impress her, but argues that three gods, Apollo, Bacchus, and Cupid, can support him and that his best personal attributes are his fidelity and his integrity. He maintains that he is not fickle, and that his beloved, by loving him, will provide the subject matter for his finest poetry. But all this promise of immortality must be considered in the light of the mythological examples that Ovid offers in the poet's defense. They consist of women who have been loved by Jupiter, the most notorious adulterer in the Olympian pantheon.

The poet here explores and exploits the traditional subject matter of love poetry, especially the concept of *fides,* or fidelity.

AMORES I. 3

Iusta precor: quae me nuper praedata puella est,
    aut amet aut faciat, cur ego semper amem.
a, nimium volui: tantum patiatur amari,
    audierit nostras tot Cytherea preces.
5   accipe, per longos tibi qui deserviat annos;
    accipe, qui pura norit amare fide.
si me non veterum commendant magna parentum

✦ ✦ ✦

1   **precor, -ārī, -atus:** *to pray for, beg, implore.*
    praedor, -ārī, -ātus: *to take as prey, catch.*
    puella: the first reference to the girl Ovid will love. We now know that the subject of his poetry will be heterosexual love. *Puella* is the traditional word used by Latin love elegists for the young woman who is the object of their desire.
2   **amet:** a jussive subjunctive, as is *faciat*.
    amem: a deliberative subjunctive in a question implying doubt or indignation.
3   **a:** exclamation expressing anguish.
    nimius, -a, -um: *too much, too great.*
    patiatur: a jussive subjunctive.
4   **audierit:** a syncopated form of the future perfect indicative.
    nostras: Ovid here employs a poetic convention in using a first person plural adjective with singular intent.
    Cytherēa, -ae (f.): refers to Venus; an epithet taken from the name of the island in the Aegean Sea known for its worship of the goddess.
    prex, -cis (f.): *prayer.*
5   **dēserviō, -īre:** *to devote oneself, serve zealously.* Here, a present subjunctive used in a relative clause of characeristic. Ovid refers to a standard idea of Latin love elegy that the lover is enslaved by his lover or by his emotion.
6   **accipe:** this ANAPHORA draws attention to the poet's offering himself as a devoted, skilled lover.
    noscō, -ere, nōvī, nōtum: *to learn.* Here it is a syncopated form of the perfect subjunctive *noverit*. Like *deserviat* (5), it too occurs in a relative clause of characteristic.
7   **si:** *etsi.*
    commendō, -āre, -āvī, -ātum: *to recommend, make agreeable or attractive.* This is the first protasis in a series of four simple conditions all using the present indicative.

nomina, si nostri sanguinis auctor eques,
  nec meus innumeris renovatur campus aratris,
10   temperat et sumptus parcus uterque parens,
  at Phoebus comitesque novem vitisque repertor
    hac faciunt et me qui tibi donat Amor
  et nulli cessura fides, sine crimine mores,
    nudaque simplicitas purpureusque pudor.
15 non mihi mille placent, non sum desultor amoris:

✢ ✢ ✢

8 **si ... eques:** another phrase in which an *est* is needed to complete its meaning.
  nostri: another poetic use of the plural with singular intent.
9 **aratrum, -ī (n.):** *a plow.*
10 **temperō, -āre, -āvī, -ātum:** *to moderate, regulate.*
  sumptus, -ūs (m.): *expenditure.*
  parcus, -a, -um: *frugal, thrifty.*
11 **comitesque novem:** refers to the nine Muses. Here begins the apodosis to balance the four conditions set forth in the protasis. It first names four deities (Apollo, the Muses, Bacchus, Love) and continues with four honorable human qualities (fidelity, character, simplicity, modesty).
  vītis, -is (f.): *the grapevine.*
  repertor, -ōris (m.): *originator, discoverer.* Here it refers to Bacchus.
12 **hac faciunt:** an unusual idiomatic construction meaning either "act on my behalf" or "are on my side."
  faciunt: there are a total of eight subjects for this verb: *Phoebus* (11), *comitesque* (11), *repertor* (11), *Amor* (12), *fides* (13), *mores* (13), *simplicitas* (14), *pudor* (14).
14 **purpureus, -a, -um:** *radiant, glowing, blushing.*
  pudor, -ōris (m.): *modesty.* Note the ASSONANCE and ALLITERATION drawing attention to this culminating qualification. In light of what Ovid has already said and will go on to say in this poem, this phrase is a good example of Ovid's playful self-mockery.
15 **dēsultor, -ōris (m.):** *a circus rider who leaps from horse to horse.* Ovid uses the word here to suggest an inconstant or fickle lover. It provides a very graphic image of a lover leaping from partner to partner.

tu mihi, si qua fides, cura perennis eris;
   tecum, quos dederint annos mihi fila sororum,
vivere contingat teque dolente mori;
   te mihi materiem felicem in carmina praebe:
20   provenient causa carmina digna sua.
   carmine nomen habent exterrita cornibus Io
et quam fluminea lusit adulter ave

✦ ✦ ✦

16 **qua:** *aliqua.*
    si . . . fides: another ELLIPSIS of *sum,* probably *sit.*
17 **fīlum, -ī (n.):** *thread, yarn.*
    sororum: refers to the Fates, the three sisters: Clotho, who spun; Lachesis, who measured; and Atropos, who severed the thread of life at one's birth.
18 **contingat:** a jussive subjunctive, here used impersonally.
    mori: present infinitive of *morior*; a second complementary infinitive with *contingat.*
19 **māteriēs, -ēi (f.):** *material, subject matter.*
20 **prōveniō, -īre, -vēnī, -ventum:** *to come into being, arise.*
    causa . . . sua: CHIASTIC word order.
    dignus, -a, -um: *worthy.*
21 **habent:** this verb has three subjects—*Io* (21); the clause *quam . . . ave* (22) with an understood antecedent *ea;* and the clause *quaeque . . . tenuit* (23–24), also with an understood antecedent *ea.*
    exterreō, -ēre, -uī, -itum: *to frighten, terrify.*
    Io: Io was a maiden beloved by Jupiter who, in order to hide her from Juno, transformed Io into a heifer. Juno, suspecting Jupiter's infidelity, asked for the heifer and set Argus with his hundred eyes to watch over her. Jupiter sent Hermes to kill Argus and later released Io from her disguised shape.
22 **quam:** a reference to Leda, also beloved by Jupiter, who wooed her in the guise of a swan.
    flūmineus, -a, -um: *of or pertaining to a river.*
    lusit: from *ludō, lūdere, lūsī, lūsum.*
    adulter, -erī (m.): *an adulterer.*

quaeque super pontum simulato vecta iuvenco
    virginea tenuit cornua vara manu.
25   nos quoque per totum pariter cantabimur orbem
    iunctaque semper erunt nomina nostra tuis.

✦ ✦ ✦

23 **quaeque:** refers to the maiden Europa whom Jupiter deceived in the guise of a bull.
pontus, -ī (m.): *the sea.*
vecta: from *vehō, vehere, vexī, vectum*—to carry.
iuvencus, -ī (m.): *a young bull.*

24 **virginea ... manu:** because this line is not symmetrical, it is a variation of a GOLDEN LINE—a single verb accompanied by two adjective/noun pairs. When Ovid chooses to include here three mythologial characters loved by Jupiter, he may in fact reveal a truth about the poet as lover. Io is described with the word *exterrita*, the phrase depicting Leda uses the verb *lusit*, and Jupiter is described as an *adulter* in conjunction with Leda and as *simulato* in the Europa couplet. These stories do not illustrate eternal fidelity.
vārus, -a, -um: *bent outwards.*

25 **nos:** refers both to Ovid and to his yet-to-be-revealed lover.

26 **nomina nostra:** here probably with singular intent referring specifically to the poet.

16 ✦ OVID

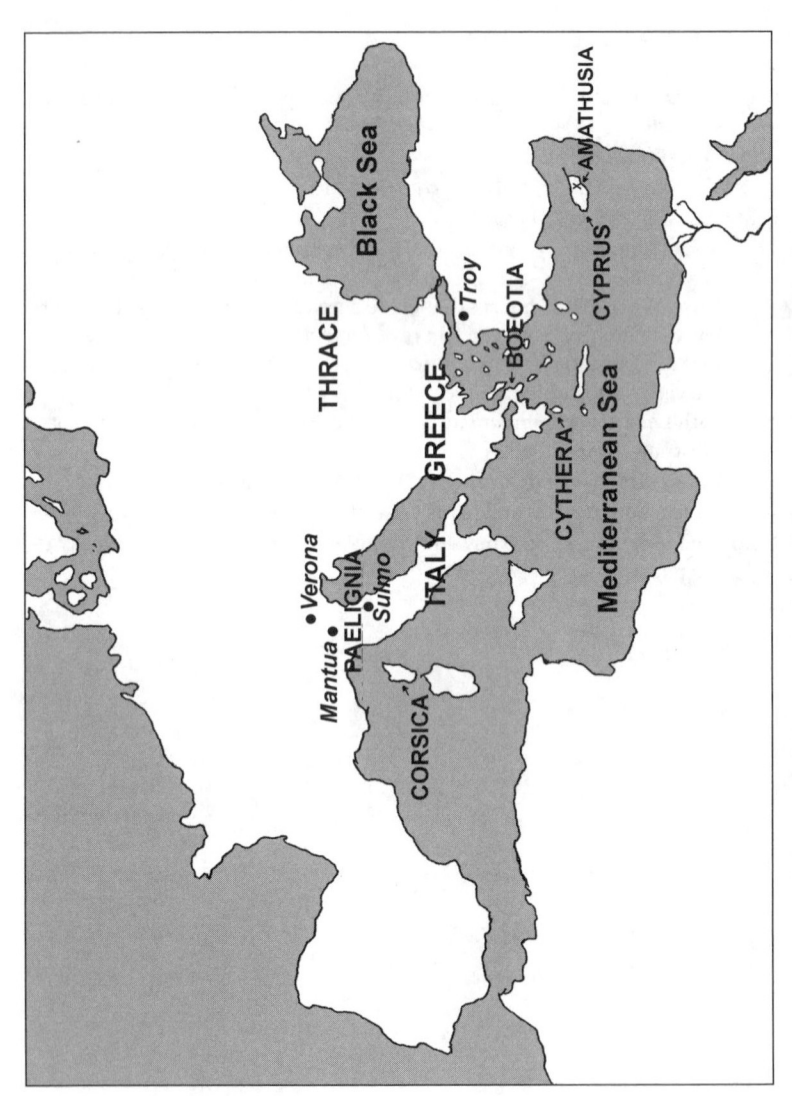

Map of Places in the Amores (except I. 1)

AMORES I. 9

Ovid addresses this poem to a man called Atticus, with the pretense that Atticus has accused the poet of devoting himself to making love and thus of leading a lazy and non-productive life. Ovid argues that the lover is a soldier and that the rigors of warfare are identical to those of love. He gives several examples of how these parallels work, and, typically, provides three mythological examples of famous warriors, Achilles, Hector, and Mars himself, who were also lovers.

Again, the poet inverts an established theme of elegiac poetry, because the conventional poetic treatment of Love and War contrasted rather than equated the two. While the traditional lover preferred *otium* to *negotium,* Ovid playfully suggests that the earnest lover is as busy as the soldier and has no time for leisure.

AMORES I. 9

Militat omnis amans, et habet sua castra Cupido;
    Attice, crede mihi, militat omnis amans.
quae bello est habilis, Veneri quoque convenit aetas:
    turpe senex miles, turpe senilis amor.
5 quos petiere duces animos in milite forti,
    hos petit in socio bella puella viro:
pervigilant ambo, terra requiescit uterque;
    ille fores dominae servat, at ille ducis.

✧ ✧ ✧

1   **mīlitō, -āre, -āvī, -ātum:** *to be a soldier, serve as a soldier.* Ovid employs a METAPHOR here, the lover as soldier/warrior. Roman poets often felt that the lover fought a kind of war either with his mistress, a rival, or his own overpowering emotion.
    amans, -ntis (m., f.): *a lover.*
    Cupido: Cupid is not so much seen by Ovid as an enemy but rather the general under whom the soldier/lover serves.
2   **Attice:** it is unusual for Ovid to have an addressee in his love elegies. It is not known, with any certainty, who Atticus was.
3   **habilis, -e:** *suitable, fit.*
    conveniō, -īre, -vēnī, -ventum: *to be suitable or adapted for.*
    aetas: the age that suits the best soldiering and lovemaking is youth, according to Ovid.
4   **turpis, -e:** *loathsome, repulsive, shameful.*
    turpe senex miles: supply a missing *est*. The neuter predicate adjective works like a noun.
    senīlis, -e: *old, aged.*
5   **petiere:** the alternate spelling for the 3rd person plural perfect active indicative, a common usage in Ovid.
6   **bella:** a wordplay of both sound and sense. The striking ASSONANCE with *puella* and the hint of *bellum* draw attention to the replacement of the general Cupid by the girl.
7   **ambō, -ae, -ō:** *both.*
    terra: poetic use of the ablative of place where without a preposition.
8   **ille, ille:** the first refers to the lover (*amans*) and the second to the soldier (*miles*).
    foris, foris (f.): *door, double door.*

AMORES I. 9 ✦ 19

militis officium longa est via: mitte puellam, → *Imperative*
   strenuus exempto fine sequetur amans;   10
ibit in adversos montes duplicataque nimbo
   flumina, congestas exteret ille nives,
nec freta pressurus tumidos causabitur Euros → *Deponent (Fut)*
   aptave verrendis sidera quaeret aquis.
quis nisi vel miles vel amans et frigora noctis → *Gerundive* 15
   et denso mixtas perferet imbre nives?
mittitur infestos alter speculator in hostes,
   in rivale oculos alter, ut hoste, tenet.
ille graves urbes, hic durae limen amicae
   obsidet; hic portas frangit, at ille fores.   20

(Ablative absolute — annotation on *exempto fine*)
(*Distributed* — annotation on *ille...hic...hic...ille*)

✦ ✦ ✦

9   **mitte:** here in the sense of dispatching, sending away or ahead.
10 **eximō, -ere, -ēmī, -emptum:** *to take away.*
11 **duplicō, -āre, -āvī, -ātum:** *to double in size or amount.*
     nimbus, -ī (m.): *cloudburst, rainstorm.*
12 **congestus, -a, -um:** *piled up.*
     exterō, -ere, -trīvī, -trītum: *to wear down, trample on.*
     nix, nivis (f.): *snow.*
13 **fretum, -ī (n.):** *strait, sea.*
     premō, -ere, pressī, -ssum: *to press on, push.*
     causor, -ārī, -ātus: *to plead as an excuse or reason.*
     tumidos: used in an active sense of causing the sea to swell.
     Eurus, -ī (m.): *the east wind.*
14 **aptave ... sidera:** constellations, which would suggest favorable conditions for sailing.
     aptus, -a, -um: (+ dat.) *appropriate, fitting, suited.*
     -ve (conj.): *or.*
     verrō, -ere, versum: *to pass over, skim, sweep, row.*
     sīdus, -eris (n.): *constellation.*
15 **frīgus, -oris (n.):** *cold, chill.*
16 **et ... nives:** a variation on a GOLDEN LINE in INTERLOCKED WORD ORDER.
     perferō, -ferre, -tulī, -lātum: *to suffer, endure, undergo.*
17 **speculātor, -ōris (m.):** *a scout, spy.*
18 **rīvalis, -is (m.):** *a rival.*
20 **obsideō, -ēre, -sēdī, -sessus:** *to beseige.*
     at ille fores: there is an ELLIPSIS in this phrase. Supply another *frangit.*

saepe soporatos invadere profuit hostes
    caedere et armata vulgus inerme manu.
sic fera Threicii ceciderunt agmina Rhesi,
    et dominum capti deseruistis equi.
25 nempe maritorum somnis utuntur amantes
    et sua sopitis hostibus arma movent.
custodum transire manus vigilumque catervas
    militis et miseri semper amantis opus.
Mars dubius, nec certa Venus: victique resurgunt,
30   quosque neges umquam posse iacere, cadunt.
ergo desidiam quicumque vocabat amorem,
    desinat: ingenii est experientis Amor.

21 **sopōrō, -āre, -āvī, -ātum:** *to put asleep.*
    invādō, -ere, -vāsī, -vāsum: *to attack, set on.*
    prōsum, -desse, -fuī, -futūrus: *to be advantageous, helpful, useful.*
22 **armata . . . manu:** CHIASMUS.
23 **ferus, -a, -um:** *fierce, savage, wild.*
    Thrēicius, -a, -um: *from Thrace,* a region northeast of Greece.
    Rhēsus, -ī (m.): *a Thracian who fought on the side of the Trojans.* Odysseus and Diomedes sneaked into his camp at night, slaughtered his men, and stole his famous white chariot horses.
    sic . . . Rhesi: a variant of a GOLDEN LINE in INTERLOCKED WORD ORDER.
24 **deserō, -ere, -uī, -tum:** *to abandon, leave.* Here, an APOSTROPHE enveloped by the vocative *capti . . . equi.*
25 **nempe (conj.):** *to be sure, yet, certainly.*
    somnis: perhaps a sleepiness induced by too much strong wine at dinner.
26 **sōpītus, -a, -um:** *sleepy.* Recalls the *soporatos hostes* of 21.
27 **transeō, -īre, -īvī, -ītum:** *to cross, go across.* The subject of a missing *est* to be supplied in line 28.
    vigil, -ilis (m.): *guard, sentry.*
29 **dubius, -a, -um:** *uncertain, wavering.*
    resurgō, -ere, -surrexī, -surrectum: *to rise up again.*
30 **neges:** a subjunctive in a relative clause of characteristic.
31 **dēsīdia, -ae (f.):** *idleness, inactivity, leisure.*
    quicumque: presumably *Atticus* of line 2.
32 **desinat:** a jussive subjunctive.
    ingenii . . . experientis: genitive of quality or description.

AMORES I. 9 ✦ 21

ardet in abducta Briseide magnus Achilles
   (dum licet, Argeas frangite, Troes, opes);
35 Hector ab Andromaches complexibus ibat ad arma,
   et galeam capiti quae daret, uxor erat;
   summa ducum, Atrides visa Priameide fertur
     Maenadis effusis obstipuisse comis.
   Mars quoque deprensus fabrilia vincula sensit:
40   notior in caelo fabula nulla fuit.

✦ ✦ ✦

33 **abdūcō, -ere, -dūxī, -ductum:** *to carry off.*
    Brīsēis, -idis (f.): *Achilles's slave and lover* whom Agamemnon stole but later returned. Ablative of cause with *in*.
    Achillēs, -is (m.): *Greek hero of the Trojan War, son of Peleus and Thetis.* When Agamemnon stole Briseis, Achilles sulked in his tent, refusing to fight and later even refused to take her back. He was eventually killed in battle by the Trojan Paris.
34 **Argēus, -a, -um:** *Greek.*
    frangite: APOSTROPHE.
    Trōs, -ōis (m.): *Trojan.*
35 **Hector, -oris (m.):** *prince of Troy, eldest son of Priam.* He fought valiantly to save Troy but was defeated and killed by Achilles.
    Andromachē, -ēs (f.): *wife of Hector.*
36 **galea, -ae (f.):** *helmet.*
    daret: subjunctive in a relative clause of characteristic.
37 **summa:** a nominative neuter plural standing in apposition to the masculine singular *Atrides*.
    Atrīdēs, -ae (m.): *a descendant of Atreus,* usually used of Agamemnon.
    Priamēis, -idos (f.): *Cassandra,* daughter of Priam, king of Troy. She was carried off as a prize of war by Agamemnon; however, both the hero and his lover were murdered by Clytemnestra, his wife, when they reached Greece.
38 **Maenas, -adis (f.):** *a female worshipper of Bacchus, a Bacchante, Maenad.* The association here is due most likely to the loose, flowing hair common to both the Maenads and Cassandra, a sign of madness in both.
    obstipēscō, -ere, -stipuī: *to be amazed, astonished.*
    coma, -ae (f.): *hair.*
39 **Mars . . . sensit:** refers to the story of Mars and Venus who were caught in an adulterous affair by means of a fine mesh net forged by Venus's husband, Vulcan.
    dēprendō, -dere, -dī, -sum: *to catch, discover.*
    fabrīlis, -e: *of or pertaining to a metal worker, skilled, fabricated.*
    vinculum, -ī (n.): *chain, bond.*

ipse ego segnis eram discinctaque in otia natus;
mollierant animos lectus et umbra meos;
impulit ignavum formosae cura puellae,
iussit et in castris aera merere suis.
45   inde vides agilem nocturnaque bella gerentem:
qui nolet fieri desidiosus, amet.

✦ ✦ ✦

41   **segnis, -e:** *inactive, sluggish.*
discinctus, -a, -um: *undisciplined, easygoing.*
ōtium, -ī (n.): *leisure.*
natus: perfect participle of *nascor*, used as an adjective.
42   **molliō, -īre, -īvī, -ītum:** *to soften, weaken, enfeeble.*
lectus et umbra: HENDIADYS. The two nouns carry the meaning of a single, modified noun, a shady couch.
43   **impellō, -ere, -pulī, -pulsum:** *to push, urge on.*
ignavum: modifies an assumed *me*.
formōsus, -a, -um: *beautiful.*
44   **in castris ... suis:** reminiscent of *sua castra* (1). This wording returns the reader to the original intent of the poem.
aes, aeris (n.): *money, pay.*
45   **vides:** perhaps addressing *Atticus*.
agilis, -e: *active, busy.*
46   **amet:** a jussive subjunctive.

AMORES I. 11

In poem I. 5 Ovid finally tells us that his mistress's name is Corinna. *Amores* I. 11 is addressed to Corinna's maid Nape. In it, the poet flatters Nape, calling her *docta, cognita utilis,* and *ingeniosa,* in order to obtain her aid in carrying to Corinna a message in which the poet requests a night with her. Ovid suggests that Nape's own experiences with love oblige her to support his suit. Having gained Nape as his ally, the poet provides detailed instructions on how and when his message can best be delivered. His repeated requests that the maid use all haste are emphasized when he directs her to elicit from Corinna a simple, single word reply: "come." In a final humorous appeal for divine aid in his mission, the poet promises to dedicate his message tablets to Venus, should he be successful.

Throughout this poem, the poet argues that he desperately needs Corinna; surprisingly, he presents this argument to her maid, for he provides no clue to what is actually written on the tablets. He again exploits the traditional subject matter of elegiac love poetry: here, the theme of "carpe diem" is used to convince the girl to enjoy love while there is still time.

AMORES I. 11

Colligere incertos et in ordine ponere crines
    docta neque ancillas inter habenda Nape
inque ministeriis furtivae cognita noctis
    utilis et dandis ingeniosa notis,
5   saepe venire ad me dubitantem hortata Corinnam,
    saepe laboranti fida reperta mihi,

✦ ✦ ✦

1   **colligō, -ere, -lēgī, -lectum:** *to gather.*
    incertus, -a, -um: *disarranged, not fixed.*
2   **docta:** Ovid begins with a compliment to Corinna's maid in an attempt to win her favor and support.
    ancillas: placed before the preposition.
    neque ... habenda: note that this participle is negative, i.e., Nape is no common handmaid like others. It is another flattery on Ovid's part.
    Napē, -ēs (f.): one of Corinna's personal maids who acts as a go-between for Ovid and his mistress. His flattery continues as he addresses her as more than a simple hairdresser—a conspirator.
3   **ministerium, -ī (n.):** *office, duty.*
    furtīvus, -a, -um: *clandestine, secret.* Although this genitive modifies *noctis*, its placement attracts its meaning also to *ministeriis*.
4   **utilis:** predicate adjective with *cognita*. Suppy a missing *esse* to join the two.
    ingeniōsus, -a, -um: *clever.*
    nota, -ae (f.): *a note.*
5   **Corinnam:** the first time we have seen Ovid's mistress's name.
6   **saepe:** ANAPHORA serving to emphasize Ovid's meaning here as well as to unite the couplet.
    laboranti: perhaps meant to recall the activities of both soldiers and lovers as expressed in *Amores* I. 9.
    fīdus, -a, -um: *faithful, loyal.*
    reperiō, -īre, repperī, repertum: *to find, discover.*

accipe et ad dominam peraratas mane tabellas
    perfer et obstantes sedula pelle moras.
nec silicum venae nec durum in pectore ferrum
10   nec tibi simplicitas ordine maior adest;
credibile est et te sensisse Cupidinis arcus:

✤ ✤ ✤

7 **dominam:** refers to Nape's mistress who is Ovid's as well.
perārō, -āre, -āvī, -ātum: *to plow through, inscribe.*
tabella, -ae (f.): these are the pair of wooden tablets, each half covered on one side with wax, in which Ovid's message was engraved with a writing stylus. The tablets were then tied together with the message concealed in the middle. The METAPHOR from plowing suits since a metal plow furrows through the earth just as the stylus scratches its way through the surface of the wax leaving behind its message. It is also a fine example of Ovid's applying a rather ordinary word to a novel situation.

8 **obstō, -āre, -itī, -ātum:** *to stand in the way, block the path.*
sēdulus, -a, -um: *attentive, persistent.*
pelle: the third imperative in two lines and the second in this line emphasizes the haste Ovid feels to communicate with his mistress. The imperatives combined with *obstantes . . . moras* give a graphic image of the poet's urgency.

9 **silex, -icis (m.):** *hard rock or stone, flint.*
vēna, -ae (f.): *blood vessel, vein;* the first element in a TRICOLON CRESCENDO.
ferrum, -ī (n.): *iron, steel.*

10 **tibi:** dative of possession with a compound of *sum.*
adest: singular verb with multiple subjects: *venae* (9), *ferrum* (9), and *simplicitas* (10).

11 **arcus, -ūs (m.):** *a bow.*
Cupidinis arcus: reminiscent of *Amores* I. 9 when Ovid sees himself as a soldier in Cupid's army, as well as of I. 1 when Ovid first feels the sting of Cupid's arrows. In employing the METAPHOR here Ovid includes Nape as a fellow soldier/lover, creating an even closer link with her and garnering yet more favor.

in me militiae signa tuere tuae.
si quaeret quid agam, spe noctis vivere dices;
cetera fert blanda cera notata manu.
15 dum loquor, hora fugit: vacuae bene redde tabellas,
verum continuo fac tamen illa legat.
aspicias oculos mando frontemque legentis:
et tacito vultu scire futura licet.

✢ ✢ ✢

12 **mīlitia, -ae (f.):** *military service.*
tueor, -ērī, tuitus: *to observe, watch over, guard.* Here, the imperative singular.
13 **quaeret:** assume a missing *ea* as subject.
quid agam: present subjunctive in an indirect question. An idiomatic expression here meaning "how I am doing."
spēs, -eī (f.): *hope.*
spe noctis: this love affair, like most carried on with married women, occurs under the cover of darkness.
vivere: Ovid here suggests that his very existence is dependent on this love affair.
14 **cetera:** scan the line carefully to determine the quantity of all the final -*a*'s in this line heavy with ASSONANCE.
blandus, -a, -um: *charming, seductive.*
cēra, -ae (f.): *wax, beeswax;* but here meaning the letter inscribed in the wax.
15 **dum . . . fugit:** a variation on the *carpe diem* theme used by the lover to persuade his mistress to yield to him.
vacuae: dative with *redde* referring to his mistress.
bene: note the correspondence between the meaning of the line and the fast pace created by repeated DACTYLS.
16 **verum (conj.):** *but.*
continuō (adv.): *immediately, forthwith, without delay.*
legat: present subjunctive in an indirect command after the imperative *fac* without *ut*.
17 **aspicias:** present subjunctive after *mando* without the *ut*, as often in poetry.
mandō, -āre, -āvī, -ātum: *to order, bid.*

nec mora, perlectis rescribat multa iubeto:
20   odi, cum late splendida cera vacat.
comprimat ordinibus versus, oculosque moretur
    margine in extremo littera †rasa† meos.
quid digitos opus est graphio lassare tenendo?

✧ ✧ ✧

19 **nec mora:** supply *sit* as the verb in this negative purpose clause.
    rescribat: present subjunctive in an indirect command with the *ut* omitted.
    iubeto: a future imperative. Ovid's fourth command in the last three couplets.
20 **ōdī, odisse, ōsum:** *to hate, dislike.*
    splendidus, -a, -um: *bright, shining.*
    vacō, -āre, -āvī, -ātum: *to be empty, vacant, unfilled.* Note the slow rhythm in the first half of the line created by repeated SPONDEES reflecting the poet's displeasure.
21 **comprimō, -ere, -pressī, -pressum:** *to pack closely or densely.* Here, a jussive subjunctive.
    versus: these are not necessarily verses of poetry but simply lines of writing. The image contrasts with *splendida cera vacat* (20).
    moretur: subject is *littera* (22); another jussive subjunctive. The abrupt change of subject here suggests the eagerness with which the lover addresses Nape.
22 **margō, -inis (m.):** *margin.*
    extrēmus, -a, -um: *farthest.*
    rādō, -ere, rāsī, -sum: *to rub out or erase; to scratch* but here assumed to mean "inscribed" by the context, although an erasure may suggest a carefully thought-out composition. In either case the poet is suggesting that he wants an extensive reply from his lover. The daggers show that modern editors are uncertain whether *rasa* is the correct reading.
    meos: The exaggerated separation of the adjective from its noun lends even more intensity to the lover's eagerness for a response.
23 **graphium, -ī (n.):** *stylus*—a sharp, pointed instrument used for incising letters onto waxed writing tablets.
    lassō, -āre, -āvī, -ātum: *to tire, exhaust.*

hoc habeat scriptum tota tabella "veni."
25 non ego victrices lauro redimire tabellas
nec Veneris media ponere in aede morer.
subscribam VENERI FIDAS SIBI NASO MINISTRAS
DEDICAT. AT NUPER VILE FUISTIS ACER.

✣ ✣ ✣

24 **habeat:** a jussive subjunctive.
veni: from first fearing that the wax tablets will return to him empty in line 20, to requesting that Corinna fill them as full as possible with writing in lines 21–22, Ovid at last decides that he would prefer the tablets to return with but one word written on them.
25 **victrix, -īcis:** *victorious*.
lauro: this was the plant used to crown victorious generals and it also crowned their dispatches reporting their victories to the Roman Senate.
redimiō, -īre, -iī, -ītum: *to wreathe, encircle*.
26 **Veneris . . . morer:** Ovid here mimics the custom of triumphant generals who dedicated their laurels to Jupiter in his temple on the Capitoline Hill.
morer: potential subjunctive.
27 **sibi:** dative with *fidas* referring to the subject *Naso*.
Naso: Publius Ovidius Naso, nominative.
28 **vīlis, -e:** *worthless, common, ordinary*.
fuistis: PERSONIFICATION.
acer, -eris (n.): maple wood.

AMORES I. 12

In poem I. 11, the poet asks Nape to deliver a message to his mistress; in I. 12 we learn that Corinna has replied that she is unable to entertain her lover today. Ovid initially scolds the hapless Nape for tripping as she carried the tablets, thus bringing bad luck to his message, and even implies that she was drunk when she set out. He then devotes the major portion of this poem to a long and detailed curse directed against the wax and wood on which the poet's message was incised. Both wax and wood are described as ominous and death-bearing, and the poet castigates himself for having chosen to send a love message on such deadly materials.

When Ovid curses the writing tablets that provoked his lover's rebuke, he employs another conventional topic of lyric and elegiac poetry. Both Propertius (III. 23) and Horace (*Carm.* II. 13) had made similar protests. In this poem, Ovid's humorous and exaggerated anger is not that of a miserably disappointed lover; rather his "anger" is constructed to showcase the poet's skill and versatility and reflects his pleasure in his own clever virtuosity.

AMORES I. 12

Flete meos casus: tristes rediere tabellae;
　　infelix hodie littera posse negat.
omina sunt aliquid: modo cum discedere vellet,
　　ad limen digitos restitit icta Nape.
5　missa foras iterum limen transire memento
　　cautius atque alte sobria ferre pedem.

✦ ✦ ✦

1　**flete:** the appeal for sympathy in an otherwise lighthearted treatment establishes exaggerated emotional outburst as the poet's main device in this poem.
rediere: the 3rd person plural perfect active alternate form.
tabella, -ae (f.): *writing tablet.*
2　**infēlix, -icis:** *unhappy, ill-fated.*
littera: the singular is used here to denote the whole of the writing.
posse negat: an indirect statement with the subject understood.
3　**modo (adv.):** *just now, recently.*
vellet: imperfect subjunctive used in a *cum*-circumstantial clause. Here it means "starting to."
4　**ad ... Nape:** the unusual initial SPONDEE and the repetitions of *i* and *t* mimic and intensify Nape's stumbling.
digitos: a Greek accusative (used of the part of the body affected, i.e., the toes) with the perfect participle *icta*.
restō, -āre, -itī: *to linger, remain; to stop.*
iciō, -ere, īcī, ictum: *to strike.*
5　**memento:** a future active imperative which, with this verb, will translate as the present tense.
6　**altē (adv.):** *at a great height.*
sōbrius, -a, -um: *sober, not intoxicated.* Perhaps the first time Nape set out on her mission she was not completely sober. If so, her tripping on the threshold would more likely suggest human frailty rather than divine intervention. Ovid here paints a quite different picture of this same maid from that of I. 11.

ite hinc, difficiles, funebria ligna, tabellae,
   tuque, negaturis cera referta notis,
quam, puto, de longae collectam flore cicutae
10   melle sub infami Corsica misit apis.
at tamquam minio penitus medicata rubebas:

✦ ✦ ✦

7   **hinc:** *from here, from this place.*
    difficiles ... tabellae: two vocative plural pairs in CHIASTIC word order personifying the tablets.
    lignum, -ī (n.): *wood.*
8   **tuque:** vocative singular personifying the *cera referta*.
    negaturis ... notis: Ovid continues the vocative reprimand in CHIASTIC word order intensifying his displeasure by the use of ASSONANCE.
    cēra, -ae (f.): *wax.*
    nota, -ae (f.): *note, mark.*
    cera referta: vocative singular.
9   **puto:** suggests that Ovid may not be completely serious in what he says about the wax. Note the SYSTOLE in this metrical foot which scans as a DACTYL.
    colligō, -ere, -lēgī, -lectum: *to gather together, collect.*
    cicūta, -ae (f.): *poisonous hemlock (Conium maculatum).* Hemlock was given to criminals as poison. The most well-known individual to die from hemlock poisoning was Socrates. The plant was also considered to be an antaphrodisiac and thus might have contributed to the cause of Corinna's refusal.
10 **mel, mellis (n.):** *honey.*
    infāmis, -e: *infamous, disgraced.* Corsican honey was infamous for being bitter, due, according to ancient sources, to the large number of box trees, yew trees, and thyme on the island (McKeown, 328).
    Corsicus, -a, -um: *of or belonging to the island of Corsica* off the western coast of Italy, north of Sardinia.
    apis, -is (f.): *a bee.*
11 **minium, -ī (n.):** *cinnabar, a bright red dye.*
    medicō, -āre, -āvī, -ātum: *to dye.*
    rubeō, -ēre: *to turn bright red.* Directed to the wax which, unlike ordinary wax that was dyed black, was red.

32 ✦ OVID

       ille color vere sanguinulentus erat.
   proiectae triviis iaceatis, inutile lignum,
       vosque rotae frangat praetereuntis onus.
15   illum etiam, qui vos ex arbore vertit in usum,
       convincam puras non habuisse manus.
   praebuit illa arbor misero suspendia collo,
       carnifici diras praebuit illa cruces;
   illa dedit turpes raucis bubonibus umbras,

✦ ✦ ✦

12   **color, -ōris (m.):** *color, pigment.*
      vērē (adv.): *truly, indeed.*
      sanguinulentus, -a, -um: *blood-red, crimson.* This adjective is suggestive of the deadly power of these tablets already mentioned, *funebria ligna* (7).
13   **prōiciō, -ere, -iēcī, -iectum:** *to fling to the ground.* There is no expressed noun in this couplet for this adjective to modify. Supply a missing *tabellae.*
      trivium, -ī (n.): *the meeting place of three roads; a crossroads.*
      iaceatis: addresses the supplied *tabellae* in a jussive subjunctive. A continuation of the PERSONIFICATION.
      inūtilis, -e: *useless.*
14   **frangat:** another jussive subjunctive.
16   **convincō, -ere, -vīcī, -victum:** *to prove, demonstrate.*
17   **suspendium, -ī (n.):** *hanging* (as a means of execution or suicide.)
      collum, -ī (n.): *the neck.*
18   **carnifex, -ficis (m.):** *an executioner.*
      dīrus, -a, -um: *awful, dreadful, frightful.*
      crux, -ucis (f.): *a wooden frame or cross on which criminals were hanged or impaled.*
19   **turpis, -e:** *loathsome, repulsive, shameful.*
      turpes ... umbras: CHIASTIC word order.
      raucus, -a, -um: *harsh-sounding, raucous.*
      būbō, -ōnis (m.): *the horned owl;* its call sounded funereal and was considered a bad omen.

20   vulturis in ramis et strigis ova tulit.
          his ego commisi nostros insanus amores
             molliaque ad dominam verba ferenda dedi?
          aptius hae capiant vadimonia garrula cerae,
             quas aliquis duro cognitor ore legat;
25   inter ephemeridas melius tabulasque iacerent,
             in quibus absumptas fleret avarus opes.
          ergo ego vos rebus duplices pro nomine sensi:

✦ ✦ ✦

20   **vultur, -uris (m.):** *a vulture.* These are birds of prey and hence were believed to be evil.
       rāmus, -ī (m.): *a branch.*
       strix, -igis (f.): *an owl, screech-owl.* The Romans believed these birds attacked infants in their cradles (Barsby, 137).
21   **his:** note the first position prominence in this clause.
       nostros . . . amores: poetic use of the plural.
       insānus, -a, -um: *frenzied, mad.*
23   **aptus, -a, -um:** (+ dat.) *fit, suitable, appropriate.*
       capiant: a potential subjunctive.
       vadimōnium, -ī (n.): *a legal term referring to an agreement of both parties in a legal suit to appear in court on an appointed day.*
       garrulus, -a, -um: *loquacious.* This word contrasts with the one-word reply Ovid had hoped for in I. 11.
24   **aliquis . . . ore:** INTERLOCKED WORD ORDER (SYNCHESIS).
       cognitor, -ōris (m.): *a legal representative, attorney.*
       legat: subjunctive by attraction, dependent on the subjunctive in line 23.
25   **ephēmeris, -idos (f.):** *a record book, day book.*
       iacerent: a potential subjunctive expressing past time.
26   **absumō, -ere, -sumpsī, -sumptum:** *to use up, spend, squander.*
       fleret: imperfect subjunctive again by attraction, dependent on *iacerent* (25).
       avārus, -a, -um: *greedy, avaricious, miserly.*
27   **duplex, -icis:** *two-faced, deceitful.* The adjective is used here both in its figurative sense in that the tablets have not delivered the message the poet had hoped for and in its literal sense since there are two halves to the tablets.

auspicii numerus non erat ipse boni.
quid precer iratus, nisi vos cariosa senectus
30   rodat, et immundo cera sit alba situ?

✦ ✦ ✦

28 **auspicium, -ī (n.):** *portent, fortune, luck*—with *boni,* a genitive of quality (descriptive genitive).
29 **precor, -ārī, -ātus:** *to pray for, implore, beg.* Here, a deliberative subjunctive.
   cariōsus, -a, -um: *decayed.*
   senectūs, -ūtis (f.): *old age.*
30 **rōdō, -ere, rōsī, -sum:** *to eat away, erode.* Here, an optative subjunctive, as is *sit.*
   immundus, -a, -um: *unclean, foul.*

AMORES II. 19

In this final poem of Book II of the *Amores*, Ovid develops yet another variation of a theme that pervades all three books: the constant impediments and ups and downs in any love affair, especially one with a married woman. He has previously explored such topics as the inability to come to his beloved because of the efforts of a zealous and careful doorkeeper or those of a eunuch-chaperon, his own promiscuity, his beloved's flirtations with another man, and geographic separation. In II. 19, constructing a highly ironic paradox, Ovid rebukes Corinna's husband for not guarding her closely enough, and urges him to tighten his guard of her, lest Ovid lose interest in her. Ovid chooses this topic to demonstrate his versatility: he is a master of the art of *variatio* or variation, a canonical standard of Latin elegiac poetry. By poem III. 12, Ovid has fully explored every possibility for variation in a love poem, and his apparently fictitious affair has come to an end.

In poem II. 19 Ovid also employs the rhetorical device of *suasoria* or persuasive argument. The poet begins by addressing Corinna's husband, rebuking him for his carelessness (1–8). Ovid explains that he needs to be frustrated and hurt in order to love. Next, he devotes a section describing the wisdom of Corinna, who plays both easy to seduce *and* hard to get in order to keep him interested (9–18). Lines 19–36 provide an extended comment on Corinna's successful techniques, accompanied by two mythological examples. Finally (37–60), the poet returns to his *suasoria*, again rebuking the husband and summing up his argument emphatically (60):

> me tibi rivalem si iuvat esse, veta!
> If you want me for your rival, forbid me!

AMORES II. 19

Si tibi non opus est servata, stulte, puella,
  at mihi fac serves, quo magis ipse velim.
quod licet, ingratum est; quod non licet, acrius urit:
  ferreus est, si quis quod sinit alter, amat.
5 speremus pariter, pariter metuamus amantes,
  et faciat voto rara repulsa locum.

✢ ✢ ✢

1   In the first two lines of the elegy, Ovid establishes the paradox that drives the poem—a clever variation of the theme of the excluded lover. Here it is the very exclusion of the lover that makes him desire the girl he loves. In the first eight lines Ovid addresses his lover's husband.
   servata . . . puella: ablatives after *opus est* expressing need.
   stulte: typically in elegy a foolish husband, one who does not guard his wife carefully.
   puella: In elegiac poetry, a *puella*, is more than just a girl—the word can be used for both wife and mistress.

2   **at:** here best translated as *at least*.
   fac serves: an informal construction for *fac ut serves*, an indirect command.
   quo magis velim: a relative clause of result.

3   **ūrō, -ere, ussī, ūssus:** *to burn, to inflame with passion*.

4   **ferreus . . . amat:** contains a HYPERBATON.
   ferreus: suggests a man whose feelings lack refinement and has a heart as hard as iron.

5   **speremus . . . metuamus:** note the CHIASTIC word order and the emotional contrast. The lover is always poised between hope and fear. Both verbs are hortatory subjunctives. This line contains the paradox that first appears in line 2.
   pariter (adv.): *at the same time*.

6   **vōtum, -ī (n.):** *desire*.
   repulsa, -ae (f.): *refusal, denial*. An occasional rebuff makes the lover work even harder to win the girl's affections.

quo mihi fortunam, quae numquam fallere curet?
　　nil ego quod nullo tempore laedat amo.
viderat hoc in me vitium versuta Corinna,
10　　quaque capi possem callida norat opem.
a, quotiens sani capitis mentita dolores
　　cunctantem tardo iussit abire pede!
a, quotiens finxit culpam, quantumque licebat
　　insonti, speciem praebuit esse nocens!

✦ ✦ ✦

7　**quo mihi fortunam:** an idiomatic use of the dative of reference—*of what use to me is fortune?*
　　fallō, -ere, fefellī, falsum: *deceive, trick; to fail.*
　　curet: subjunctive in a relative clause of characteristic. The poet here suggests that perfect good fortune is boring.
8　**quod . . . laedat:** another relative clause of characteristic. Note the HYPERBATON in this line. The object of *amo,* the last word in the line, is *nil,* the first word in the line.
9　**vitium, -ī (n.):** *defect, fault; vice, moral failing.*
　　versutus, -a, -um: *shrewd, clever, ingenious.*
　　Corinna, -ae (f.): Ovid's beloved, his *puella,* whom he first names in *Amores* I. 5.
10　**qua:** the antecedent for this feminine relative pronoun is *ops*. This line encompasses a HYSTERON PROTERON.
　　possem: subjuctive in a relative clause of characteristic.
　　callidus, -a, -um: *clever, resourceful.*
　　noscō, -ere, nōvī, nōtum: *to learn; to know.* Here the syncopated third person plural pluperfect active.
　　ops, opis (f.): *ability, ruse, trick.*
11　**a, quotiens:** when repeated in line 13, creates an ANAPHORA.
　　mentior, -īrī, -ītum: *to pretend, tell a lie.* Supply a missing *est* to complete this verb form. This protestation is age-old.
12　**cunctor, -ārī, -ātus:** *to linger, hesitate.* The SPONDEES in the first half of the PENTAMETER reinforce the poet's reluctance to leave.
13　**fingō, -ere, finxī, fictus:** *to invent, feign.* Corinna pretends to be unfaithful—she plays Ovid's game.
14　**insons, -ntis:** *guiltless, innocent.*
　　speciēs, -iēī (f.): *appearance, impression.*
　　nocens, -entis: *hurtful, injurious; guilty.* Here a predicate nominative after *esse*. This use of the nominative is a "Hellenizing construction" that Ovid employs several times in his poetry according to McKeown. (*Ovid. Amores Volume III. A Commentary on Book Two,* 413).

15   sic ubi vexarat tepidosque refoverat ignes,
            rursus erat votis comis et apta meis.
       quas mihi blanditias, quam dulcia verba parabat!
            oscula, di magni, qualia quotque dabat!
       tu quoque, quae nostros rapuisti nuper ocellos,
20   saepe time simulans, saepe rogata nega,
       et sine me ante tuos proiectum in limine postes
            longa pruinosa frigora nocte pati.
       sic mihi durat amor longosque adolescit in annos;
            hoc iuvat; haec animi sunt alimenta mei.

✦ ✦ ✦

15 **refoveō, -ēre, -ōvī, -ōtum:** *to rekindle, restore, revive.* A compound verb first coined by Ovid. The two pluperfect verbs in this line, following *ubi*, indicate repeated actions.
16 **cōmis, -is, -e:** *loving, affable.*
17 **quas, quam:** These accusative relative adjectives are exclamatory and introduce relative clauses of characteristic in the indicative, emphasizing the factual and hence believable nature of the assertions.
18 **di magni:** a rare and colloquial interjection.
19 **tu quoque:** Having addressed Corinna's husband in lines 1–9, Ovid now speaks directly to her.
    ocellus, -ī (m.): *a little eye.*
20 **saepe . . . saepe:** ANAPHORA. The repetition underscores the need for Corinna to have constant vigilance in playing the game of love.
21 **sine:** here the present imperative of *sinō.*
22 **pruīnōsus, -a, -um:** *frosty.* Part of a TRANSFERRED EPITHET in INTERLOCKED WORD ORDER. Logically the *longa* should be modifying *nocte* rather than *frigora.*
23 **dūrō, -āre, -āvī, -ātum:** *to endure, persevere.*
    adolescō, -ere, -ēvī: *to grow, increase.*
24 **hoc:** neuter nominative singular representing the assertion in line 23 — Ovid's love endures and grows.
    iuvō, -āre, iuvī, iutum: *to give pleasure to, to please.*
    haec: neuter nominative plural standing collectively for the list of clever tricks used by Corinna to seduce Ovid in lines 11–23.
    alimentum, -ī (n.): *nourishment, food.* This word foreshadows the food METAPHOR that follows in lines 24–25. Love, according to Ovid, must be hungry, not fat, lest its nourishment be oversweet and boredom ensue.

25   pinguis amor nimiumque patens in taedia nobis
            vertitur et, stomacho dulcis ut esca, nocet.
        si numquam Danaen habuisset aenea turris,
            non esset Danae de Iove facta parens;
        dum servat Iuno mutatam cornibus Io,
30   facta est quam fuerat, gratior illa Iovi.
        quod licet et facile est quisquis cupit, arbore frondes
            carpat et e magno flumine potet aquam.
        siqua volet regnare diu, deludat amantem.

✦ ✦ ✦

25 **taedium, -ī (n.):** *weariness, tediousness.*
26 **esca, -ae (f.):** *food.*
27 **Danaē, -es (f.):** *Danae.* She was shut up in a tower by her father Acrisius lest she bear him a son who would kill him. She was impregnated by Jupiter, who entered her tower disguised as a shower of gold. She bore Perseus, who accidentally killed Acrisius thus fulfilling the oracle's prophecy. Ovid alludes to this story in *Met.* IV. 611ff.
    aeneus, -a, -um: *bronze.*
    turris, -is (f.): *tower.*
29 **cornu, -ūs (n.):** *horn.*
    Iō, Iūs (f.): *Io,* daughter of Inachus, king of Argos. Jupiter saw her and desired her. To prevent Juno from discovering Io, Jupiter changes her into a cow. In bovine form she wandered all over Asia Minor until she reached Egypt where she was changed back to human form by Jupiter and gave birth to a son, Epaphus. Ovid tells her story in *Met.* I. 588ff. In this line, *Io* is in the accusative case.
30 Contains both HYPERBATON and HYPERBOLE—i.e., Io was even more attractive to Jupiter as a cow.
31 **quod . . . est:** object of *quisquis cupit.*
32 **carpō, -ere, -sī, -tum:** *seize, pluck.* A jussive subjunctive as is *potet.* The references here to drinking water from a large river and to gathering leaves from a tree are analogous to the proverbial saying "bringing coals to Newcastle (a major coal mining center)." A girl who is easy to get is no challenge.
    pōtō, -āre, -āvī, -ātum: *to drink.*
33 **qua:** note the alternate form, replacing *quae,* for this feminine nominative singular pronoun and the reference to the royal power of the beloved.
    deludō, -ere, -sī, -sum: *to mock, deceive, delude.* Ovid wants Corinna to appear to be unfaithul to him, not to be so truly.

(ei mihi, ne monitis torquear ipse meis!)
35 quidlibet eveniat, nocet indulgentia nobis:
       quod sequitur, fugio; quod fugit, ipse sequor.
    At tu, formosae nimium secure puellae,
       incipe iam prima claudere nocte forem;
    incipe, quis totiens furtim tua limina pulset,
40   quaerere, quid latrent nocte silente canes,
    quas ferat et referat sollers ancilla tabellas,
       cur totiens vacuo secubet ipsa toro.
    mordeat ista tuas aliquando cura medullas,
       daque locum nostris materiamque dolis.
45 ille potest vacuo furari litore harenas,

✦ ✦ ✦

34 **torqueō, -ēre, torsī, tortum:** *to rack, torture.*
35 **quidlibet:** although an impersonal verb, best to translate as *whatever you like.*
   indulgentia, -ae (f.): *gentleness, fondness.*
36 **sequitur, fugio ... fugit, ipse sequor:** note the humorous CHIASMUS. Ovid wants to do the chasing, not to be chased.
38 **tu:** Ovid again addresses Corinna's husband, rebuking him for taking Corinna's fidelity for granted.
   formōsus, -a, -um: *beautiful.*
   incipe: along with the *incipe* of line 39, forms an ANAPHORA.
39 **totiens (adv.):** *so often.*
41 **sollers, -tis:** *clever, skillful.* Ovid tells the tale of another *ancilla*, Nape, and her skill at carrying tablets in *Amores* I. 11 and 12.
   tabella, -ae (f.): *writing tablet.*
42 **secubō, -āre, -uī:** *to sleep by oneself. secubare* is used to describe sexual abstinence. *Secubus* is practised in the worship of Isis and Ceres, and in elegy.
43 **mordeō, -dēre, momordī, morsum:** *to bite, devour.* Here a jussive subjunctive.
   iste, ista, istud: *that of yours.*
   aliquandō (adv.): *at last.*
44 **dolus, -ī (m.):** *trickery, stratagem, treachery.* The three books of the *Amores* provide numerous examples of Ovid's *doli*.
45 **furor, -ārī, -ātum:** *to steal, purloin.* Lines 45 and 46 comprise a protracted HYSTERON PROTERON. The *si quis* clause of line 46 leads to the resolution clause *ille potest* of line 45. Stealing sands from the seashore is another pointless task like gathering leaves from trees or water from a stream.

uxorem stulti si quis amare potest.
iamque ego praemoneo: nisi tu servare puellam
 incipis, incipiet desinere esse mea.
multa diuque tuli; speravi saepe futurum,
50 cum bene servasses, ut bene verba darem.
lentus es et pateris nulli patienda marito;
 at mihi concessi finis amoris erit!
scilicet infelix numquam prohibebor adire?
 nox mihi sub nullo vindice semper erit.
55 nil metuam? per nulla traham suspiria somnos?
 nil facies, cur te iure perisse velim?

✦ ✦ ✦

47 **praemoneō, -ēre, -uī, -itum:** *to forewarn, admonish beforehand.* Ovid again addresses the husband.
48 **incipis, incipiet:** POLYPTOTON.
49 **futurum:** supply a missing *esse*.
50 **servasses:** a pluperfect subjunctive in a circumstantial clause to express the improbability of the husband guarding his wife more carefully and thus rendering the game of love less interesting and less alluring.
 ut bene verba darem: a colloquial construction meaning *to deceive*. Here it forms a result clause.
51 **nulli ... marito:** a dative of agent with the gerundive. A husband was forbidden by Augustan law to tolerate his wife's adultery.
52 **concedō, -ere, -cessī, -cessum:** *to assent to, permit.* Ovid now threatens that the husband's sluggishness will force him to end the affair.
53 **scīlicet:** *naturally, of course.* The word is bitter and ironic.
54 **sub:** here, denoting a restriction—*under the risk of*.
 vindex, -icis (m., f.): *an avenger, one who takes vengeance.*
55 **suspirium, -ī (n.):** *sigh.* Sighing in one's sleep is typical behavior for a lover.
56 **pereō, -īre, -ī, -itum:** *to perish, die.* Since according to his argument, Ovid still has no real reason for rebuking the husband, he pretends to be even more angry.

42 ✦ OVID

        quid mihi cum facili, quid cum lenone marito?
           corrumpit vitio gaudia nostra suo.
        quin alium, quem tanta iuvat patientia, quaeris?
60   me tibi rivalem si iuvat esse, veta.

✦ ✦ ✦

57   **quid mihi cum:** a colloquial expression meaning *what's in it for me?*
       lēnō, -ōnis (m.): *brothel keeper, pimp.* A very strong, if poetic, accusation since according to the law against adultery made by Augustus, a husband could be prosecuted for pimping. In *Amores* III. 12 Ovid, using this same noun, brags about his success advertising women.
58   **corrumpō, -umpere, -ūpī, -uptum:** *to spoil, destroy.*
       vitiō: The CHIASMUS here places the lovers' joy amidst the husband's moral failing.
59   **quīn** (adv.): *why not?*
60   **me:** subject of the infinitive *esse*. Note the ELLIPSIS—another *me* is expected after *veta*.

AMORES III. 12

In *Amores* III. 12 Ovid addresses his audience, placing them among his rivals for Corinna. While the poem appears to be self-reflective in the style of a soliloquy, Ovid upsets this misapprehension in the final couplet of the poem (lines 43–44):

> *et mea debuerat falso laudata videri*
> *femina; credulitas nunc mihi vestra nocet.*

> My praise of my woman ought to have seemed false;
> your gullibility is injurious to me.

Ovid's audience, he argues in this poem, has been seduced by the power of his poetry; it is through his poetic genius that Corinna has become so desirable, through his eloquence that she is now *vendibilis*, a woman who can be bought. He has become her *leno*, her pimp.

In much of the poem (lines 19–42), as J. C. McKeown notes, Ovid, once a star pupil in the art of rhetoric, employs the rhetorical technique of *refutatio* or refutation (*Amores 3.12*, 164–69). He provides twenty-three mythological references to illustrate the kinds of stories that poets tell in order to prove his major point—that to believe in his descriptions of Corinna is to be taken in by the same kind of fiction that underlies the myths to which he alludes. The last reference Ovid makes, to the power of Amphion's lyre to move rocks and build walls, is a telling conclusion to Ovid's argument. He is, in effect, telling his audience, as McKeown writes, that while elegists generally complain of losing their mistresses in spite of the fame they have granted them in his poetry, "[he] laments that it is precisely because he has made Corinna famous in his poetry that he has lost her love" (*Amores 3.12*, 173). The poet has himself moved stones with his poetry and made his audience believe in his fictional beloved to such a degree that they are now, he claims, her slaves.

AMORES III. 12

    Quis fuit ille dies, quo tristia semper amanti
        omina non albae concinuistis aves?
    quodve putem sidus nostris occurrere fatis,
        quosve deos in me bella movere querar?
5   quae modo dicta mea est, quam coepi solus amare,
        cum multis vereor ne sit habenda mihi.
    fallimur, an nostris innotuit illa libellis?
        sic erit: ingenio prostitit illa meo.
    et merito: quid enim formae praeconia feci?
10   vendibilis culpa facta puella mea est.

✧ ✧ ✧

1   **quō:** *in consequence, on which.*
2   **non albae ... aves:** LITOTES. Birds in the Roman world were closely associated with the gods and as such were thought to be their messengers.
    concinnō, -āre, -āvī, -ātum: *to set in order, give rise to.*
3   **putem:** present tense of a potential subjunctive.
    occurō, -ere, occurrī, occusum: *to block the path or progress of.*
4   **querar:** another present tense potential subjunctive.
5   **quae:** *she who.*
6   **sit:** present subjunctive in a clause of fearing; as such, the *ne* does not signal a negative clause.
    habenda: with *sit* a passive periphrastic expressing necessity or obligation.
    mihi: a dative of agent with the passive periphrastic.
7   **fallō, -ere, fefellī, falsum:** *to deceive, trick.* A poetic use of the plural here.
    innotescō, -escere, -uī: *to become known, famous, celebrated.*
    libellus, -ī (m.): *small book or volume.* Catullus refers to his corpus of poems as a *libellus*, reflecting the poet's intention to write a short, well-crafted book of poetry.
8   **prostō, -āre, -itī, -itum:** *to prostitute, offer oneself for hire, expose oneself.*
9   **meritō** (adv.): *deservedly.*
    quid: here the adverb, *why? what reason?*
    praeconium, -ī (n.): *the action of announcing in public.*
10   **vendibilis, -is, -e:** *attractive for sale, easily sold.*

me lenone placet, duce me perductus amator,
    ianua per nostras est adaperta manus.
an prosint, dubium, nocuerunt carmina certe:
    invidiae nostris illa fuere bonis.
15 cum Thebae, cum Troia foret, cum Caesaris acta,
    ingenium movit sola Corinna meum.
aversis utinam tetigissem carmina Musis,
    Phoebus et inceptum destituisset opus!
Nec tamen ut testes mos est audire poetas:
20   malueram verbis pondus abesse meis.

✦ ✦ ✦

11 **me leone ... me duce:** parallel ablatives absolute.
lēnō, -ōnis (m.): *brothel keeper, pimp.* In *Amores* II. 19, Ovid complains of husbands who are too lenient, using this same noun. Here he brags about his success advertising women.
placet: assume *she* as the subject.
perdūcō, -ere, -xī, -ctum: *to bring, conduct.*
12 **adaperiō, -īre, -uī, -tum:** *to open wide, open up.*
13 **prōsum, prōdesse, prōfuī, prōfutūrus:** *to benefit, be helpful or useful to.* Present subjunctive in an indirect question; *carmina* is its subject.
dubium: part of an impersonal expression—*it is doubtful*—introducing the indirect question.
14 **invidia, -ae (f.):** *ill will, jealousy, envy.* A double dative; *invidiae* a dative of purpose and *nostris bonis* a dative of reference.
15 **Thebae, Troia, Caesaris acta:** these are all subjects of epic poetry, which Ovid has eschewed in favor of elegy, prompted by his Corinna of line 16.
foret: imperfect subjunctive of *esse* in a *cum* concessive clause.
acta: here, the past participle used substantively.
17 **utinam:** a particle introducing an optative subjunctive—*I wish that, if only.*
Musis: the goddesses whom poets traditionally invoked to favor their work. Here, Ovid is wishing them away.
18 **Phoebus:** the lyre-playing god who cared for poetry and music.
destituō, -ere, -uī, -ūtum: *to abandon, disregard.*
19 **testis, -is (m.):** *a witness.* Ovid now employs a legal term to establish his argument as a poet. Following *ut* it stands in apposition to *poetas*—"poets as witnesses."
20 **pondus, -eris (n.):** *weight.*

> per nos Scylla patri caros furata capillos
> > pube premit rabidos inguinibusque canes;
> nos pedibus pinnas dedimus, nos crinibus angues;
> > victor Abantiades alite fertur equo.
25 > idem per spatium Tityon porreximus ingens
> > et tria vipereo fecimus ora cani;

✦ ✦ ✦

21 **per nos:** Here begins Ovid's catalogue of myths, all of which are well known because of the art of the poet. This is the legal proof of which he speaks.
Scylla, -ae (f.): This reference is to the story of *Scylla*, daughter of Nisus, who, because of her love for King Minos who is beseiging her city, cut off her father's protective lock of hair and thus betrayed his kingdom. Minos rejected Scylla for this deed and while Scylla clings to Minos's ship in despair, her father, now an osprey, attacks her and she is herself transformed into a bird. Ovid relates this story in *Met.* VIII. 1–151.
patri: a dative case dependent on *caros*.
furor, -ārī, -ātus: *to steal.*
22 **pūbēs, -is (f.):** *the pubic region.*
premō, -ere, -ssī, -ssum: *to press on, conceal.*
rabidus, -a, -us: *raging, violent, mad.*
inguen, -inis (n.): *the groin.* This reference is to the more commonly known story of the siren Scylla, recounted in both the *Odyssey* and the *Aeneid*, who lured ships to the rocks. Circe punished Scylla for loving Glaucus by turning her into a monster whose body from the waist down was composed of raging wild dogs.
23 **pinna, -ae (f.):** *feather.*
pedibus pinnas: a reference to Perseus who was supplied with winged shoes by Mercury.
anguis, -is (m.): *snake, serpent.* A reference to Medusa, the snake-haired Gorgon slain by Perseus.
24 **Abantiadēs, -ae (m.):** *Perseus,* named here for his descent from his great grandfather, Abas. The collation of the Perseus and Bellerophon story dates from late antiquity.
āles, -itis: *winged, having wings.*
25 **Tityos, -ī (m.):** *Tityus,* a giant whose punishment for his attempted rape of Latona was to be spread out over nine acres in Hades and for vultures to pluck away at his liver nightly which grew back during the daytime.
porrigō, -igere, -exī, -ectum: *to stretch out, extend.*
26 **cani:** Cerberus.

fecimus Enceladon iaculantem mille lacertis,
　　ambiguae captos virginis ore viros.
　Aeolios Ithacis inclusimus utribus Euros;
30　　proditor in medio Tantalus amne sitit;
　de Niobe silicem, de virgine fecimus ursam;

✦ ✦ ✦

27　**Enceladus, -ī (m.):** *Enceladus,* one of the race of Giants who was imprisoned under Mt. Etna as punishment for his having attacked the gods.
　iaculor, -ārī, -ātus: *to throw, shoot, hurl a javelin.*
　lacertus, -ī (m.): *upper arm.*
28　**ambiguus, -a, -um:** *undecided, uncertain, wavering.* The Sirens encompass both Good and Evil—their enchanting power to allure also brings death.
　virginis: the luring Sirens.
　viros: a second direct object of *fecimus,* line 27.
29　**Aeolius, -a, -um:** *of or relating to Aeolus, the ruler of the winds.*
　Ithacus, -a, -um: *of Ithaca.* Alludes especially to Ulysses.
　uter, utris (m.): *a leather bag.*
　Eurus, -ī (m.): *the east wind.*
30　**prōditor, -ōris (m.):** *a betrayer, traitor.*
　Tantalus, -ī (m.): *Tantalus.* For betraying the secrets of the gods, Tantalus was condemned to stand in the underworld in a pool of water that always receded when he tried to quench his thirst from it and to watch as fruit hanging above him withdrew whenever he tried to grasp it.
　amnis, amnis (m.): *a river, stream.*
　sitiō, -īre: *to feel thirsty, be thirsty.*
31　**Niobē, -ēs (f.):** was turned to stone after the slaying of all her children by Apollo and Artemis on account of Niobe's boasting. She represents the image of grief with ever-flowing water cascading down her hillside.
　silex, -icis (m.): *hard rock or stone; flint.*
　ursa, -ae (f.): *a she-bear.* A reference to Callisto, a nymph in the train of Diana who was changed into a bear by Zeus and then into the constellation Ursa Major.

concinit Odrysium Cecropis ales Ityn.
Iuppiter aut in aves aut se transformat in aurum
aut secat inposita virgine taurus aquas.
35 Protea quid referam Thebanaque semina, dentes,
qui vomerent flammas ore, fuisse boves;
flere genis electra tuas, auriga, sorores;

✦ ✦ ✦

32 **ales, -itis (m.):** *a large bird.* An Athenian bird sings of Thracian Itys—a reference to the nightingale, the transformed Philomela, an Athenian woman. Ovid uses a grandiose PLEONASM here.
Odrysius, -a, -um: *Thracian.*
Cecropis, -idis: *of Athens.* This reference employs the patronym of Cecrops, an early king of Athens.
Itys, -os (m.): Itys, the son of Procne and Tereus, killed by his mother in revenge for his father's infidelity.

34 **secō, -āre, -āvī, -ātum:** *to cut.*
virgine: *Europa.*
taurus, -ī (m.): *a bull.*

35 **Proteus, -eī (m.):** the legendary *sea god* able to change his own shape at will. Here, a Greek masculine accusative *-a.*
quid: here, the adverb.
Thēbānus, -a, -um: *of or relating to the city Thebes.*
sēmen, -inis (n.): *seed.*
dentes: these are the teeth of the dragon, slain by Cadmus, from which sprang armed men to populate the city of Thebes.

36 **qui:** antecedent is *boves.*
vomō, -ere, -uī, -itum: *to vomit, spew out.* Here, an imperfect subjunctive relative clause imbedded in an indirect statement.
boves: these are the fierce bulls that Jason, under the influence of Medea's secret herbs, yoked to plow the earth from which sprang an army of men.

37 **flere:** a second infinitive in the indirect discourse dependent on *referam,* line 35.
gena, -ae (f.): *cheek.* Here, an ablative of place.
electrum, -ī (n.): *amber.*
auriga: a reference to Phaeton whose sisters, the Heliades, wept tears of amber while mourning their brother's death and were themselves turned into poplar trees.

> quaeque rates fuerint, nunc maris esse deas,
> aversumque diem mensis furialibus Atrei,
40 duraque percussam saxa secuta lyram?
> exit in inmensum fecunda licentia vatum,
> obligat historica nec sua verba fide:
> et mea debuerat falso laudata videri
> femina; credulitas nunc mihi vestra nocet.

✦ ✦ ✦

38 **ratis, ratis (f.):** *boat, ship.* A reference to Aeneas's ships that were changed into sea nymphs to escape being destroyed by Turnus.
fuerint: another subjunctive, here perfect tense, in a relative clause embedded in indirect discourse.
39 **furiālis, -is, -e:** *frenzied, mad.*
Atreus, -ī (m.): murdered his brother Thyestes after discovering an adulterous affair between his wife and his brother. The reference here is to Atreus's serving the children born of that affair to his brother as dinner.
40 **dūrus, -a, -um:** *hard.*
percutiō, -ere, -cussī, -cussum: *to strike, beat.*
saxum, -ī (n.): *stone, rock, boulder.* The reference here is to the story of Amphion, the founder of Thebes, who, while walking around the city playing his lyre, charmed the stones to form a wall.
41 **inmensum, -ī (n.):** *infinite space, immeasurable expanse.*
43 **falsō (adv.):** *with intent to deceive, untruthfully.* Here modifying *laudata*.
44 **nocet:** having begun by extolling the power and influence of his poetry, Ovid, in the end, places the blame for Corinna's attractiveness on the credulity of his readers.

AMORES III. 15

In this last poem of the three books, Ovid addresses Venus and tells her that she must find a new love poet. He declares that his poetry has made him as distinguished to Sulmo as Vergil is to Mantua or Catullus to Verona, ranking himself among the greatest of the Roman poets. The poet says farewell to Cupid and to Venus. He proclaims that Bacchus now calls him to a greater work, most likely a tragedy, since Bacchus was the patron god of the theater. The poet in fact did write a single tragedy, the *Medea*, now lost. *Amores* III. 15 concludes with the traditional wish that his elegies survive him.

This poem looks back to I. 1 where the poet described his "accidental" birth as a love elegist. But, it is also a reply to III. 1. In that poem, the poet constructed a mock dialogue between elegy and tragedy in which tragedy argues that Ovid is now ready to write more serious poetry, whereas elegy claims him for herself. In reply, the poet asks tragedy for a little more time for his love poetry, although he recognizes that he will soon have to assume a greater task. This last poem of the elegies is also reminiscent of Horace, *Odes* III. 30, in which Horace announces that his odes will be more lasting than any material monument.

AMORES III. 15

    Quaere novum vatem, tenerorum mater Amorum:
        raditur haec elegis ultima meta meis;
    quos ego composui, Paeligni ruris alumnus,
        (nec me deliciae dedecuere meae)
5   si quid id est, usque a proavis vetus ordinis heres,
        non modo militiae turbine factus eques.
    Mantua Vergilio gaudet, Verona Catullo;

✦ ✦ ✦

1   **vātēs, -is (m.):** *prophet, poet.* The oldest word for poet but one that had fallen out of favor. It was restored to prominence by the Augustan poets.
    tener, -era, -erum: *tender, sensitive.*
    mater Amorum: refers to Venus.
2   **rādō, -ere, rāsī, -sum:** *to scrape, graze.*
    elegī, -ōrum (m.): *elegiac verses.*
    meta: used of the turning posts at either end of a circus. Chariots competing in races would try to make the turn at the end of the circus as closely as possible, often grazing the post with the chariot.
3   **Paelignus, -a, -um:** *of or pertaining to the mountainous region in central Italy, east of Rome*; Ovid's province by birth.
    alumnus, -ī (m.): *a "son" or "foster son"; a product of a particular region or environment.*
4   **deliciae:** refers to the elegies, but also used by Catullus of his beloved in poems 2 and 3.
    dēdecet, -ēre, -uit: *to disgrace, dishonor.*
5   **proavus, -ī (m.):** *a forefather, ancestor.*
    vetus ordinis heres: this phrase gives us some important biographical information about Ovid and his family: that Ovid is an *eques* by birth, not by a recent reward for military service; as well as a glimpse of the poet's fascination with genealogy, which is more obvious in his stories of the *Metamorphoses*.
6   **modo (adv.):** *just now, recently.*
    mīlitia, -ae (f.): *military service.*
    turbō, -inis (m.): *a whirlwind.*
7   **Mantua, -ae (f.):** *birthplace of the poet Vergil in the north of Italy.*
    Vērōna, -ae (f.): like Vergil's, Catullus's birthplace also lay in the far north of the Italian penninsula.

Paelignae dicar gloria gentis ego,
   quam sua libertas ad honesta coegerat arma,
10   cum timuit socias anxia Roma manus.
atque aliquis spectans hospes Sulmonis aquosi
   moenia, quae campi iugera pauca tenent,
"quae tantum" dicet "potuistis ferre poetam,
   quantulacumque estis, vos ego magna voco."
15 culte puer puerique parens Amathusia culti,
   aurea de campo vellite signa meo:
corniger increpuit thyrso graviore Lyaeus;

✢ ✢ ✢

9 **honestus, -a, -um:** *honorable.* Ovid speaks here from the point of view of a Paelignian, proud of his region's uprising in its struggle to maintain equality when threatened by Rome.
10 **anxius, -a, -um:** *anxious, distressed, worried.*
11 **Sulmō, -ōnis (m.):** *the town in Paelignia where Ovid was born.*
   aquōsus, -a, -um: *watery, wet.* Because Paelignia was a mountainous region it was filled with running streams.
12 **iūgerum, -ī (n.):** *a measurement of land equal approximately to two-thirds of an acre and measuring 240 feet by 120 feet.*
14 **quantuluscumque, -acumque, -umcumque:** *however small.*
15 **cultus, -a, -um:** *refined, sophisticated, elegant.* The final *-e* is short making this the vocative singular modifying *puer.*
   puer: Cupid; prompts a memory of I. 1, where, described with the adjective *saeve,* he was declared to be the reason for these poems having been written.
   Amathusius, -a, -um: *of or pertaining to a town in the southern part of Cyprus,* sacred to Venus, hence an epithet for Venus.
16 **aurea:** modifies *signa* but its first position in the line places it close to *Amathusia* who was often thought of as golden-haired.
   vellō, -ere, vulsī, vulsum: *to pull up.* When used with *signa* forms a military term meaning "to break camp"; reminiscent of I. 9.
17 **corniger, -era, -erum:** *having horns.* Bacchus is often referred to as "bull-horned."
   increpō, -āre, -uī, -itum: *to rattle, clang.*
   thyrsus, -ī (m.): *a wand,* usually covered with vine leaves and carried by worshippers of Bacchus.
   Lyaeus, -ī (m.): another name for *Bacchus* highlighting his role as the patron god of the theater who provides relaxation and release from care. Here Ovid invokes him for his own release from elegy.

pulsanda est magnis area maior equis.
imbelles elegi, genialis Musa, valete,
20   post mea mansurum fata superstes opus.

✦ ✦ ✦

18 **magnis ... equis:** CHIASTIC word order.
    area maior: a reference to the poet's future work, most probably the *Medea* but possibly a hint at the epic-scale *Metamorphoses*.
19 **imbellis, -e:** *not suited for war, unwarlike*. Here, a PERSONIFICATION with *elegi*.
    genialis, -e: *creative*.
20 **superstes, -itis:** *surviving after death*.

The Metamorphoses

INTRODUCTION TO THE METAMORPHOSES

Ovid's *Metamorphoses*, a poem of fifteen books, is written in dactylic hexameters, the meter of the three great epic poems of antiquity, the *Iliad*, the *Odyssey*, and the *Aeneid*. While its meter suggests that the *Metamorphoses* is an epic, the subject matter, as well as its structure, places the poem in a category of its own. The focus on love seems more appropriate for elegy than for epic; the length and scope of the poem are more epic than elegiac. The poem consists of several hundred metamorphoses, or transformations, described in over 250 tales that begin with the creation of the world and of man, and end in the time of Augustus, first of the Roman emperors. The range of narratives includes the lives and loves of the gods, divine wrath, stories from the *Iliad*, the *Odyssey*, and the *Aeneid*, and accounts of important mythological and human families.

Ovid sets forth the plan for his massive undertaking in the first four lines of the poem:

> In nova fert animus mutatas dicere formas
> corpora; di, coeptis (nam vos mutastis et illas)
> adspirate meis primaque ab origine mundi
> ad mea perpetuum deducite tempora carmen!

> I plan to tell of forms changed into new bodies; you gods
> (for you yourselves have made these changes)
> look favorably on what I am beginning and spin out my
>   song to be continuous
> from the first origin of the world to my own times.

Met. I. 1–4

Most of the tales explain the origin *(aition)* of a natural phenomenon, such as a particular flower, tree, or bird, the name of a river or sea, the reason for a particular custom or tradition such as the color of the fruit of the mulberry tree or the wearing of the laurel wreath. The final transformation of the poem is that of Julius Caesar into a god and a star, and Ovid ends the poem, as he promises in his prelude, in his own time, the age of Augustus, first of the Roman emperors.

The idea of metamorphosis was extremely popular in Greek poetry, especially the poetry of the Hellenistic period. The poet Callimachus, writing in Alexandria in the third century B.C., wrote a narrative elegy of some four thousand lines in four books, which he called *Aitia*, or causes. (Ovid also used this meter for his love poetry: see the Appendix on meter.) Callimachus described the loves of the gods and the origin of many local religious practices. Other Alexandrian poets also wrote about metamorphoses, and, although these works are largely lost to us, Ovid had access to them and consulted these poets for information and inspiration. In Ovid, a metamorphosis most often transforms a human into a plant, animal, or stone; in the case of Pygmalion's statue, a stone into a woman. But in each instance the transformation affects only the physical body; the basic character of the individual survives the metamorphosis and usually determines it; Daphne, for example, who is changed into a laurel tree to escape the pursuing god Apollo, as a tree still shrinks from Apollo's advances; Baucis and Philemon, devoted to the gods and completely faithful to one another, are transformed into a pair of intertwined trees.

The poem may be divided into three major sections (Anderson [1996], 13): Books 1–6 are chiefly concerned with stories about gods and men; Books 7–11 primarily with stories that focus on human beings and their destructive passions; and Books 12–15 with stories that tell of Troy, Rome, and the deification of the great Roman heroes. In this textbook, the stories of Creation, Apollo and Daphne, and Pyramus and Thisbe come from the first section; the tales of Daedalus and Icarus, of Philemon and Baucis, of Orpheus and Eurydice, and of Pygmalion are from the second. Yet often the stories defy classification or categorization and the tremendous appeal of Ovid's great work throughout the ages is due, in large measure, to the complex and varied narrative.

Although the overarching theme that unifies the poem is metamorphosis, Ovid does seem to use two devices to create a kind of unity within the three sections of this complex tapestry of stories. Sometimes one story, like a frame, encompasses a series of tales, such as the cycle of stories told by the daughters of Minyas to pass the time while they stay at home, having refused to join in the worship of Bacchus; the story of Pyramus and Thisbe is told by one of the Minyeides. In addition, Ovid repeats patterns of thematically related stories; so, for example, stories like the Apollo and Daphne episode also consider the disastrous passions of the gods for mortal females.

To find a central theme for such a complex poem is difficult. The poem is about endless change and the helplessness of human beings in a world where the gods are generally cruel or indifferent. Like his Alexandrian predecessors, Ovid is fascinated more by the narrative potential inherent in myth than in its possible truths; he loves to tell stories for their own sake. Some of his stories are serious and moving, or full of pathos such as the poignant tale praising the simple piety of Philemon and Baucis. Other stories, however, have a far less serious tone, even when the subject matter itself is tragic; the poet recounts the loss of Daedalus's son in a dramatic story which appears to be about parental grief but the pathos is undermined by the larger context of the story (see the introduction to Daedalus and Icarus below). The story of the doomed love of Pyramus and Thisbe is not as serious as it first seems; neither is the story of the "pious" Pygmalion simply the tale of a righteous and religious man. No single label fits this remarkable collection of stories.

With the loss of a number of collections of mythological tales that Ovid had available to him, the *Metamorphoses* remains the only source now for many classical myths. For centuries, it has provided and continues to provide inspiration for poets, novelists, musicians, playwrights, and artists. Perhaps no other single work of literature except the Bible has had a similar impact.[1]

---

[1] For a listing of literary, musical, and artistic works based on myth, especially the *Metamorphoses*, see Jane Reid, *The Oxford Guide to Classical Mythology in the Arts 1300–1900s*, 2 vols., Oxford and New York, 1993.

Creation

CREATION
Met. I. 1–88

Lines 1–4 of *Metamorphoses* Book I comprise a short but programmatic prologue to the entire work. Ovid tells his readers that the overall theme of the poem will be *mutatas...formas*, changed bodies or forms. He invokes the gods to help him to compose a continuous poem, i.e., a long poem with a unifying theme (*ad mea perpetuum deducite tempora carmen*). Although his poem will be long and continuous, it will not be a traditional epic focusing on the adventures of a single hero (Achilles, Odysseus, Aeneas). Rather, it is a collection of carefully crafted stories that range from the creation of the world to the reign of Augustus. In these first four lines Ovid aligns himself with Homer and Vergil, but also with the Hellenistic canon established by the poet Callimachus, who decried the *deducite carmen* established by epic, preferring instead the short, beautifully crafted poem. In the *Metamorphoses*, Ovid will have his cake and eat it too, varying his style from epic to elegy to suit his subject matter.

At the beginning of his creation story, Ovid tells us, the world was single in appearance (*unus...vultus*) called *chaos*; sea, earth, and sky were not yet distinguishable (lines 5–20). In line 21 the poet introduces a creator (*deus...et melior natura*, a god or better nature) who begins to order a world where the elements were at war. In line 32, Ovid again alludes to a nameless creator (*quisque fuit ille deorum*, whoever it was of the gods) who begins to play an active role in forming the world into coherent parts and as *mundi fabricator*, maker of the world, begins to establish order and discourage conflict in earth, sea, and sky. This maker creates the stars and constellations. Finally man is formed. Though the poet at first leaves man's origin as uncertain (I. 76–88), he ends the account of man's creation with Prometheus as possible creator, leaving the world of philosophy for the realm of myth that will so dominate the rest of his poem. Prometheus orders man to look to heaven for guidance (lines 85–86); as McKim notes, man spends much of the rest of the *Metamorphoses* disobeying this command (*Myth against Philosophy*, 102).

The world is revealed as unstable and chaotic soon after lines 1–85. Ovid describes the declining ages from the peace and tranquility of the golden age, to the violence of the age of iron (I. 89–150), followed by battle of the gods and giants, the impiety of mankind, and Jupiter's eradication by a catastrophic flood of the entire human race save for a single couple, Deucalion and Pyrrha, who repopulate the earth.

By beginning his fifteen-book epic with this description of creation, Ovid is positioning himself as part of a continuum of ancient writers who have treated this topic. His Roman model does not resemble that of the Roman poet Lucretius, whose *De Rerum Natura* is a philosophical account of the world. Rather, it is more similar to, though much longer than, the brief creation story in Vergil's *Eclogue* VI, 31ff. Like Vergil, Ovid, as his *Metamorphoses* will affirm, is not interested in establishing a real cosmogony, but rather offers this "scientific" account of the world's beginning in order, as some argue, to provide a contrast to "the imaginative abandon of the bulk of the *Met*." (McKim, 97). That "bulk" consists of over two hundred mythological tales, skillfully linked by a variety of devices (for example, tales told by an internal storyteller differentiated from the narrator of the whole, or related though not necessarily sequential themes). Most depict a chaotic world of erratic, often violent actions, first by gods and then by men: a world that is in constant flux.

To underscore the world's chaos, Ovid places the philosopher Pythagoras in Book XV, part of whose speech revisits the topic established in Book I.

Furthermore, in the final book of the poem, the instability of all forms is propounded by Pythagoras as a law of nature (XV. 252–53: *nec species sua cuique manet, rerumque nouatrix / ex aliis alias reparat natura figuras*, "and none maintains its own appearance, but the innovatress of things, / nature, restores one shape from another"). Pythagoras's precept is phrased in a way that pointedly recalls the description of chaos at the opening of the poem, *nulli sua forma manebat*, "no part maintained its form" (I. 17). What appeared there as an aberrant precosmic state is now alleged to be the constant and universal condition of nature. As Tarrant observes, "the point is underscored verbally by the shift in tense from *manebat* in I. 17, describing what was not yet the case, to the timeless *manet* of XV. 252" (*Chaos in Ovid's Metamorphoses*, 351).

Here, at the end of his poem then, Ovid again overturns the concept that the outcome of creation is the disappearance of chaos from the world.

THE CREATION
Met. I. 1–88

In nova fert animus mutatas dicere formas
corpora; di, coeptis (nam vos mutastis et illas)
adspirate meis primaque ab origine mundi
ad mea perpetuum deducite tempora carmen!
5   Ante mare et terras et quod tegit omnia caelum
unus erat toto naturae vultus in orbe,

✦ ✦ ✦

1   **in nova:** Ovid deliberately constrasts his opening words to those of Homer's "man of many devices" of the *Odyssey*, "wrath" of the *Iliad*, and the "arms and the man" of Vergil's *Aeneid*. This underscores his intention to write a different kind of epic poem.
    mutatas ... formas: Ovid's first and clever transformation. In this first line he has transformed the Greek *metamorphoses* into its Latin variant employing the same sounds as the Greek.
2   **corpora:** this exaggerated delay of the noun from its adjective, *nova*, brings emphasis and completes the expression of the poem's main theme—forms changed into new bodies.
    di: here, an invocation to the gods above for help in the poet's enterprise, not to the Muses.
    coeptis: a dative case dependent on *adspirate*, line 3.
    mutastis: Ovid uses the syncopated perfect tense here as he will do often throughout this poem.
3   **adspīrō, -āre, -āvī, -ātum:** *to favor, aid, inspire.*
    mundus, -ī (m.): *the universe, the world, the earth.*
4   **dēdūcō, -ere, -dūxī, -ductum:** *to draw out, spin.* This central verb has its flanking adjectives and noun pairs spinning around it in INTERLOCKED WORD ORDER as a graphic representation of the poet's art.
    carmen, -inis (n.): *poetry, song.*
5   **mare ... terras ... caelum:** This TRICOLON introduces the three divisions of the universe yet to be given form and which will be Ovid's focus in this passage.
    quod: a PROLEPSIS. The relative pronoun precedes its antecedent *caelum*.

quem dixere chaos: rudis indigestaque moles
nec quicquam nisi pondus iners congestaque eodem
non bene iunctarum discordia semina rerum.
10   nullus adhuc mundo praebebat lumina Titan,
nec nova crescendo reparabat cornua Phoebe,
nec circumfuso pendebat in aere tellus
ponderibus librata suis, nec bracchia longo
margine terrarum porrexerat Amphitrite;

✣ ✣ ✣

7   **dixere:** the third person plural perfect active alternate form. The subject is, presumably, the *di* of line 2 whom Ovid calls upon in his invocation.
chaos, -ī (n.): *a formless state.*
rudis, -e: *crude, rough.* The first of many words over the next two and a half lines denoting negativity.
indigestus, -a, -um: *confused, disorderly.*
8   **pondus, -eris (n.):** *weight.*
9   **iunctarum ... rerum:** Ovid employs a CHIASMUS here to highlight the disjointed nature of the universe at this point.
discors, -rdis: *discordant, incongruous.*
10 **mundus, -ī (m.):** the heavens, dative case with the compound verb *praebebat.*
Tītān, -nos (m.): an unspecified member of the race of gods preceding the array of Olympians. Ovid establishes a pattern in line 10 that he carries forward to line 12 of placing the subject at line end and splitting the verb over the 3rd and 4th foot.
11 **crescendo:** here, an ablative gerund denoting means. Note the similarities in structure and sound between lines 10 and 11.
reparō, -āre, -āvī, -ātum: *to renew, revive, restore.*
Phoebē, -ēs (f.): one of the race of Titans, here identified with the moon.
12 **circumfundō, -fundere, -fūdī, -fūsum:** *to surround, spread round, envelop.*
pendeō, -ēre, pendī: *to hang, hang down, fall.*
aēr, aēris (m.): *air.*
tellūs, -ūris (f.): *land, country.*
13 **lībrō, -āre, -āvī, -ātum:** *to hold suspended, poise.*
14 **margine:** ablative of place where.
porrigō, -igere, -exī, -ectum: *to stretch out, extend.*
Amphitrītē, -ēs (f.): the wife of Neptune and so, by extension, a PERSONIFICATION of the sea.

68 ✣ OVID

15   utque erat et tellus illic et pontus et aer,
          sic erat instabilis tellus, innabilis unda,
          lucis egens aer; nulli sua forma manebat,
          obstabatque aliis aliud, quia corpore in uno
          frigida pugnabant calidis, umentia siccis,
20   mollia cum duris, sine pondere, habentia pondus.
            Hanc deus et melior litem natura diremit.
          nam caelo terras et terris abscidit undas
          et liquidum spisso secrevit ab aere caelum.
          quae postquam evolvit caecoque exemit acervo,

✣ ✣ ✣

15   **ut ... sic:** *while ... at the same time* (implies a contrast).
        illīc (adv.): *there, in that place.*
        pontus, -ī (m.): *sea.*
16   **innabilis, -e:** *not able to be swum in, unswimmable.* An adjective unique to Ovid.
17   **egeō, -ēre, -uī:** *to be without, lack.*
        nulli: dative of reference.
18   **alius, alia, aliud:** *one (thing) ... another (thing).*
        aliis: the dative with a compound verb.
19   **calidis:** rather than use a preposition with the adversary after *pugnabant*, Ovid here uses the dative case without a preposition, as he does with *siccis*.
        umeō, -ēre: *to be wet or moist.* Here the present participle used substantively.
20   **duris:** Ovid uses the preposition here with an ablative case noun rather than the dative case as in the previous line.
21   **līs, lītis (f.):** *quarrel, dispute, disagreement.*
        dirimō, -imere, -ēmī, -emptum: *to separate, break up.*
22   **caelo:** an ablative of separation, as is *terris*.
        abscīdō, -dere, -dī, -sum: *to separate, cut off.* Subject is the unspecified *deus* of line 21.
23   **spissus, -a, -um:** *thick, dense.*
        secernō, -ernere, -rēvī, -rētum: *to isolate, cut off.*
        caelum: this final word, echoing the *caelo* at the beginning of the phrase in line 22, encloses the division of the universe into three realms as set forth in line 5, in the opening of this passage.
24   **quae:** neuter plural relative pronoun referring back to the three elements—*terras* (22), *undas* (22), *caelum* (22).
        evolvō, -ere, -vī, -utum: *to free, release.*
        caecus, -a, -um: *blind.*
        acervus, -ī (m.): *a disordered mass, chaos.*

25   dissociata locis concordi pace ligavit:
        ignea convexi vis et sine pondere caeli
        emicuit summaque locum sibi fecit in arce;
        proximus est aer illi levitate locoque;
        densior his tellus elementaque grandia traxit
30   et pressa est gravitate sua; circumfluus umor
        ultima possedit solidumque coercuit orbem.
            Sic ubi dispositam quisquis fuit ille deorum
        congeriem secuit sectamque in membra coegit,
        principio terram, ne non aequalis ab omni
35   parte foret, magni speciem glomeravit in orbis.
        tum freta diffundi rapidisque tumescere ventis
        iussit et ambitae circumdare litora terrae;
        addidit et fontes et stagna inmensa lacusque

✦ ✦ ✦

25 **dissociō, -āre, -āvī, -ātum:** *to separte, break apart.*
    locis: a locative followed by *concordi pace,* an ablative of means.
27 **ēmicō, -āre, -uī, -ātum:** *to spring up.*
28 **proximus:** Ovid is leading us through a hierarchy of the creation of the universe in an ordered manner starting from the highest point, the sun.
    illi: a dative case with *proximus.*
29 **densior . . . tellus:** supply a missing *est.*
    elementum, -ī (n.): *one of the four basic substances of the universe (earth, air, water, fire), an element.*
    grandis, -is, -e: *large, massive.*
30 **circumfluus, -a, -um:** *that flows around.*
    ūmor, -ōris (m.): *moisture.*
31 **ultima:** modifying an understood *loca.*
    coerceō, -ēre, -uī, -itum: *to bound, enclose.*
33 **congeriēs, -ēī (f.):** *heap, pile, mass.*
    secō, -āre, -uī, -tum: *to cut, sever.*
34 **principiō (adv.):** *in the beginning, to start with.*
    ne: here introducing a purpose clause and, combined with *non,* part of a LITOTES.
    aequalis, -is, -e: *symmetrical, even.*
35 **glomerō, -āre, -āvī, -ātum:** *to form or gather into a ball.*
    speciem: object of *in.* PROLEPSIS.
36 **diffundō, -undere, -ūdī, -ūssum:** *to spread out, diffuse.*
    tumescō, -ere: *to become swollen or inflated, to swell.*
37 **ambiō, -īre, -uī, -ītum:** *to surround, encircle.* With *circumdare* forms a PLEONASM.

fluminaque obliquis cinxit declivia ripis,
40   quae, diversa locis, partim sorbentur ab ipsa,
in mare perveniunt partim campoque recepta
liberioris aquae pro ripis litora pulsant.
iussit et extendi campos, subsidere valles,
fronde tegi silvas, lapidosos surgere montes,
45   utque duae dextra caelum totidemque sinistra
parte secant zonae, quinta est ardentior illis,
sic onus inclusum numero distinxit eodem
cura dei, totidemque plagae tellure premuntur.
quarum quae media est, non est habitabilis aestu;
50   nix tegit alta duas; totidem inter utramque locavit
temperiemque dedit mixta cum frigore flamma.

✦ ✦ ✦

39   **oblīquus, -a, -um:** *slanting.*
dēclīvis, -is, -e: *sloping, falling, declining.*
rīpa, -ae (f.): *river bank.*
40   **dīversus, -a, -um:** *set apart, separate.* Presumably modifying *flumina,* line 39.
locis: an ablative of respect.
sorbeō, -ēre, -uī, -itum: *to drink up, absorb.*
ipsa: modifying an understood *terra.*
41   **campo:** here, the poetic usage referring to the expanse of the sea, not of the land.
45   **duae:** note the HYPERBATON in the exaggerated separation of this adjective from its noun *zonae* in the next line.
totidem: *as many, the same number of.*
46   **secō, -āre, -āvī, -ātum:** *to cut, split up, subdivide.*
ardens, -ntis: *burning, blazing, hot.*
47   **onus inclusum:** this enclosed, heavy burden is the Earth.
distinguō, -ere, -nxī, -nctum: *to divide up, mark off, separate.*
48   **plaga, -ae (f.):** *territory, region, expanse.*
49   **quarum:** agrees with an understood *zonae* as does the feminine *quae,* and *duas,* and *utramque* of line 50.
50   **nix, nivis (f.):** *snow.*
totidem: here, *two.*
utramque: modifies an understood *zona.*
51   **temperiēs, -ēī (f.):** *mild climate, moderation.*
mixta ... flamma: ablative absolute.

Inminet his aer, qui, quanto est pondere terrae
pondus aquae levius, tanto est onerosior igni.
illic et nebulas, illic consistere nubes
55 iussit et humanas motura tonitrua mentes
et cum fulminibus facientes fulgura ventos.
His quoque non passim mundi fabricator habendum
aera permisit; vix nunc obsistitur illis,
cum sua quisque regat diverso flamina tractu,
60 quin lanient mundum; tanta est discordia fratrum.

✢ ✢ ✢

52 **imineō, -ēre:** *to hang poised over.*
qui: subject of *est*, line 53.
pondus, -eris (n.): *weight.* Here an ablative of comparison with *levius.*
53 **pondus aquae:** subject of *est*, line 52.
igni: ablative of comparison with *onerosior.*
54 **nebula, -ae (f.):** *mist, fog.*
consistō, -ere, -stitī: *to settle, stand.*
nūbēs, nūbis (f.): *cloud.*
55 **motura:** a future active participle expressing intent. Its accusative subject is *tonitrua.* Its accusative object is *mentes.*
tonitrus, -ūs (m.): *thunder.* This noun has an alternate accusative neuter plural form that Ovid has chosen to use here.
56 **fulmen, -inis (n.):** *thunderbolt.*
facientes: Ovid varies his structure slightly in this line employing a present participle rather than the future participle as in line 55. This participle modifies the accusative *ventos* and its object is *fulgura.*
fulgur, -uris (n.): *lightening, lightning, flash.* Caused here by the winds, not Jupiter.
57 **his:** dative of agent with the future passive participle *habendum.*
passim (adv.): *here and there, scattered about.*
mundus, -ī (m.): *heavens, universe, world, earth.*
fabricator, -ōris (m.): *maker, fashioner.*
58 **vix (adv.):** *hardly, scarcely, barely.*
obsistō, -ere, -stitī, -stitum: *to stand in the way of, block, impede.* Here used impersonally.
59 **regat:** present subjunctive in a *cum* causal clause.
flāmen, -minis (n.): *wind, breeze.*
tractus, -ūs (m.): *tract, expanse, extent.*
60 **quīn (conj.):** *so as to prevent, so that . . . not.*
laniō, -āre, -āvī, -ātum: *to tear, mangle.*
fratrum: these are the winds that Ovid now describes in detail.

Eurus ad Auroram Nabataeaque regna recessit
Persidaque et radiis iuga subdita matutinis;
vesper et occiduo quae litora sole tepescunt,
proxima sunt Zephyro; Scythiam septemque triones
65 horrifer invasit Boreas; contraria tellus
nubibus adsiduis pluviaque madescit ab Austro.
haec super inposuit liquidum et gravitate carentem
aethera nec quicquam terrenae faecis habentem.
Vix ita limitibus dissaepserat omnia certis,

✦ ✦ ✦

61 **Eurus, -ī (m.):** *the east wind.* Ovid begins his description of the four winds with the east wind in the nominative case and balances it with the west in the dative. He then gives us the north in the nominative and counters it with the south in the ablative. Each wind is attached to a region of the Roman world.
Aurōra, -ae (f.): *the dawn, sunrise.*
Nabataeus, -a, -um: *a people of northern Arabia.*
recēdō, -ere, -ssī, -ssum: *to withdraw, retire.*
62 **Persidis, -is:** *Persian.*
iugum, -ī (n.): *mountain heights.*
subditus, -a, -um: *situated beneath.*
mātūtīnus, -a, -um: *of the early morning, eastern.*
63 **vesper (irreg.) (m.):** *the evening, the west.*
occiduus, -a, -um: *setting, going down, western.*
tepescō, -ere, -uī: *to grow warm.*
64 **Zephyrus, -ī (m.):** *a west wind.*
Scythia, -ae (f.): *Scythia,* a region north and east of the Black Sea.
triōnēs, -ōnum (m. pl.): *oxen used for plowing.* When used with *septem* refers to the constellation Ursa Major and, by extension, to the north.
65 **horrifer, -era, -erum:** *dreadful, freezing.*
Boreās, -ae (m.): *the north wind, the north.*
66 **pluvia, -ae (f.):** *rain.*
madescō, -ere, -uī: *to become wet or soaking.*
Auster, -trī (m.): *the south wind, the south.*
68 **aethera:** a Greek accusative singular form.
quisquam, quicquam: *anyone/thing, anyone/thing whatever.*
faex, -cis (f.): *dregs.* Here, a partitive genitive with *quicquam.*
69 **dissaepiō, -īre, -psī, -ptum:** *to separate off*

70   cum, quae pressa diu fuerant caligine caeca,
        sidera coeperunt toto effervescere caelo;
        neu regio foret ulla suis animalibus orba,
        astra tenent caeleste solum formaeque deorum,
        cesserunt nitidis habitandae piscibus undae,
75   terra feras cepit, volucres agitabilis aer.
            Sanctius his animal mentisque capacius altae
        deerat adhuc et quod dominari in cetera posset:
        natus homo est, sive hunc divino semine fecit
        ille opifex rerum, mundi melioris origo,
80   sive recens tellus seductaque nuper ab alto
        aethere cognati retinebat semina caeli.

✣ ✣ ✣

70 **quae:** look to the next line for the antecedent of this pronoun—PROLEPSIS.
    cālīgō, -inis (f.): *darkness.*
    caecus, -a, -um: *blind.*
71 **effervescō, -ere, efferuī:** *to become violently agitated, seethe.*
72 **animalibus:** here, an ablative with *orba.*
    orbus, -a, -um: *bereft, deprived, destitute.*
73 **astrum, -ī (n.):** *star, heavenly body.*
    solum, -ī (n.): *earth, soil, base, floor.*
    formaeque: nominative.
74 **nitidus, -a, -um:** *bright, radiant, shining.*
    piscis, -is (m.): *fish.*
75 **fera, -ae (f.):** *wild animal.*
    volucris, -cris (f.): *bird.*
    agitābilis, -is, -e: *mobile.*
76 **sanctus, -a, -um:** *sacrosanct, holy, sacred, pure.*
    capax, -ācis: *capable.*
77 **dēsum, -esse, -fuī:** *to be lacking or wanting.*
    dominor, -ārī, -ātus: *to rule, be master.*
    posset: subjunctive in a relative clause of purpose.
78 **natus homo est:** a simple, direct phrase for a profound event.
    sive: *whether, or if.*
    sēmen, -inis (n.): *seed, origin.*
79 **opifex, -ficis (m.):** *craftsman, artisan.*
    orīgō, -inis (f.): *rise, beginnings*
81 **cognātus, -a, -um:** *related by birth, kindred.*
    retineō, -ēre, -uī, -tentum: *to hold, grasp, cling.*

> quam satus Iapeto, mixtam pluvialibus undis,
> finxit in effigiem moderantum cuncta deorum,
> pronaque cum spectent animalia cetera terram,
> 85 os homini sublime dedit caelumque videre
> iussit et erectos ad sidera tollere vultus:
> sic, modo quae fuerat rudis et sine imagine, tellus
> induit ignotas hominum conversa figuras.

✦ ✦ ✦

82 **quam:** looks back to *tellus,* line 80, for its antecedent.
satus, -a, -um: *sprung (from a parent).*
Iapetus, -ī (m.): one of the Titans, father of Prometheus, whom Ovid here describes as the creator of mankind.
pluviālis, -is, -e: *rainy.*
83 **fingō, -ere, -nxī, -ctum:** *to make, form, fashion.*
moderor, -ārī, -ātus: *to control, manipulate.*
84 **cum:** introducing a concessive clause.
85 **sublimis, -is, -e:** *lofty, directed upwards.*
vidēre: assume a missing *hominem* as subject of this infinitive.
86 **ērigō, -ere, -rexī, -rectum:** *to raise oneself.*
88 **ignōtus, -a, -um:** *unfamiliar, unknown.*
conversus, -a, -um: *turned, changed.*

Apollo and Daphne

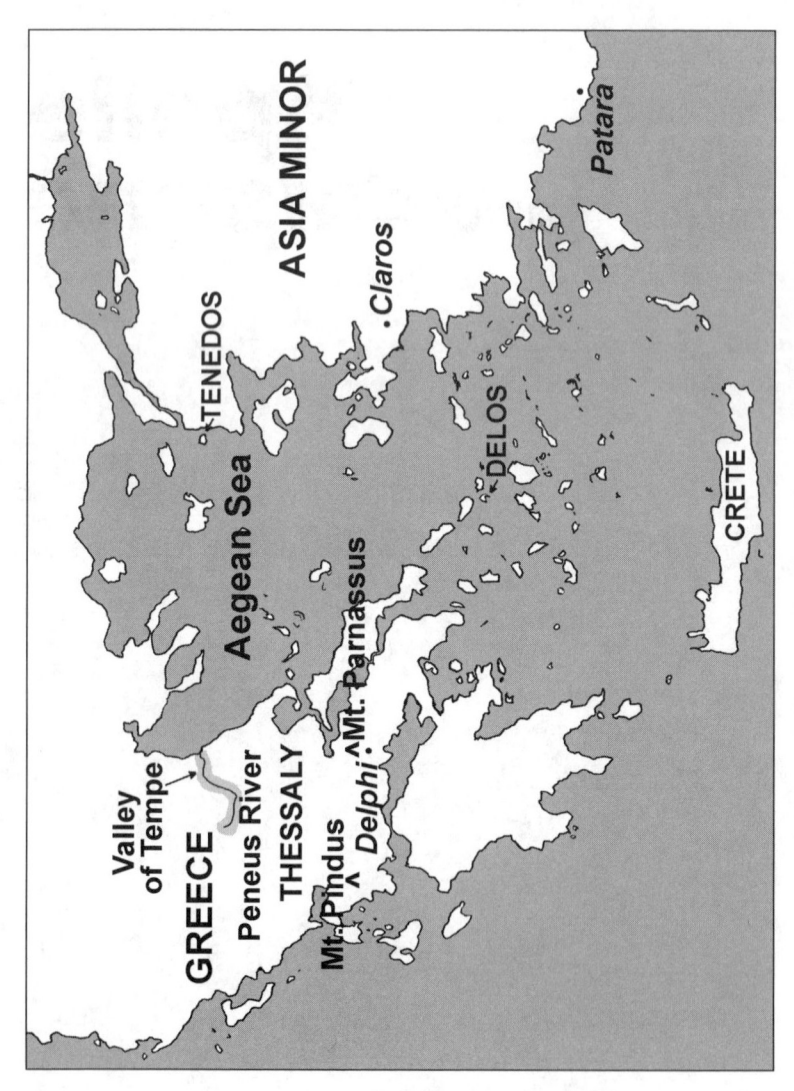

Map of Places in Apollo and Daphne

APOLLO AND DAPHNE
Met. I. 452–567

This is the first love story of the *Metamorphoses*. It follows the opening narratives of the poem, which describe the Creation, the Ages of Man, and the Flood. From the aftermath of the flood comes a snake-like creature called Python, which Apollo killed with his bow and arrow. Apollo's victory over Python was commemorated by the Pythian Games, although the wreath-crowns given the victors as prizes were made of oak leaves, not laurel, since the laurel tree was not yet known. The story of Apollo and Daphne is, in part, about the origin of the laurel, and the ending of the story connects the Rome of Ovid to the past by explaining the practice of awarding Roman victors a laurel wreath. This association with the past, so revered by Romans, was especially important to the emperor Augustus. By linking himself with the founder of Rome, Aeneas, and to the heroic deeds and practices of the past, he justified and glorified his own new role as *princeps*.

This myth of transformation includes many internal transformations of its own. When Apollo, full of boastful pride because of his victory over Python, claims to be a better archer than Cupid, the god of love immediately strikes him with an arrow so that he is consumed with love for the woodland nymph Daphne, daughter of the river god Peneus. At the same time, Cupid strikes Daphne with an arrow that has the opposite effect, so that she is immediately revolted and terrified by the god's advances. Ovid describes Daphne as if she were the love object of an elegiac lover; at the same time, as she flees the god, he compares her to a hare running for its life from a hound, in language reminiscent of epic. The god's pursuit of his unwilling victim is both tragic and comic; this blending of perspectives is typical of Ovid throughout the poem. Daphne, terrified by the fear of rape, is pitiful; the god, reduced to the status of a desperate mortal lover who pleads that his love be acknowledged and accepted, is comic. Both god and nymph have been transformed from their normal states, and as the nymph's capture becomes imminent, she prays to her father for help, and is willingly changed into a laurel tree rather than suffer the god's violent embrace.

The Apollo and Daphne episode is followed by the story of Zeus and Io, another in the series of narratives concerned with acts of rape, either attempted or performed, by the gods.

Perhaps no tale by Ovid has been so enormously popular for artists and writers. The subject of wall paintings and mosaics in antiquity, it has been reinterpreted by artists as diverse as Botticelli, Bernini, Dürer, Rubens, and Sargent, by musicians such as Handel and Scarlatti, and by poets including Spenser, Dryden, and Milton.

APOLLO AND DAPHNE
Met. I. 452–567

Primus amor Phoebi Daphne Peneia, quem non
fors ignara dedit, sed saeva Cupidinis ira,
Delius hunc nuper, victa serpente superbus,
455   viderat adducto flectentem cornua nervo

✦ ✦ ✦

452 **Phoebus, -ī (m.):** one of many appellations for Apollo. This one refers to him as the god of light. There is an ELLIPSIS in this line: supply a form of *esse* to join the two nominative phrases: *Primus amor* and *Daphne Peneia*.

Daphnē, -ēs (f.): nominative singular in apposition to *amor*.

Pēnēius, -a, -um: a patronymic referring to Daphne as the daughter of the river deity *Peneus*. Peneus is the name of a principal river in Thessaly, which rises in Mt. Pindus and flows through the Vale of Tempe, noted for its beauty. *Daphne Peneia* make up nearly half the syllables of the line and establish Daphne's importance in this story.

quem non: antecedent is *amor*. This is an uncommon occurrence of two monosyllables at a line end. Following the uncommon fifth foot bucolic DIAERESIS, they represent a break with the introductory information and signal the beginning of the story.

453 **fors, -tis (f.):** *chance, luck.*

saeva Cupidinis ira: Ovid, like Vergil (*Aeneid* I. 4–12) begins a section of his epic with reference to the wrath of the gods, but Cupid's wrath is far less disastrous than Juno's. The adjective *saeva* is one Ovid uses to describe Cupid at *Amores* I. 1.5.

454 **Dēlius, -iī (m.):** a standard epithet for Apollo derived from Delos, the island of his birth.

serpens, -ntis (f., m.): *snake, serpent.* Here, feminine.

superbus: introduces Apollo in this episode as arrogant and haughty, qualities that incite Cupid's wrath.

455 **cornua:** a SYNECDOCHE referring to the bow by naming its basic parts. Bows were generally made from naturally bent horns held together with a central piece of metal.

nervus, -ī (m.): *string of a musical instrument or bow.* The drawn-out bowstring stretches from one end of the bow to the other just as the words describing that string, *adducto . . . nervo*, lie at either end of the phrase expressing the bow.

> "quid" que "tibi, lascive puer, cum fortibus armis?"
> dixerat: "ista decent umeros gestamina nostros,
> qui dare certa ferae, dare vulnera possumus hosti,
> qui modo pestifero tot iugera ventre prementem
> 460 stravimus innumeris tumidum Pythona sagittis.

✧ ✧ ✧

456 **que:** a simple connective interrupting the flow of the quotation and helping the line to move with a light and energetic rhythm.
lascīvus, -a, -um: *naughty, unrestrained, mischievous.*
tibi: take with *quid* and translate loosely as "what do you want with."
armis: weapons common both to Apollo and Cupid—arrows.
457 **umerus, -ī (m.):** *the shoulder.*
gestāmen, -inis (n.): *load, burden.*
nostros: Ovid's use of the plural with singular intent.
458 **dare ... dare:** ANAPHORA used to swell Apollo's arrogance.
fera, -ae (f.): *wild animal.*
possumus: another use of "we" for "I."
459 **qui:** taken with the *qui* of line 458 creates an ANAPHORA emphasizing the prowess of Apollo as a hunter. Because the first *qui* introduces two clauses, his boast here forms a variation of a TRICOLON CRESCENDO.
pestifer, -era, -erum: *deadly, pernicious, pestilential.*
iūgerum, -ī (n.): *a measurement of land equal approximately to two-thirds of an acre and measuring 240 feet by 120 feet.*
venter, -tris (m.): *the belly or underside.*
premō, -ere, pressī, -ssum: *to press on, push, cover.*
460 **sternō, -ere, strāvī, strātum:** *to strew, lay low, spread over an area, throw down.*
tumidus, -a, -um: *swollen.*
Pythōn, -ōnis (m.): the Python, a serpent that Apollo killed near Delphi. The Pythian games were inaugurated in honor of this achievement. Ovid recounts that story just prior to the Apollo/Daphne episode. Here, a Greek masculine accusative singular form ending in *-a*.
sagitta, -ae (f.): *arrow.*
innumeris tumidum Pythona sagittis: HYPERBOLE in CHIASTIC word order.

tu face nescio quos esto contentus amores
inritare tua, nec laudes adsere nostras!"
filius huic Veneris "figat tuus omnia, Phoebe,
te meus arcus" ait; "quantoque animalia cedunt
465   cuncta deo, tanto minor est tua gloria nostra."
dixit et eliso percussis aere pennis
inpiger umbrosa Parnasi constitit arce

✦ ✦ ✦

461 **fax, facis (f.):** *torch, firebrand*.
  nescio quos: with *amores*. A dismissive, haughty remark. The *-o* of *nescio* is short by SYSTOLE.
  esto: future singular imperative.
  contentus, -a, -um: *content, satisfied*.
462 **inrītō, -āre, -āvī, -ātum:** *to provoke, rouse*.
  tua: ablative singular modifying *face*, 461. The HYPERBATON creates suspense and sustains interest throughout the clause.
  laus, laudis (f.): *praise*.
  adserō, -ere, -uī, -tum: *to lay claim to*.
463 **Venus, -eris (f.):** Venus, the goddess most associated with love and sexual attraction.
  fīgō, -ere, -xī, -xum: a concessive subjunctive; translate as "although," or "even though."
464 **te meus arcus:** supply a missing *figet* to balance *figat* from line 463. It is a practice common to Ovid to omit duplicate words in parallel constructions. Although the first clause is subjunctive, this second will be future indicative.
  arcus, -ūs (m.): *a bow*.
  quanto ... tanto: these correlatives used as ablatives of degree of difference introduce a comparison of the sort "*by as much as ... by just so much....*"
466 **ēlīdō, -ere, -sī, -sum:** *to expel, force out, drive forth*.
  eliso percussis aere pennis: SYNCHESIS and multiple SPONDEES graphically exaggerate Cupid's flying motions.
  āēr, āeris (m.): *air*. Here, a three syllable word (both *e*'s are short).
  penna, -ae (f.): *wing, feather*.
467 **inpiger, -era, -erum:** *tireless, energetic, quick*.
  umbrosus, -a, -um: *shady*.
  Parnāsus, -ī (m.): a mountain in Greece at the base of which is Delphi; sacred to both Apollo and the Muses.
  constō, -āre, -itī: *to take up a position*.

eque sagittifera prompsit duo tela pharetra
diversorum operum: fugat hoc, facit illud amorem;
470 quod facit, auratum est et cuspide fulget acuta,
quod fugat, obtusum est et habet sub harundine plumbum.
hoc deus in nympha Peneide fixit, at illo
laesit Apollineas traiecta per ossa medullas;

✦ ✦ ✦

468 **eque:** *ex que = et ex.*
sagittifer, -era, -erum: *loaded with arrows.*
prōmō, -ere, -psī, -ptum: *to bring forth, draw forth, produce.*
pharetra, -ae (f.): *quiver.* Note that the words describing the quiver, *sagittifera ... pharetra*, surround the weapons within.
469 **dīversus, -a, -um:** *differing, distinct.*
fugō, -āre, -āvī, -ātum: *to cause to flee, drive away, repel.*
hoc ... illud: the first of several ANTITHESES Ovid sets up in the next few lines to demonstrate the very different effects Cupid's arrows have on Apollo and Daphne.
470 **quod facit:** with *quod fugat* (471) forms an ANAPHORA used to draw attention to the ANTITHESIS. Although parallel in form these two lines reflect the opposite effects of the two arrows.
aurātus, -a, -um: *golden.*
cuspis, -idis (f.): *spear, lance; sharp point, tip.*
fulgeō, -ēre, fulsī: *to glisten, gleam.*
acūtus, -a, -um: *sharp, pointed.*
471 **obtūsus, -a, -um:** *dull, blunt.*
harundō, -inis (f.): *the shaft of an arrow.*
472 **nympha, -ae (f.):** *nymph, a demi-goddess.* Although this word most often refers to a woodland spirit, here it may also carry its original Greek meaning of unmarried girl.
Pēnēis, -idos: *daughter of the river god Peneus.* Here, a Greek feminine ablative adjective modifying *nympha*.
illo: completes another ANTITHESIS begun with *hoc*.
473 **Apollineus, -a, -um:** *of or pertaining to Apollo.*
trāiciō, -ere, -iēcī, -iectum: *to pierce, transfix.*
medulla, -ae (f.): *marrow*; often representing the inmost soul. This wound will have a dramatic effect on Apollo, changing him from an epic-scale hero into a frustrated elegiac lover, just as Cupid's arrow does to Ovid himself in *Amores* I. 1.

protinus alter amat, fugit altera nomen amantis
475   silvarum latebris captivarumque ferarum
exuviis gaudens innuptaeque aemula Phoebes:
vitta coercebat positos sine lege capillos.
multi illam petiere, illa aversata petentes
inpatiens expersque viri nemora avia lustrat

✣ ✣ ✣

474 **alter ... altera:** graphic CHIASMUS succinctly pointing out the ANTITHESIS.
amans, -tis (m.): *a lover.* This line, full of ASSONANCE, completes the fourth ANTITHESIS within five lines. The same words (*alter, amo*), in varying forms, are employed to describe two different effects on two different characters. The phrase *nomen amantis* constitutes a PLEONASM for Apollo.
475 **latebra, -ae (f.):** *hiding place.*
476 **exuviae, -ārum (f.):** *skin torn from a hunted animal, spoils.*
innuptus, -a, -um: *unmarried.*
aemula, -ae (f.): *a female imitator.*
Phoebē, -ēs (f.): *Diana*, twin sister to Apollo; the virgin goddess most associated with forests and the hunt. Here, a Greek genitive singular ending.
477 **vitta:** a headband was worn by both married and unmarried women; but married women wore their hair tied up while unmarried women let it hang loose (*sine lege*) as Daphne does here.
coerceō, -ēre, -uī, -itum: *to restrain, restrict, control.*
478 **petiere:** the third person plural perfect active alternate form. Here meaning *to seek the hand of in marriage, to court.*
āversor, -ārī, -ātus: *to turn away from in disgust, to reject.*
petentes: an accusative plural present participle used here as a substantive to represent Daphne's suitors.
479 **inpatiens, -ntis:** *impatient.*
expers, -ertis: *lacking experience or knowledge.*
nemus, -oris (n.): *wood, sacred grove.*
āvius, -a, -um: *uncharted, remote, distant.*
lustrō, -āre, -āvī, -ātum: *to move through or around, traverse, roam.*

84 ✦ OVID

480   nec, quid Hymen, quid Amor, quid sint conubia curat.
       saepe pater dixit: "generum mihi, filia, debes,"
       saepe pater dixit: "debes mihi, nata, nepotes";
       illa velut crimen taedas exosa iugales
       pulchra verecundo suffuderat ora rubore
485   inque patris blandis haerens cervice lacertis
       "da mihi perpetua, genitor carissime," dixit
       "virginitate frui! dedit hoc pater ante Dianae."

✦ ✦ ✦

480 **quid ... quid ... quid:** sets up a TRICOLON emphasizing strongly Daphne's lack of interest in marriage.
Hymēn: *the god of marriage* and, by extension, marriage.
cōnūbium, -ī (n.): *the rite or ceremony of marriage.*
481 **gener, -erī (m.):** *a son-in-law.*
482 **saepe pater dixit:** ANAPHORA drawing attention to Peneus's words which embody the purpose of Roman marriage, to produce children.
generum ... debes, debes ... nepotes: graphic CHIASMUS.
nāta, -ae (f.): *daughter.*
483 **velut:** *just as, in the same way that*; often introduces a SIMILE. Here, with *crimen*.
taedas: these were the pine torches carried in marriage processions that escorted a bride to her husband's house the night of the wedding. Here, a METONYMY referring to the marriage state.
exōsus, -a, -um: *hating, despising. odi* and its compounds have either an active or passive meaning; here, present active.
iugālis, -e: *matrimonial, nuptial.*
484 **pulchra ... rubore:** a GOLDEN LINE—a five-word line made up of a central verb flanked by an adjective/noun pair in INTERLOCKED WORD ORDER on each side.
ora: an accusative plural direct object.
verēcundus, -a, -um: *modest.*
suffundō, -ere, -fūdī, -fūsum: *to pour into, overspread; to color, redden, blush.*
rubor, -ōris (m.): *redness.*
485 **blandus, -a, -um:** *charming, seductive, caressing.*
cervix, -īcis (f.): *the neck.*
lacertus, -ī (m.): *the upper arm from elbow to shoulder.* The word order here may portray Daphne with her arms entwined about her father's neck.
486 **genitor, -ōris (m.):** *father.*
487 **virginitās, -tātis (f.):** *maidenhood.*
Dianae: at the age of three, Diana is said to have asked for and been granted the gift of Virginity from her father, Jupiter (see Calimachus *Hymn to Artemis, I*).

ille quidem obsequitur, sed te decor iste quod optas
esse vetat, votoque tuo tua forma repugnat:
490 Phoebus amat visaeque cupit conubia Daphnes,
quodque cupit, sperat, suaque illum oracula fallunt,
utque leves stipulae demptis adolentur aristis,
ut facibus saepes ardent, quas forte viator
vel nimis admovit vel iam sub luce reliquit,
495 sic deus in flammas abiit, sic pectore toto

✣ ✣ ✣

488 **obsequor, -sequī, -secūtus:** *to comply, humor, gratify.*
te: APOSTROPHE—heightens sympathy for Daphne and her impossible situation: beauty that attracts unwanted male advances.
decor, -ōris (m.): *beauty, good looks.*
489 **vōtum, -ī (n.):** *vow, oath.* Here, a dative after a compound verb. The preponderance of harsh *t* sounds and the juxtapositions of *vetat, voto* and *tuo, tua* all reinforce Daphne's hopeless situation.
repugnō, -āre, -āvī, -ātum: *to resist, fight against.*
490 **Daphnes:** here an objective genitive dependent on *conubia*. This noun has a Greek declension: *Daphnē, Daphnēs, Daphnae, Daphnēn, Daphnē.*
491 **suaque... fallunt:** Apollo, the god most associated with prophecy, is unable to see the futility of his own desire. He is self-deceived.
ōrāculum, -ī (n.): *oracle, divine utterance.*
492 **utque:** introduces a SIMILE.
stipula, -ae (f.): *stubble, the stalks left in the field after a harvest.*
dēmō, -ere, dempsī, demptum: *to remove, take away.*
adoleō, -ēre, -uī, adultum: *to burn.*
arista, -ae (f.): *harvest.*
493 **ut:** ANAPHORA and ASYNDETON introducing a second SIMILE about burning.
saepēs, -is (f.): *hedge.*
494 **vel... vel:** the correlatives balance the line creating a parallel structure just as *sic, sic* will do in the next line.
sub luce: translate idiomatically as *at dawn.*
495 **sic... sic:** these resolve the earlier two SIMILES introduced by *utque* (492) and *ut* (493).
abeō, -īre, -iī, -itum: *to change, be transformed into.*

uritur et sterilem sperando nutrit amorem.
spectat inornatos collo pendere capillos
et "quid, si comantur?" ait. videt igne micantes
sideribus similes oculos, videt oscula, quae non
500 est vidisse satis; laudat digitosque manusque
bracchiaque et nudos media plus parte lacertos;
si qua latent, meliora putat. fugit ocior aura

✦ ✦ ✦

496 **urō, -ere, ussī, ustum:** *to burn, inflame with passion*; parallel to *Amores* I. 1.26 when Ovid, the lover, is struck with one of Cupid's arrows.
sterilis, -e: *futile*; an appropriate adjective as Apollo's love for Daphne is all in vain. Unlike the *stipulae* in line 492, which make the fields more fertile, Apollo burns with a love that will never be fruitful; it will never be rewarded or fulfilled.
sperando: here a simple ablative gerund.
nūtriō, -īre, -īvī, -ītum: *to encourage, foster.*
497 **collum, -ī (n.):** *the neck.*
pendeō, -ēre, pependī: *to hang.*
498 **comō, -ere, -psī, -ptum:** *to adorn, arrange*. Here, a subjunctive in a future-less-vivid condition with the apodosis understood.
499 **sīdus, -eris (n.):** *star, constellation*. Here, dative with *similes*.
osculum, -ī (n.): *mouth, lips.*
500 **... que ... que:** with the third *-que* immediately in 501 create POLYSYNDETON isolating and highlighting each part as Apollo runs his eyes over her body.
501 **brācchium, -ī (n.):** *arm.*
nudos ... lacertos: a CHIASTIC arrangement of words drawing attention to her partially exposed arms that excite the young god. *media* and *parte* are ablatives of comparison with the adverbial *plus,* which modifies *nudos*. Translate roughly *her arms more than half naked.*
502 **qua:** variant form of *aliquae* after *si*. Ovid leaves out the details but provides ample room for imagination.
ōcior, ōcius: *swifter, faster.*
aura, -ae (f.): *a breeze.*

illa levi neque ad haec revocantis verba resistit:
"nympha, precor, Penei, mane! non insequor hostis;
505 nympha, mane! sic agna lupum, sic cerva leonem,
sic aquilam penna fugiunt trepidante columbae,
hostes quaeque suos: amor est mihi causa sequendi!
me miserum! ne prona cadas indignave laedi
crura notent sentes et sim tibi causa doloris!

✦ ✦ ✦

503 **illa levi:** completes the INTERLOCKED phrase begun with *ocior aura* (502). The ENJAMBMENT between lines 502–3 helps to reflect the speed and intention with which Daphne flees her pursuer.
504 **precor, -ārī, -ātus:** *to pray for, implore, beg.* It is of note that Apollo, a god, is here reduced to praying to a maiden.
Pēnēi: here, a Greek vocative ending in short *-i*. The multiple CAESURAE, in this line as well as in the next several lines describing Apollo's pursuit of the maiden, suggest intermittent utterances during the chase. We can almost hear him gasping for air as he pursues her.
insequor, -sequī, -secūtus: *to pursue.*
505 **sic:** the first of three phrases that, introduced with this same adverb, create a TRICOLON CRESCENDO full of IRONY because, although he claims not to be, Apollo behaves exactly like the wolf, the lion, and the eagle, all predatory hunters.
agna, -ae (f.): *a ewe lamb.*
cerva, -ae (f.): *a deer.*
506 **aquila, -ae (f.):** *an eagle.*
penna, -ae (f.): *a wing; feather.*
columba, -ae (f.): *a dove,* a bird especially associated with Venus.
508 **me miserum:** an accusative of exclamation typical of the elegiac lover (see *Amores* I. 1.25).
cadas: an optative subjunctive, as are *notent* and *sim* (509), introduced by *ne*.
indignus, -a, -um: *not deserving.*
laedō, -ere, laesī, laesum: *to harm, injure.* Here, the present passive infinitive after *indignave*.
509 **crūs, crūris (n.):** *the lower leg, shin.*
notō, -āre, -āvī, -ātum: *to mark.*
sentis, -is (m.): *a briar or bramble.*
sim...doloris: nearly the same structure as *amor...sequendi* (507). Because of its separation from the negative particle *ne*, the clause sounds positive and foreshadows the true ending of the chase.

88 ✦ OVID

510   aspera, qua properas, loca sunt: moderatius, oro,
curre fugamque inhibe, moderatius insequar ipse.
cui placeas, inquire tamen: non incola montis,
non ego sum pastor, non hic armenta gregesque
horridus observo. nescis, temeraria, nescis,
515   quem fugias, ideoque fugis: mihi Delphica tellus
et Claros et Tenedos Patareaque regia servit;
Iuppiter est genitor; per me, quod eritque fuitque

✦ ✦ ✦

510 **qua:** adverb formed from the relative pronoun—*in which direction, where.*
     moderatius: the comparative of the adverb.
511 **inhibeō, -ēre, -uī, -itum:** *to restrain, check.*
512 **cui:** dative with *placeas.*
     inquīrō, -ere, -quīsīvī, -sītum: *to inquire, ask.*
     non: introduces a TRICOLON CRESCENDO with ASYNDETON. His TRICOLON here reflects the one in lines 505–506.
     incola: the verb for this phrase is found in the next line—*sum.*
513 **pastor, -ōris (m.):** *a shepherd.*
     hīc: *here, in this place.*
     armentum, -ī (n.): *a herd.*
     grex, gregis (m.): *a flock.*
514 **horridus, -a, -um:** *rough in manner, rude, uncouth; hairy.*
     nescis ... nescis: repetition for emphasis.
     temerārius, -a, -um: *thoughtless, reckless, hasty.*
515 **fugias:** subjunctive in an indirect question.
     tellūs, -ūris (f.): *land, country.*
516 **et ... et ... -que:** POLYSYNDETON emphasizes just how many places on earth recognize the greatness of this deity.
     Claros, -ī (f.): a small town, sacred to Apollo, on the central coast of Asia Minor.
     Tenedos, -ī (f.): an island in the Aegean, sacred to Apollo.
     Patarēus, -a, -um: *of or related to Patara,* a coastal city in southern Asia Minor with an oracle of Apollo.
     rēgia, -ae (f.): *royal palace, court.*
517 **Iuppiter est genitor:** Apollo comically tries to place himself back into the realm of deities even while he is possessed by very human emotions and in hot pursuit of Daphne.
     per me: ANAPHORA and ENJAMBMENT drawing yet more attention to the boast.

estque, patet; per me concordant carmina nervis.
certa quidem nostra est, nostra tamen una sagitta
520   certior, in vacuo quae vulnera pectore fecit!
inventum medicina meum est, opiferque per orbem
dicor, et herbarum subiecta potentia nobis.
ei mihi, quod nullis amor est sanabilis herbis
nec prosunt domino, quae prosunt omnibus, artes!"
525   Plura locuturum timido Peneia cursu
fugit cumque ipso verba inperfecta reliquit,

✦ ✦ ✦

518 ...-que: the third in a series creating POLYSYNDETON that isolates and emphasizes each of the three verbs and adds weight to Apollo's boast about his prophetic powers. Nonetheless he is unable to foresee his own failure in this chase.
concordō, -āre, -āvī, -ātum: *to agree, harmonize.*
nervus, -ī (m.): *a string of a musical instrument.* Here, an ablative, probably of place where without the preposition.

519 **nostra:** nominative but difficult to see because of ELISION; modifies *sagitta*.
nostra: ablative of comparison with *certior* (520).
una: Cupid's.
sagitta, -ae (f.): *arrow.* Take with both clauses in the line.

521 **inventum, -ī (n.):** *discovery, invention.*
medicina: Apollo is known as the god of healing. It is IRONIC that just as his power of foresight has earlier failed him, so too do his powers fail to heal the wound caused by Cupid's arrow.
opifer, -era, -erum: *aid-bringing, helper.*

522 **herba, -ae (f.):** *plant, herb.*
sūbiciō -ere, -iēcī, -iectum: *to subject to, put under the control of.* Supply *est*.
potentia, -ae (f.): *power, influence.*

523 **ei:** interjection used to express anguish, *oh!*
mihi: dative of reference.
quod: take with the interjection and translate *alas, that*.
sānābilis, -e: *curable.* For the elegiac lover, love is a disease, often incurable.

525 **plura:** neuter accusative plural object of *locuturum*.
locuturum: future active participial direct object of *fugit*. Modifies *him* (*Apollo*).

526 **inperfectus, -a, -um:** *unfinished.*

tum quoque visa decens; nudabant corpora venti,
obviaque adversas vibrabant flamina vestes,
et levis inpulsos retro dabat aura capillos,
530 auctaque forma fuga est. sed enim non sustinet ultra
perdere blanditias iuvenis deus, utque monebat
ipse Amor, admisso sequitur vestigia passu.
ut canis in vacuo leporem cum Gallicus arvo
vidit, et hic praedam pedibus petit, ille salutem;

✦ ✦ ✦

527 **tum ... decens:** supply *est* to complete the perfect passive with *visa*.
corpora: often used in poetry in the plural to stand for the whole person.
venti: the first of three words (with *flamina*, 528 and *aura*, 529) used in three lines referring to the movement of air and its effects on Daphne's body and clothing. Note the parallel structure of the lines, particularly 528–29.
528 **obvius, -a, -um:** *opposing, confronting.*
vibrō, -āre, -āvī, -ātum: *to wave, flutter.*
flāmen, -inis (n.): *wind, breeze.*
529 **inpellō, -ere, -pulī, -pulsum:** *to push, drive, set in motion.*
530 **auctaque ... est:** the ASSONANCE of *a* sounds smoothes the line and with the ELISION quickens the pace of her flight, which only serves to make her more desirable and attractive to the god. The mid-line break in sense allows but a brief pause in the narrative for both reader and pursuer.
ultra: *further, beyond that point.*
531 **blanditia, -ae (f.):** *charm, flattery.*
532 **Amor:** because of the *ipse*, this must be translated as *Cupid*.
admisso: *having been given full rein, at full speed.*
533 **ut canis:** a SIMILE of epic proportions. Apollo gains strength in the SIMILE and resumes his former stature of the skilled, proven hunter. The god seems here to become the actual enemy of real prey; this he had earlier in line 504 claimed not to be.
cum: conjunction.
Gallicus, -a, -um: *of Gaul.*
arvum, -ī (n.): *field, ploughed land.*
534 **hic ... ille:** *hic* refers to the nearer of the two possible antecedents, the *Gallicus (canis)*, and *ille* to the hare, the farther of the two. They form a parallel ANTITHESIS.
praeda, -ae (f.): *prey.*

535   alter inhaesuro similis iam iamque tenere
        sperat et extento stringit vestigia rostro,
        alter in ambiguo est, an sit conprensus, et ipsis
        morsibus eripitur tangentiaque ora relinquit:
        sic deus et virgo est hic spe celer, illa timore.
540   qui tamen insequitur pennis adiutus Amoris,
        ocior est requiemque negat tergoque fugacis
        inminet et crinem sparsum cervicibus adflat.

✦ ✦ ✦

535 **alter**: the beginning of another ANTITHESIS.
    inhaereō, -rēre, -sī, -sum: *to stick, cling, attach*. Here, the masculine dative future active participle with *similis*.
    iam iamque: adds speed to the meter and vividness to the SIMILE.
536 **vestigia:** recalls the *vestigia* of line 532 that referred directly to Daphne. Here, refers not just to the impression left by the foot but to the foot itself.
    rostrum, -ī (n.): *muzzle, snout*.
537 **alter:** completes the ANTITHESIS begun in line 535.
    ambiguum, -ī (n.): *uncertainty, doubt*.
    an sit conprensus: an indirect question introduced by *an*.
    conprendō, -ere, -dī, -sum: *to seize, catch hold of*.
538 **morsus, -ūs (m.):** *a bite*.
    eripitur: this passive form carries a reflexive meaning—*snatches itself away*. This is a line filled with harsh sounds that reflect the frightening situation.
539 **hic ... illa:** another ANTITHESIS with parallel structure. In this instance, because of the clear genders, *hic* and *illa* are not *the former* and *the latter*, but rather *he* and *she*.
    spēs, -eī (f.): *hope, expectation*.
540 **adiuvō, -āre, -iūvī, -iūtum:** *to help, assist*.
541 **ōcior, -ius:** *swifter*. The subject is the *qui*-clause in line 540.
    requiēs, -ētis (f.): (*requiem*, acc.) *rest, relaxation*.
    tergo: dative after *inminet* (542).
    fugax, -ācis: *fleeing, running away*—the one who is fleeing, i.e., Daphne. The rapid succession of increasingly longer clauses helps to give the effect of speed and of the ever-gaining Apollo.
542 **inmineō, -ēre:** *to press closely on, to be almost on*.
    spargō, -ere, sparsī, sparsum: *to scatter, strew*.
    cervix, -īcis (f.): *neck*.
    adflō, -āre, -āvī, -ātum: *to breathe onto, blow onto*.

　　　　　viribus absumptis expalluit illa citaeque
　　　　　victa labore fugae spectans Peneidas undas
545　　　"fer, pater," inquit "opem! si flumina numen habetis,
547　　　qua nimium placui, mutando perde figuram!"
　　　　　vix prece finita torpor gravis occupat artus,
　　　　　mollia cinguntur tenui praecordia libro,
550　　　in frondem crines, in ramos bracchia crescunt,
　　　　　pes modo tam velox pigris radicibus haeret,

✦ ✦ ✦

543　**absumō, -ere, -sumpsī, -sumptum:** *to use up, squander, spend.*
　　expallescō, -ere, -paluī: *to turn pale.*
　　citus, -a, -um: *rapid, speedy.*
544　**victa:** modifies the subject, Daphne.
　　Peneidas undas: direct object of *spectans*. Refers to her father, the river.
545　**fer:** imperative singular.
　　flumina: nominative plural subject of *habetis*. Since her father was the divinity of the river, she refers to him as the water itself.
547　**qua:** refers to *figuram*; ablative of means or instrument. The lack of a line 546 is due to uncertainties and inaccuracies in the ancient texts.
　　nimium: *excessively, extremely, very much.*
548　**torpor, -ōris (m.):** *numbness, heaviness.*
　　artus, -ūs (m.): *limb of a tree or body.*
549　**tenuis, -e:** *fine, thin.*
　　praecordia, -ōrum (n.): *chest, heart, breast.*
　　liber, -brī (m.): *the inner bark of a tree.*
550　**frons, -dis (f.):** *foliage, leafy boughs.*
　　crescunt: with both clauses of the line.
551　**vēlox, -ōcis:** *swift, speedy.* The strong, principal CAESURA of this line falls between two ANTONYMS, *velox* || *pigris*, which graphically reflect the change brought about by Daphne's ongoing metamorphosis.
　　piger, -gra, -grum: *sluggish, inactive.*
　　rādix, -īcis (f.): *a root*; here, ablative with *haeret*.
　　haereō, -ēre, haesī, haesum: *to cling.* The many SPONDEES and multiple consonant clusters slow down the pace of the line perhaps mimicing Daphne's feet, which become slow and stuck to the ground.

ora cacumen habet: remanet nitor unus in illa.
Hanc quoque Phoebus amat positaque in stipite dextra
sentit adhuc trepidare novo sub cortice pectus
555   conplexusque suis ramos ut membra lacertis
oscula dat ligno; refugit tamen oscula lignum.
cui deus "at, quoniam coniunx mea non potes esse,
arbor eris certe" dixit "mea! semper habebunt
te coma, te citharae, te nostrae, laure, pharetrae;

✦ ✦ ✦

552   **cacūmen, -cūminis (n.):** *top or tip of a tree.*
nitor, -ōris (m.): *brilliance, brightness, splendor, elegance.* Though this word is modified with the adjective *unus*, it may nonetheless have a dual reference: to the sheen of the new leaves and to her former glowing beauty. Note the metrical contrast to line 551 where the line is heavily SPONDAIC; here the line is all DACTYLIC.
553   **hanc:** refers to Daphne in her new appearance as the laurel.
stīpes, -itis (m.): *tree trunk; woody branch.*
554   **cortex, -icis (m.):** *outer bark of a tree.*
555   **membrum, -ī (n.):** *part of the body; limb of a tree or body.*
lacertus, -ī (m.): *upper arm.* With *suis*, the CHIASTIC word order places Apollo's arms around the branches/limbs.
556   **lignum, -ī (n.):** *wood, firewood.* Note double use of the word in different cases in this line.
refugit: her transformation has been purely physical. Even in her new guise, Daphne remains true to her former character, shrinking still from Apollo's attention.
559   **te ... te ... te ... :** the pronouns are given great prominence in this line. Ovid employs ANAPHORA to introduce a TRICOLON CRESCENDO, each element of which contains a well-known Apollonian attribute.
coma, -ae (f.): *hair.*
cithara, -ae (f.): *lyre.*
laurus, -ī (f.): *foliage of the laurel (bay) tree; the bay tree.*
pharetra, -ae (f.): *quiver.*

560   tu ducibus Latiis aderis, cum laeta Triumphum
        vox canet et visent longas Capitolia pompas;
        postibus Augustis eadem fidissima custos
        ante fores stabis mediamque tuebere quercum,
        utque meum intonsis caput est iuvenale capillis,
565   tu quoque perpetuos semper gere frondis honores!"

✧ ✧ ✧

560 ducibus: dative with *adsum*. A general celebrating a triumph would wear a garland made of bay and carry a branch of it—the bay being a sign of victory.

Latius, -a, -um: a poetic adjective for Rome, taken from the name of the ancient territory in which Rome was founded. Ovid here links a contemporary Augustan practice to a divine past.

Triumphum: the sacred and glorious procession by which a Roman general was welcomed back to the city of Rome and honored for victories on the battlefield.

561 longas: the procession included officials of the government, spoils captured from the defeated people, sacrificial white bulls, prisoners of war, musicians, and the general and his troops.

Capitolia: used poetically in the plural. The Capitoline was one of the seven hills of Rome, on which sat the great temple to Jupiter Optimus Maximus and the sacred citadel. The procession, which began in the Campus Martius, ended at the Temple of Jupiter on the Capitoline where the general performed a ritual sacrifice and dedicated his laurel/bay wreath.

562 postibus Augustis: ablative with *stabis* (563) without a preposition.

fīdus, -a, -um: *faithful, loyal.*

563 foris, -is (f.): *door;* most frequently in the plural because doors on Roman houses were double doors made of two halves.

tueor, -ērī, tuitus: *to observe, watch over, guard*. Here, the second person singular, future deponent alternate *-re* ending instead of the more common *-ris*.

quercum: over the door to Augustus's house on the Palatine Hill hung a garland of oak leaves called the civic crown.

564 intonsus, -a, -um: *unshorn, uncut.*

iuvenālis, -e: *youthful.*

565 semper: the *Laurus nobilis* or Mediterranean bay tree is an evergreen tree; it never loses its leaves.

gere: second person singular imperative.

finierat Paean: factis modo laurea ramis
adnuit utque caput visa est agitasse cacumen.

✢ ✢ ✢

566 **finierat:** pluperfect indicative formed with the syncopated perfect stem.
Paeān, -nis (m.): yet one more appellation for Apollo; this one suggests his capacity to heal, although he has healed no one in this story. This word is also used of a hymn of praise to Apollo.
laurea, -ae (f.): *the laurel/bay tree.*
567 **adnuō, -ere, -uī, -ūtum:** *to nod, to nod in approval.*
visa est: offers an element of doubt—either she *was seen* or *seemed* to use her treetop as a head to nod her consent to Apollo's words.
agitō, -āre, -āvī, -ātum: *to shake, brandish.*
cacūmen: it is significant that the line ends not with *caput* but with *cacumen*. Daphne's metamorphosis is complete. She has lost all semblance of human form and henceforth will be a tree.

Pyramus and Thisbe

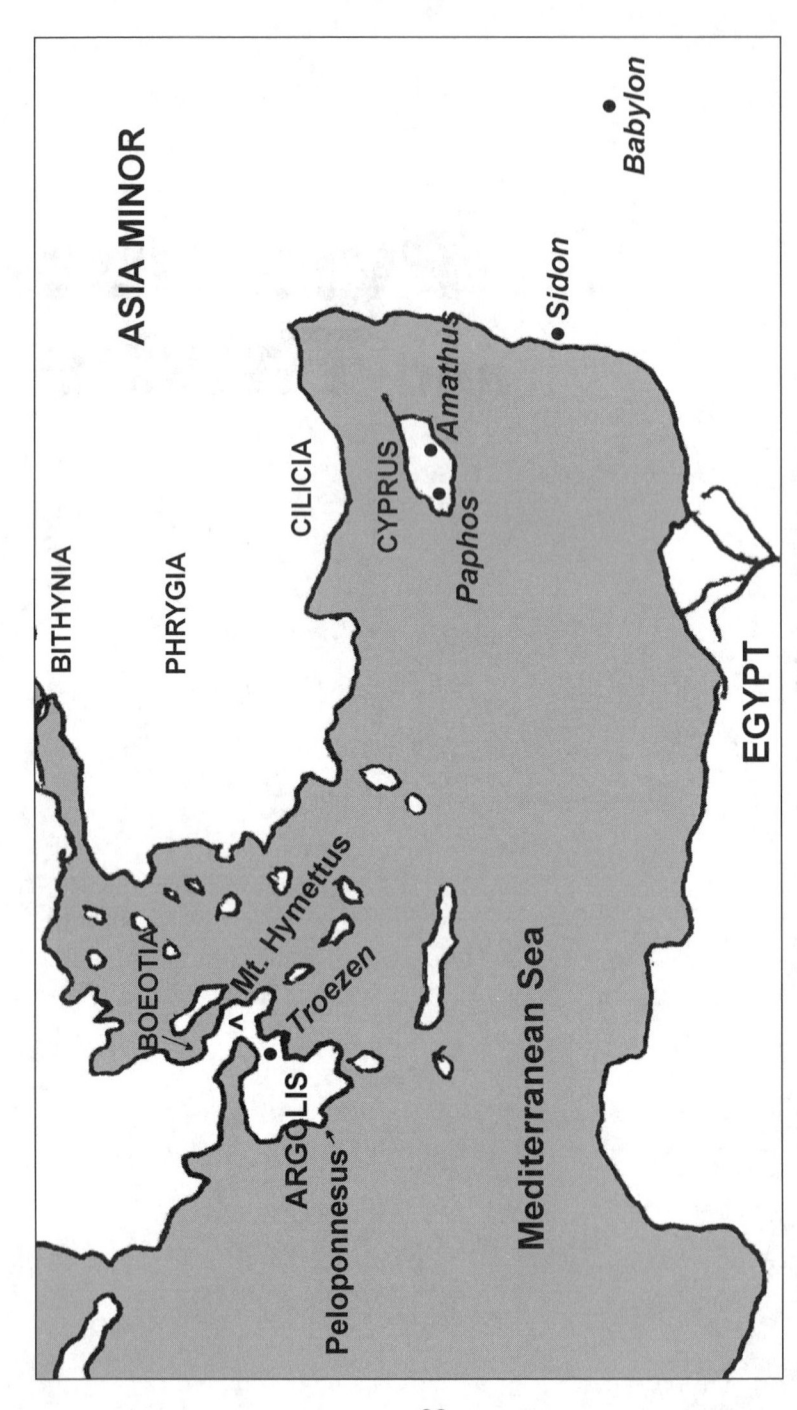

Map of Places in Pyramus and Thisbe, Philemon and Baucis, and Pygmalion

PYRAMUS AND THISBE
Met. IV. 55–166

The episode of Pyramus and Thisbe is a story within a story. It is the first of four told by the three daughters of Minyas, who have chosen to ignore the festival of Bacchus and the priest's call to all women to honor the divinity of the god in wild revels. These daughters have denied the divinity of Bacchus and pursue, while remaining at home, their never-ending tasks of spinning and weaving. By the time the Minyeides have finished their stories, each an account of a metamorphosis, the god whom they have denied and whose holy day they have profaned takes his revenge by changing them into bats.

Ovid sets the scene for Pyramus and Thisbe in the environs of Babylon and gives the two lovers exotic Oriental names. In this tale of forbidden love, the parents will not allow them to marry. The wall that separates their two houses becomes a symbol of this prohibition. But through a chink in the wall they communicate and make plans to meet near a tomb outside the city. Thisbe arrives first and is frightened away by a lioness, who, having just killed a prey, bloodies the cloak that Thisbe has left behind. Pyramus, finding the cloak, concludes that Thisbe is dead and, remorseful and grief-stricken, kills himself. When Thisbe returns she finds him dead and the white berries on the tree next to his body changed to red. She kills herself with his sword so that she may join him in death; in her final words she prays to their parents that they be buried together.

The Pyramus and Thisbe story provided inspiration for the English poet Chaucer and the Italian poet Petrarch. This pair of young, star-crossed lovers also becomes the model for Shakespeare's *Romeo and Juliet*, Schmidt and Jones' *Fantastiks*, and Leonard Bernstein's *West Side Story*, among others. Ovid imbued his tragic tale with a tone that is light and sentimental, and even on occasion mocking and irreverent (see lines 122–24, for example, or consider Thisbe's long speech, lines 141–65). Shakespeare, who knew Latin and had certainly read this story, created a comic version of it in his *Midsummer's Night's Dream* that reflects Ovid's juxtaposition of a serious subject with a light and even humorous tone. Many painters have illustrated the story, including Rembrandt and Poussin.

PYRAMUS AND THISBE
Met. IV. 55–166

"Pyramus et Thisbe, iuvenum pulcherrimus alter,
56 altera, quas Oriens habuit, praelata puellis,
contiguas tenuere domos, ubi dicitur altam
coctilibus muris cinxisse Semiramis urbem.
notitiam primosque gradus vicinia fecit,
60 tempore crevit amor; taedae quoque iure coissent,
sed vetuere patres; quod non potuere vetare,
ex aequo captis ardebant mentibus ambo.

✦ ✦ ✦

55 **Pyramus, -ī (m.):** this name comes from a river in the Roman province of Cilicia (modern Turkey near the Syrian border).
    Thisbē, -ēs (f.): *Thisbe*. As with the Apollo/Daphne passage, this story also begins with the two names of the main characters.
56 **Oriens, -entis (m.):** the setting for this story, as the two main characters' names suggest, is the East, described by Roman writers as an exotic locale.
    praeferō, -ferre, -tulī, -lātum: (+ dat.) *to prefer, esteem more.*
57 **contiguus, -a, -um:** *adjacent, neighboring.*
    tenuere: third person plural alternate perfect form—subject is *Pyramus et Thisbe* (55).
    altam: HYPERBATON. The noun that this adjective modifies, *urbem*, is held until the end of the next line. Such exaggerated separation creates suspense, holds the reader's attention, and mimics the walls that embrace the city.
58 **coctilis, -e:** *of baked bricks.*
    Semīramis, -idis (f.): the legendary queen of Assyria and builder of Babylon.
59 **nōtitia, -ae (f.):** *acquaintance.*
60 **taedae:** a METONYMY for marriage.
    coeō, coīre, coiī, coitum: *to come together, unite.* Here, a pluperfect subjunctive in a mixed contrary-to-fact clause.
61 **vetuere . . . vetare:** an ANTITHESIS involving wordplay.
62 **ex aequo:** *equally.*
    ardebant: the imperfect tense reflects the progress of their love. Note the ASSONANCE of *a* sounds in this line and the long, drawn-out rhythm caused by the succession of SPONDEES.

conscius omnis abest, nutu signisque loquuntur, *deponent*
quoque magis tegitur, tectus magis aestuat ignis.
65 *abl of* fissus erat tenui rima, quam duxerat olim,
description cum fieret, paries domui communis utrique.
id vitium nulli per saecula longa notatum—
quid non sentit amor?—primi vidistis amantes
et vocis fecistis iter, tutaeque per illud
70 murmure blanditiae minimo transire solebant.
saepe, ubi constiterant hinc Thisbe, Pyramus illinc,
inque vices fuerat captatus anhelitus oris,

✢ ✢ ✢

63 **conscius, -ī (m.):** *accomplice.*
  abest: the shift to the present indicative in the next few lines creates a more vivid scene as is customary with the historic present. Translate as past tense.
  nūtus, -ūs (m.): *nod.*
64 **quōque:** because of the long first syllable this is not the familiar adverb *quoque* but rather the adverb *quō* plus *-que*.
  magis tegitur, tectus magis: CHIASTIC arrangement around the central CAESURA that divides the line in imitation of the lovers separated by the wall.
  aestuō, -āre, -āvī, -ātum: *to blaze, seethe.*
65 **findō, -ere, fidī, fissum:** *to split.*
  rīma, -ae (f.): *crack.*
66 **fieret:** functions as a passive of *faciō*. Its subject is *paries*.
  domui: here the fourth declension dative with *communis*.
67 **vitium, -ī (n.):** *defect, fault.*
  nulli: dative of agent with *notatum*.
68 **vidistis:** APOSTROPHE bringing the lovers vividly into the narrative and placing them immediately before us.
70 **murmure...minimo:** alliterative ONOMATOPOEIA; the strong sound of *m*s graphically describes the murmurs passing through the walls.
  blanditia, -ae (f.): *flattery, charm.*
71 **hinc...illinc:** a CHIASMUS arranging the lovers on opposite sides of the wall with a strong DIAERESIS in the middle of the phrase.
72 **fuerat:** read *erat*.
  in vices: an idiomatic usage meaning *by turns, alternately.*
  anhēlitus, -ūs (m.): *gasp, panting.*

	'invide' dicebant 'paries, quid amantibus obstas?
	quantum erat, ut sineres toto nos corpore iungi,
75	aut, hoc si nimium est, vel ad oscula danda pateres?
	nec sumus ingrati: tibi nos debere fatemur,
	quod datus est verbis ad amicas transitus auris.'
	talia diversa nequiquam sede locuti
	sub noctem dixere 'vale' partique dedere
80	oscula quisque suae non pervenientia contra.
	postera nocturnos Aurora removerat ignes,
	solque pruinosas radiis siccaverat herbas:
	ad solitum coiere locum. tum murmure parvo
	multa prius questi statuunt, ut nocte silenti

✦ ✦ ✦

73 **invidus, -a, -um:** *envious, malevolent.* Here, the vocative.
    paries: APOSTROPHE personifying the wall.
74 **erat:** an imperfect indicative in place of an imperfect subjunctive meaning "would be."
    sineres: imperfect subjunctive in a consecutive clause.
75 **ad:** introduces a gerundive of purpose.
    pateres: a continuation of the condition introduced by *ut* (74).
76 **ingrātus, -a, -um:** *ungrateful, thankless.*
77 **quod:** the conjunction here meaning *that, the fact that.*
    auris, -is (f.): *ear.* Here the accusative plural *-is* ending for *i*-stem nouns.
78 **sēdēs, -is (f.):** *house, dwelling.* A nicely balanced line with the adjective/noun pair, which describes the house separated by the adverb *nequiquam* just as the wall separates the two houses.
79 **dixere:** third person plural perfect active alternate form, as are *dedere* and *coiere* (83).
80 **quisque:** nominative singular, in apposition to the subject of *dixere* and *dedere*.
81 **Aurōra, -ae (f.):** *Aurora, goddess of the dawn.*
82 **pruīnōsus, -a, -um:** *frosty.*
    radius, -ī (m.): *ray of light.*

104 ✤ OVID

85 fallere custodes foribusque excedere temptent,
    cumque domo exierint, urbis quoque tecta relinquant,
    neve sit errandum lato spatiantibus arvo,
    conveniant ad busta Nini lateantque sub umbra
    arboris: arbor ibi niveis uberrima pomis,

✦ ✦ ✦

85 **custodes:** like *patres* (61), *custodes* are also traditional obstacles to the fulfillment of love in elegy.
   foris, foris (f.): *door, double-door.*
   temptent: present subjunctive after *statuunt ut* (84), expressing intent.

86 **relinquant:** present subjunctive in a continuation of the *statuunt ut* construction begun in 84. As the lovers, driven by the power of their passions, leave behind the protection of their parents, their doorkeepers, and the city, they expose themselves to the wilderness that will destroy them in the end.
   tecta: a SYNECDOCHE.

87 **neve:** introduces a negative purpose clause, hence the continued use of the subjunctive.
   sit errandum: the passive periphrastic expressing necessity or obligation.
   spatior, -ārī, -ātus: *to walk about.* Here, a present participle referring to the two lovers. This word supplies the dative of agent for the passive periphrastic.

88 **bustum, -ī (n.):** *a tomb*—here a poetic plural with singular intent.
   Ninus, -ī (m.): king of Assyria and second husband to Semiramis; the romance between Ninus and Semiramis was legendary.
   umbra: together with *arbor* (89), *pomis* (89), *gelido* (90), and *fonti* (90), constitute the major characteristics of a *locus amoenus* (a pleasant place). Generally speaking, a *locus amoenus* represents relaxation, protection, comfort, or simple pleasures; it is the ideal setting for romance.

89 **niveus, -a, -um:** *snow-white, snowy.*
   ūber, -eris: *plentiful, abundant.*
   pōmum, -ī (n.): *a fruit.*

90   ardua morus, erat, gelido contermina fonti.
       pacta placent; et lux, tarde discedere visa,
       praecipitatur aquis, et aquis nox exit ab isdem.
       "Callida per tenebras versato cardine Thisbe
       egreditur fallitque suos adopertaque vultum
95   pervenit ad tumulum dictaque sub arbore sedit.

✦ ✦ ✦

90 **arduus, -a, -um:** *tall, lofty.* The emphatic wording in this elaborate description of the mulberry tree reminds us that it provides the essential *aition* (origin) for the tale.
    mōrus, -ī (f.): *the mulberry tree.*
    gelidus, -a, -um: *icy cold.* Here a dative after the adjective *contermina.*
    conterminus, -a, -um: *nearby, adjacent.*
91 **pactum, -ī (n.):** *agreement.* From the perfect passive participle of *pacisco*, this verb often connotes a person who is betrothed, much as the characters in this story wish to be.
    tarde: three of the six feet in this line are SPONDEES slowing down the rhythm in step with the slow-setting sun.
92 **praecipitatur:** in contrast, this line is filled with DACTYLS, which quicken the pace of the line and mimic the action of the sun here.
    isdem: an alternate ablative plural form of *idem*. This does not mean the same spot in which the sun set but rather the same region, i.e., the sea.
93 **callidus, -a, -um:** *clever, resourceful.* This quality is normally considered essential to the elegiac lover in his schemes, but here Thisbe's cleverness will lead to the tragic deaths of the two lovers.
    versō, -āre, -āvī, -ātum: *to turn.*
    cardō, -inis (m.): *hinge.*
94 **suos:** modifies a missing *patres* or more likely her *custodes* of line 85, which is used there with the same verb, *fallo*, as here.
    adoperiō, -perīre, -peruī, -pertum: *to cover over.* Her covering allows her not to be recognized and successfully to deceive the doorkeepers.
    vultum: an accusative of specification, or Greek accusative, found in poetry to denote the part of the body affected.
95 **tumulum, -ī (n.):** *a grave, tomb.*

audacem faciebat amor. venit ecce recenti
caede leaena boum spumantis oblita rictus,
depositura sitim vicini fontis in unda;
quam procul ad lunae radios Babylonia Thisbe
100 vidit et obscurum timido pede fugit in antrum,
dumque fugit, tergo velamina lapsa reliquit.
ut lea saeva sitim multa conpescuit unda,
dum redit in silvas, inventos forte sine ipsa

✦ ✦ ✦

96 **faciebat:** the shift to the imperfect tense after a series of perfect verbs stresses the continuous effect love is having on her. Love is transforming her into something she had not been before.
venit: the first syllable is short, making this the historic present tense, shifting the reader's perspective back to the maiden's immediate situation.
ecce: this adverbial demonstrative makes the reader an eyewitness.
97 **boum:** genitive plural of *bōs, bovis* with *caede recenti*.
spumō, -āre, -avī, -ātum: *to foam, froth*. Here, the final syllable is long, making this the accusative plural of the present participle with *i*-stem endings. It modifies *rictus*.
oblinō, -ere, -lēvī, -litum: *to besmear, make dirty*. Modifies *leaena*.
rictus, -ūs, (m.): *the opening of the jaws*—another Greek accusative of the part of the body affected.
98 **depositura:** future active participle agreeing with *leaena* (97) and expressing intention.
sitis, -is (f.): *thirst*.
99 **ad:** *by the light of*.
Babylonia Thisbe: a reference to the city of her birth.
100 **obscūrus, -a, -um:** *dim, dark*.
timido: her recent boldness disappears quickly with the threat from the lioness.
antrum, -ī (n.): *a cave*.
101 **lapsa:** from *labor, labī, lapsus*.
102 **conpescō, -ere, -pescuī:** *to quench*.
103 **forte:** may be taken with either *inventos* or *sine ipsa*, or both. It reminds us of the purely accidental cause of this tragedy.
ipsa: refers to Thisbe.

ore cruentato tenues laniavit amictus.
105 serius egressus vestigia vidit in alto
pulvere certa ferae totoque expalluit ore
Pyramus; ut vero vestem quoque sanguine tinctam
repperit, 'una duos' inquit 'nox perdet amantes,
e quibus illa fuit longa dignissima vita;
110 nostra nocens anima est. ego te, miseranda, peremi,
in loca plena metus qui iussi nocte venires
nec prior huc veni. nostrum divellite corpus
et scelerata fero consumite viscera morsu,

✣ ✣ ✣

104 **cruentō, -āre, -āvī, -ātum:** *to stain with blood.*
tenuis, -e: *thin, slender.*
laniō, -āre, -āvī, -ātum: *to tear, mangle.*
amictus, -ūs (m.): *cloak*; modified by *inventos* (103). This adjective/noun pair encloses the clause as the cloak earlier enclosed Thisbe.
105 **sērus, -a, -um:** *late, after the expected time.* Here, the neuter comparative adverb.
107 **tingō, -ere, -nxī, -nctum:** *to wet, soak.*
108 **reperiō, -īre, repperī, repertum:** *to find, discover.*
una duos: the ANTITHESIS created by the juxtaposition of these two words adds emphasis. Note the INTERLOCKED WORD ORDER in the remainder of the line: *una duos . . . nox . . . amantes.*
110 **nostra:** the meaning is singular, as it also is in line 112.
ego . . . peremi: the words referring to Pyramus embrace *te, miseranda,* referring to Thisbe. For the second time in this lament, for dramatic effect, Ovid's narrator draws attention to Pyramus's words by APOSTROPHE.
peremō, -ere, -ī, -ptum: *to kill.*
111 **venires:** *iubeo* is used with the imperfect subjunctive minus the expected *ut* to introduce an indirect command.
112 **divellō, -ere, -vulsī, -vulsum:** *to tear apart, tear open, tear in two.*
113 **scelerātus, -a, -um:** *wicked, accursed, impious.*
morsus, -ūs (m.): *a bite.*
et . . . morsu: is a variation of a GOLDEN LINE.

o quicumque sub hac habitatis rupe leones!
115 sed timidi est optare necem.' velamina Thisbes
tollit et ad pactae secum fert arboris umbram,
utque dedit notae lacrimas, dedit oscula vesti,
'accipe nunc' inquit 'nostri quoque sanguinis haustus!'
quoque erat accinctus, demisit in ilia ferrum,
120 nec mora, ferventi moriens e vulnere traxit.
ut iacuit resupinus humo, cruor emicat alte,
non aliter quam cum vitiato fistula plumbo
scinditur et tenui stridente foramine longas

✦ ✦ ✦

114 **quicumque:** modifies *leones*.
rūpēs, -is (f.): *rocky cliff.*
leones: vocative case.
115 **timidi:** a genitive of quality or characteristic with a *hominis* understood.
nex, necis (f.): *death.*
Thisbes: a Greek genitive ending.
116 **paciscor, -ī, pactus:** *to agree upon.*
117 **notae . . . vesti:** HYPERBATON.
118 **haustus, -ūs (m.):** *a drawn quantity of liquid, a drink.*
119 **accingō, -ere, -xī, -ctum:** *to gird, equip.*
ilia, -ium (n. pl.): *gut, groin.*
120 **nec mora:** *there was no delay.*
fervens, -ntis: *hot, fresh.*
traxit: from *traho, trahere, traxī, tractum.*
121 **resupīnus, -a, -um:** *lying on one's back.*
humus, -ī (f.): *ground, earth.*
cruor, -ōris (m.): *blood, gore.*
ēmicō, -āre, -āvī, -ātum: *to spurt, shoot forth.*
122 **non aliter quam:** an example of LITOTES, expressing the affirmative by denying the opposite. It introduces a SIMILE.
vitiō, -āre, -āvī, -ātum: *to impair, cause defects in.*
fistula, -ae (f.): *pipe, tube.*
plumbum, -ī (n.): *lead.*
123 **stridō, -ere, -ī:** *to make a high-pitched sound; to whistle, shriek, hiss.*
forāmen, -inis (n.): *a hole, aperture.*

eiaculatur aquas atque ictibus aera rumpit.
125 arborei fetus adspergine caedis in atram
vertuntur faciem, madefactaque sanguine radix
purpureo tinguit pendentia mora colore.
"Ecce metu nondum posito, ne fallat amantem,
illa redit iuvenemque oculis animoque requirit,
130 quantaque vitarit narrare pericula gestit;
utque locum et visa cognoscit in arbore formam,
sic facit incertam pomi color: haeret, an haec sit.
dum dubitat, tremebunda videt pulsare cruentum

✦ ✦ ✦

124 ēiaculor, -ārī, -ātus: *to shoot forth.*
ictus, -ūs (m.): *a blow, stroke, thrust.*
āēr, āeris (n.): *the air.* This is a three-syllable word with a Greek accusative ending.
125 fētus, -ūs (m.): *fruit or product of a plant.*
adspergō, -ginis (f.): *a sprinkling, scattering, splashing.*
āter, ātra, ātrum: *black, dark-colored, stained.*
126 faciēs, -iēī (f.): *appearance, looks.*
madefaciō, -ere, -fēcī, -factum: *to soak, drench.*
127 purpureus, -a, -um: *purple, crimson.*
pendeō, -ēre, pependī: *to hang.*
mōrum, -ī (n.): *the fruit of the mulberry tree.*
128 ecce: signals a shift in scene and character. Thisbe returns to the scene.
129 occulis animoque: ZEUGMA.
130 vitō, -āre, -āvī, -ātum: *to avoid*; here the syncopated form of the perfect subjunctive used in an indirect question.
gestiō, -īre, -īvī: *to desire eagerly, want, be anxious to.*
131 utque: a correlative with *sic* (132) meaning *although . . . still.*
132 haereō, -ēre, haesī, haesum: *to be brought to a standstill, be perplexed, hesitate.*
sit: present subjunctive in an indirect question. The DIAERESIS and the three monosyllabic words that end the line underscore Thisbe's reluctance to proceed toward the tree.
133 tremebundus, -a, -um: *trembling, quivering.*

membra solum, retroque pedem tulit, oraque buxo
135   pallidiora gerens exhorruit aequoris instar,
quod tremit, exigua cum summum stringitur aura.
sed postquam remorata suos cognovit amores,
percutit indignos claro plangore lacertos
et laniata comas amplexaque corpus amatum
140   vulnera supplevit lacrimis fletumque cruori
miscuit et gelidis in vultibus oscula figens
'Pyrame,' clamavit, 'quis te mihi casus ademit?
Pyrame, responde! tua te carissima Thisbe

✦ ✦ ✦

134 **membrum, -ī (n.):** *limb.*
  solum, -ī (n.): *earth, soil.* These two nouns follow their adjectives in a separate line. The slowed resolution of adjective with noun mimics Thisbe's own gradual realization of what has happened.
  buxus, -ī (f.): *boxwood.* The wood of the boxwood is well known for its light color.
135 **exhorreō, -ēre:** *to shudder.*
  instar (n.): *like, just like*—usually takes the genitive case. Sets up a SIMILE comparing Thisbe's shaking to trembling water.
136 **tremit:** phonetically connects Thisbe to Pyramus's *tremebunda*.
  exiguus, -a, -um: *small, slight.*
  aura, -ae (f.): *breeze.*
137 **remoror, -ārī, -ātus:** *to linger, delay.*
  amores: the plural is a standard variant in poetry, generally taken to mean *beloved.*
138 **percutiō, -ere, -cussī, -cussum:** *to beat, strike.*
  clārus, -a, -um: *loud, shrill.*
  plangor, -oris (n.): *beating, lamentation.*
  lacertus, -ī (m.): *upper arm.* Thisbe's actions here and in line 139 are the typical ritual gestures of the woman as mourner in the ancient world.
139 **coma, -ae (f.):** *hair.* Here a Greek accusative of respect.
  amplector, -ī, -plexus: *to embrace.*
140 **suppleō, -ēre, -ēvī, -ētum:** *to fill up.* HYPERBOLE stretching all imagination.
141 **vultibus:** a poetic plural.
142 **mihi:** dative of separation.
  adimō, -ere, -ēmī, -emptum: *to take away, remove.*
143 **Pyrame:** ANAPHORA adding pathos to her lament.
  responde: the first of three imperatives setting up a TRICOLON.
  tua te: ALLITERATION linking the two lovers with the same sound.

nominat; exaudi vultusque attolle iacentes!'
145 ad nomen Thisbes oculos a morte gravatos
Pyramus erexit visaque recondidit illa.
"Quae postquam vestemque suam cognovit et ense
vidit ebur vacuum, 'tua te manus' inquit 'amorque
perdidit, infelix! est et mihi fortis in unum
150 hoc manus, est et amor: dabit hic in vulnera vires.
persequar extinctum letique miserrima dicar
causa comesque tui: quique a me morte revelli
heu sola poteras, poteris nec morte revelli.

✣ ✣ ✣

144 **nōminō, -āre, -āvī, -ātum:** *to call by name.*
attollō, -ere: *to lift up, raise.*
145 **Thisbes:** it is the mention of her name, not his, that stirs him.
gravō, -āre, -āvī, -ātum: *to make heavy, weigh down.* The many SPONDEES weigh down the line just like Pyramus's eyes, which are weighed down by Death.
146 **ērigō, -ere, -exī, -ectum:** *to raise.*
recondō, -ere, -idī, -itum: *to close again.*
147 **quae:** feminine nominative singular referring to Thisbe. Along with *-que*, connects this sentence to the previous one—*and when she.*
ensis, -is (m.): *a sword.*
148 **ebur, -oris (n.):** *ivory*—through SYNECDOCHE means *a scabbard.*
tua te: modifying *manus* and referring to Pyramus, this phrase mimics line 143.
149 **perdidit:** an example of ZEUGMA.
et: the first of two correlatives *et . . . et* meaning *both . . . and.*
mihi: dative of possession with *est.*
unum: with *hoc* of line 150 means *for this one thing.*
150 **amor:** here *amor* will give her strength; in line 96 *amor* made her bold.
hic: antecedent is *amor*, giving precedence to the power of her love.
151 **persequor, -sequī, -secūtus:** *to follow all the way, accompany.*
lētum, -ī (n.): *death.*
152 **revellō, -ere, -vellī, -vulsum:** *to remove, tear away.* The two occurrences of this verb, here and in line 153, form a paradox: death, which has taken him away from her, will, in fact, not take him away from her because of her own suicide.
153 **nec:** *not even.*

112 ✦ OVID

        hoc tamen amborum verbis estote rogati,
155   o multum miseri meus illiusque parentes,
        ut, quos certus amor, quos hora novissima iunxit,
        conponi tumulo non invideatis eodem;
        at tu, quae ramis arbor miserabile corpus
        nunc tegis unius, mox es tectura duorum,
160   signa tene caedis pullosque et luctibus aptos

✦ ✦ ✦

154 **hoc . . . rogati:** a heavily spondaic line. The slow, plodding meter lends weight and importance to the request she is about to make. The passive *rogati* takes the accusative *hoc*.
      estote: this is the future plural imperative emphatically expressing a command to be carried out in the future. Thisbe directly addresses the absent fathers in an APOSTROPHE.
155 **o:** sets up a direct address.
      multum: adverbial modifying the adjective *miseri*.
      miseri: vocative case modifying *parentes* at line end. Thisbe earlier used this adjective to describe herself in line 151.
      meus: the use of the singular adjective refers to Thisbe's father as the genitive *illius* does to Pyramus's.
156 **ut:** introduces an indirect command after *rogati* (154).
      quos . . . quos: ANAPHORA. These relative pronouns are each direct objects in their own clauses. The implied antecedents, *eos* or *nos*, of these pronouns function as subjects of the passive infinitive *conponi* (157).
      novissimus, -a, -um: *last, final*.
157 **conponi:** a present passive infinitive used in an indirect statement with *invideatis*.
      invideō, -ēre, -vīdī, -vīsum: *to refuse, be unwilling*.
158 **tu . . . arbor:** PERSONIFICATION.
159 **es tectura:** an active periphrastic expressing what is about to be.
160 **tene:** imperative singular, continuation of the direct address to the tree, as is *habe* (161). The metamorphosis and *aition* are established.
      pullus, -a, -um: *dingy, somber, drab-colored*.
      luctus, -ūs (m.): *grief, mourning*.
      aptus, -a, -um: (+ dat.) *appropriate, fitting, suited*.

semper habe fetus, gemini monimenta cruoris.'
dixit et aptato pectus mucrone sub imum
incubuit ferro, quod adhuc a caede tepebat.
vota tamen tetigere deos, tetigere parentes:
165   nam color in pomo est, ubi permaturuit, ater,
quodque rogis superest, una requiescit in urna."

✤ ✤ ✤

161 **fetus:** once again a noun is held until the end of its clause to create suspense and to bring an emphatic end to the declaration.
geminus, -a, -um: *double.*
monimentum, -ī (n.): *memorial.*
cruor, -ōris (m.): *bloodshed, gore.*
162 **mucrō, -ōnis (m.):** *tip, point of a sword.*
163 **incubō, -āre, -uī, -itum:** *to throw oneself upon.*
tepeō, -ēre: *to be warm, tepid.* The line begins and ends with gruesome verbs marking her suicide.
165 **permātūrescō, -ere, -tūruī:** *to become fully ripe.*
166 **rogus, -ī (m.):** *funeral pyre.* In the plural because there were two funeral pyres.
supersum, -esse, -fuī: *to remain, be left over.*
una ... urna: Ovid ends this tale of two lovers, separated at the beginning but joined into one in death with a strong image symbolizing their union—a single urn for their combined ashes.

Daedalus and Icarus

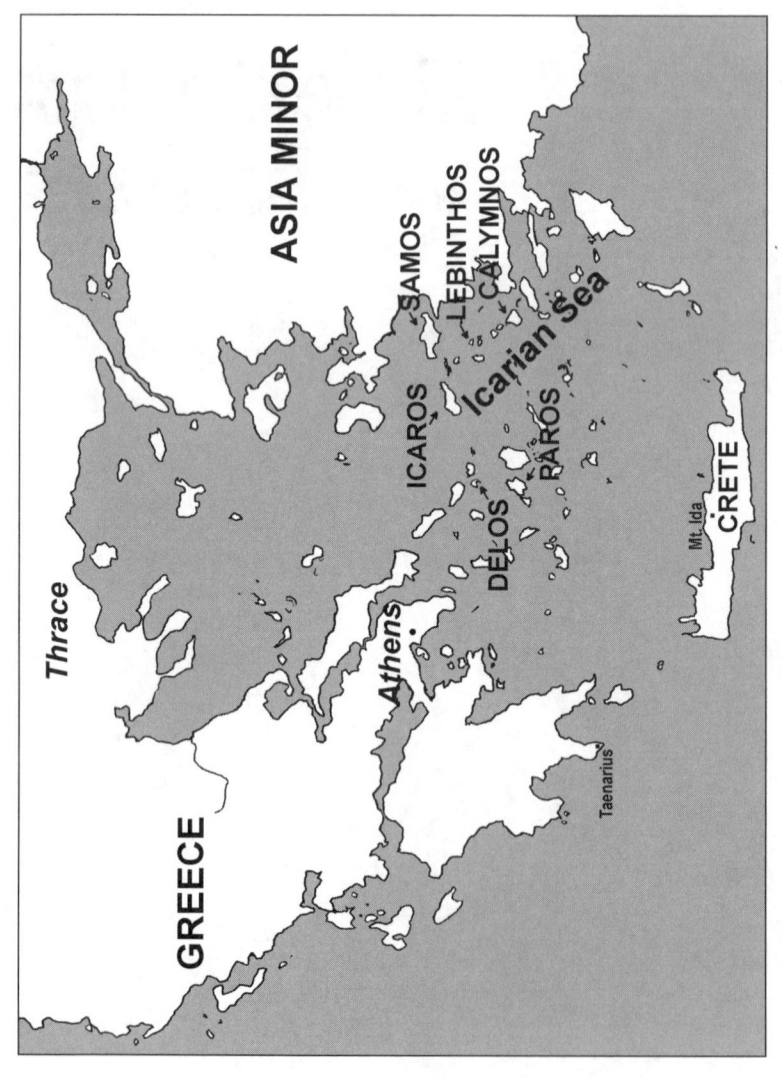

Map of Places in Daedalus and Icarus and Orpheus and Eurydice

DAEDALUS AND ICARUS
Met. VIII. 183–235

The story of Daedalus and Icarus is part of a continuous narrative begun in Book 7 about King Minos of Crete. Daedalus, introduced as an *ingenio fabrae celeberrimus artis* (a man most famous for his skill in the arts, VIII. 159), is the constructor of the labyrinth for Minos. The maze, so complex that the artist himself could scarcely find his way out of it, was built to contain the Minotaur, a monster, half man, half bull, the offspring of an unnatural union between the king's wife, Pasiphae, and a bull. Although little is said of Daedalus's sojourn in Crete, the poet describes him as discontented with his lengthy exile there. To escape, he fashions from bird feathers and beeswax wings for himself and his son Icarus, with which they seek flight.

It is not until this moment that the poet provides Daedalus's full history. After Icarus has fallen from the sky and drowned, and Daedalus has buried him, a *garrula perdix* (a chattering partridge), clapping her wings and singing with joy, confronts Daedalus as a reproach to him. The partridge was once his own twelve-year-old nephew Perdix, whom Daedalus had attempted to murder by throwing him off the Acropolis out of jealousy for the boy's artistic talent, which rivaled his own. As Perdix fell, he was saved by Athena, who transformed him into the partridge that emerges from the mud. Now the bird clearly rejoices in the justice of Daedalus's loss of his own son. This closing scene stands in stark contrast to the whole of the Daedalus and Icarus passage. The tale ostensibly describes a loving father who longs for his own land and plans to escape in flight with his son, whom he advises appropriately on the dangers of flying too high or too low. Yet the poet intends us to see the attempted murder as the reason for the long exile.

The story also illustrates an essential precept of Aristotelian philosophy, that man be moderate in all things. Both Daedalus and Icarus violate this law. Icarus flies too close to the sun, and Daedalus, by constructing wings for himself and his son, has attempted to change nature itself. This violation of the natural order of the world is doomed to fail.

Because this story epitomizes so beautifully the nature of artistic creativity, it has been a favorite topic for artists from antiquity until today. As the epigram to his novel *The Portrait of an Artist as a Young Man*, James Joyce chose from this story the words *ignotas animum dimittit in artes* (188), and he named the hero of his story Stephen Dedalus. The story has provided inspiration for numerous other writers, including Baudelaire, W. H. Auden, and Mallermé, and has been a favorite subject for artists such as Bruegel, Rubens, Tintoretto, Picasso, and Chagall.

DAEDALUS AND ICARUS
Met. VIII. 183–235

    Daedalus interea Creten longumque perosus
    exilium tactusque loci natalis amore
185 clausus erat pelago. "terras licet" inquit "et undas
    obstruat: et caelum certe patet; ibimus illac:
    omnia possideat, non possidet aera Minos."
    dixit et ignotas animum dimittit in artes
    naturamque novat. nam ponit in ordine pennas
190 a minima coeptas, longam breviore sequenti,
    ut clivo crevisse putes; sic rustica quondam

183 **Crētē, Crētēs (f.):** *Crete,* an island in the eastern Mediterranean Sea. Daedalus had fled to Crete after being condemned for murdering his nephew (*Met.* VIII. 241–59). While on the island he designed and constructed the labyrinth to hold the Minotaur. He was not permitted off the island for fear of revealing the secret of its passages. This is the accusative singular form of the noun; a direct object of *perosus.*
    perōdī, -disse, -sum: *to despise, loathe.* This verb has lost its present tense forms; therefore its perfect forms carry present meaning. Its perfect participle functions actively, so *perosus* may translate as *hating, loathing.*
184 **loci natalis:** Daedalus was an Athenian by birth.
185 **licet:** here, used as a conjunction meaning *although,* it introduces a subjunctive clause with *obstruat,* with Minos as an implied subject.
    et: here means *also.*
186 **illāc:** *by that way.*
187 **possideat:** a concessive subjunctive—*even though he possesses.*
    aera: accusative plural of *āēr.*
    Mīnōs, -ōis (m.): *Minos,* king of Crete, husband to Pasiphae, father of Ariadne, and the one who ordered the labyrinth built.
188 **ignōtus, -a, -um:** here suggesting *previously unknown.*
189 **naturamque novat:** note how throughout the line the poet employs strong ALLITERATION to underscore the importance of this man-made metamorphosis.
191 **ut:** introduces a result clause without the expected *tam* or *talis.*
    clīvus, -ī (m.): *slope, incline.*
    sic: introduces a SIMILE.

120 ✦ OVID

fistula disparibus paulatim surgit avenis;
tum lino medias et ceris alligat imas
atque ita conpositas parvo curvamine flectit,
195 ut veras imitetur aves. puer Icarus una
stabat et, ignarus sua se tractare pericla,
ore renidenti modo, quas vaga moverat aura,
captabat plumas, flavam modo pollice ceram
mollibat lusuque suo mirabile patris
200 impediebat opus. postquam manus ultima coepto
inposita est, geminas opifex libravit in alas
ipse suum corpus motaque pependit in aura;
instruit et natum "medio" que "ut limite curras,

192 **fistula, -ae (f.):** *pipe, pan-pipe.*
 dispār, -ris: *unequal, dissimilar.*
 avena, -ae (f.): *stem, stalk.*
193 **līnum, -ī (n.):** *thread, string*—probably made from the flax plant.
 et: joins both *lino* and *ceris*, as well as *medias* and *imas* in INTERLOCKED WORD ORDER.
 alligō, -āre, -āvī, -ātum: *to tie, fasten.*
194 **curvāmen, -minis (n.):** *curvature, arc.*
195 **Īcarus, -ī (m.):** *Icarus,* Daedalus's son.
 ūnā (adv.): *at the same time.*
196 **tractō, -āre, -āvī, -ātum:** *to handle, manage.*
 pericla: a syncopated form of *pericula.*
197 **renīdeō, -ēre:** *to smile with pleasure, beam.*
 modo: these correlatives lend an immediacy and visual element to the narrative. The reader is invited to watch as young Icarus chases the feathers and meddles with the wax, hindering his father's work.
 vagus, -a, -um: *shifting, moving about.*
198 **flavus, -a, -um:** *yellow.*
 pollex, -icis (m.): *the thumb.*
199 **molliō, -īre, -īvī, -ītum:** *to soften, weaken.*
 lūsus, -ūs (m.): *playing, sporting.*
200 **impediō, -īre, -īvī, -ītum:** *to hinder, impede.*
 manus ultima: i.e., the finishing touch.
201 **opifex, -ficis (m.):** *craftsman, artisan.*
 lībrō, -āre, -āvī, -ātum: *to level, balance.*
202 **pendeō, -ēre, pependī:** *to hang.*
203 **medio:** the essence of Daedalus's speech in lines 203–4 to his son is found in this first word of fatherly advice.

Icare," ait "moneo, ne, si demissior ibis,
205 unda gravet pennas, si celsior, ignis adurat:
inter utrumque vola. nec te spectare Booten
aut Helicen iubeo strictumque Orionis ensem:
me duce carpe viam!" pariter praecepta volandi
tradit et ignotas umeris accommodat alas.
210 inter opus monitusque genae maduere seniles,
et patriae tremuere manus; dedit oscula nato
non iterum repetenda suo pennisque levatus
ante volat comitique timet, velut ales, ab alto
quae teneram prolem produxit in aera nido,

✣ ✣ ✣

204 **ne:** introduces two negative purpose clauses (*gravet* and *adurat*) with ASYNDETON.
dēmissus, -a, -um: *low, close to the ground.*
205 **celsus, -a, -um:** *high, lofty.*
adūrō, -ere, -ussī, -ussum: *to burn, scorch.*
206 **Boōtes, -ae (m.):** a bright constellation in the North known as the Deer-keeper, next to the Great Bear (Ursa Major) constellation. Here, the accusative case as direct object of *spectare*.
207 **Helicē, -ēs (f.):** the Greek name for the constellation Ursa Major. Here, another accusative direct object of *spectare* (206).
stringō, -ere, -nxī, -strictum: *to unsheath.*
Ōrīōn, -onis (m.): the constellation in the South known as the Hunter. Its rising and setting are often associated with storms.
209 **ignotas:** perhaps meant to recall 188 and the *ignarus* of 196. Foreshadows the tragedy about to beset Icarus.
210 **gena, -ae (f.):** *the cheek.*
madeō, -ēre, -uī: *to grow wet.*
senīlis, -e: *old, aged.*
212 **suo:** the separation of the adjective from its noun, HYPERBATON, heightens the pathos of the scene.
213 **comitique:** dative of reference showing for whom he was concerned.
āles, -itis (m., f.): *a bird.*
214 **tener, -era, -erum:** *tender, sensitive, fragile.*
nīdus, -ī (m.): *a nest.* The exaggerated separation of the noun from its adjective, HYPERBATON, creates suspense and interest until the SIMILE is resolved. The placement of *nido* next to *aera* intensifies the height of the nest.

215   hortaturque sequi damnosasque erudit artes
et movet ipse suas et nati respicit alas.
hos aliquis tremula dum captat harundine pisces,
aut pastor baculo stivave innixus arator
vidit et obstipuit, quique aethera carpere possent,
220   credidit esse deos. et iam Iunonia laeva
parte Samos (fuerant Delosque Parosque relictae)
dextra Lebinthos erat fecundaque melle Calymne,
cum puer audaci coepit gaudere volatu
deseruitque ducem caelique cupidine tractus

✢ ✢ ✢

215 **damnōsus, -a, -um:** *destructive, ruinous.*
  ērudiō, -īre, -īvī, -ītum: *to teach, instruct.*
217 **harundō, -dinis (f.):** *a reed, sharpened reed, arrow.* Here, a rod for fishing.
218 **baculum, -ī (n.):** *walking stick, staff.*
  stīva, -ae (f.): *the shaft of a plough handle.*
  innītor, -ī, -nixus: *to lean on, rest on.*
  arātor, -ōris (m.): *a ploughman.*
219 **obstipescō, -ere, -stipuī:** *to be amazed, astonished.*
  possent: subjunctive in a relative clause of characteristic explaining why Daedalus and Icarus are believed to be gods.
220 **Iūnōnius, -a, -um:** *of or pertaining to Juno.*
  laevus, -a, -um: *left, lefthand.*
221 **Samos, -ī (f.):** an island in the eastern Mediterranean off the coast of Asia Minor between Ephesus and Miletus. Its temple to Juno, built in the sixth century B.C., was the largest in the Greek world at the time.
  Dēlos, -ī (f.): a small (two square miles) island in the Aegean revered as the birthplace of Apollo and Diana.
  Paros, -ī (f.): another island in the Aegean most known for its fine white marble and as the birthplace of the seventh-century Greek poet Archilochus.
222 **Lebinthos, -ī (f.):** an island in the Sporadic chain, off the east coast of mainland Greece.
  fēcundus, -a, -um: *fertile, fruitful.*
  Calymnē, -ēs (f.): an island off the coast of Asia Minor near Rhodes. It is known for its honey. Note Greek ending.
223 **volātus, -ūs (m.):** *flying, flight.*

225   altius egit iter. rapidi vicinia solis
      mollit odoratas, pennarum vincula, ceras;   *apposition*
      tabuerant cerae: nudos quatit ille lacertos,
      remigioque carens non ullas percipit auras,
      oraque caerulea patrium clamantia nomen
230   excipiuntur aqua, quae nomen traxit ab illo.
      at pater infelix, nec iam pater, "Icare," dixit,
      "Icare," dixit "ubi es? qua te regione requiram?"
      "Icare," dicebat: pennas adspexit in undis
      devovitque suas artes corpusque sepulcro
235   condidit, et tellus a nomine dicta sepulti.

✦ ✦ ✦

226 **mollit:** reminiscent of the young boy mischievously softening the wax, with the warmth of his own thumb in line 199. Now the sun softens the wax.
227 **tabescō, -ēre, tābuī:** *to melt gradually.*
228 **rēmigium, -ī (n.):** *oars, wings.*
229 **caeruleus, -a, -um:** *blue, greenish blue.* HYPERBATON separates this adjective from its noun in the next line. This tightly constructed phrase (*oraque . . . aqua*) consists of a double CHIASMUS entwined with a SYNCHESIS, perhaps to reflect the contorted spiraling fall of Icarus from the sky.
230 **excipiō, -ere, -cēpī, -ceptum:** *to accept, receive.*
    quae: the antecedent is *aqua*, the body of water known as the Icarian Sea.
234 **dēvoveō, -ēre, -ōvī, -ōtum:** *to curse.*
235 **sepeliō, -īre, -īvī, sepultum:** *to bury.* Here, the genitive singular of the perfect participle with *nomine*, and referring to the boy, Icarus.
    tellus: this is the island Icaria near Samos. Once again Ovid ends his tale with a reference to an *aition* (origin).

Philemon and Baucis

PHILEMON AND BAUCIS
Met. VIII. 616–724

Ovid places this story of piety and loyalty to the gods immediately after a series of tales that illustrate how the gods reward or punish mortals through metamorphosis. At a dinner party where storytelling provides the evening's entertainment, Pirithous scoffs at the notion that the gods are powerful enough to change the shapes of things. Lelex, a companion of the hero Theseus, in direct response to Pirithous's remarks, tells of the transformations of Philemon and Baucis in order to demonstrate the power and justice of the gods. This story, in turn, is followed by another about Erysichthon's illicit love and consequent metamorphosis, with a long digression on his egregiously impious act of cutting down a tree sacred to the goddess Ceres.

We do not know the precise origin of Ovid's story of Philemon and Baucis. It is, however, one of a number of stories from the ancient world that illustrate the importance of the unwritten law of hospitality: hosts had a moral obligation to provide food, drink, and shelter to guests without questioning their identity. Stories of visits from divinities who test mortals' application of this rule appear in both Judaic and Graeco-Roman culture. In Genesis, for example, the stories of God's visit to Abraham and Sarah, Chapter 18, and the visit to Lot of two angels, Chapter 19, provide important variations of this story. We have no evidence that Ovid read Genesis; he, however, probably knew the *Hecale,* a lost poem by the Greek poet Callimachus that describes how a poor old woman gave hospitality to the hero Theseus. Ovid considered this basic story important enough to include additional variations of it in *Metamorphoses* I. 212ff. and *Fasti* V. 495ff.

Ovid's narrative of the pious Philemon and Baucis is enhanced through the emphasis of their simple home and humble food. He painstakingly lists the steps for preparing the meal and the courses served by the humble hosts to the great gods Jupiter and Mercury, who appear in human guise. This lengthy description highlights the spontaneous, unqualified generosity of the mortal husband and wife. The couple give all they have to their guests, long before they perceive that they are entertaining divinities. Their simple piety receives the highest reward: they are granted their request to die together. Their transformations into trees, she into a linden and he into an oak, assure for them a kind of immortality: the oak and linden will henceforth be reminders of the pious couple's generosity.

This tale portrays a kind of love rarely seen in the *Metamorphoses*, for just as Baucis and Philemon love and honor the gods without reservation, so do they love each other truly, faithfully, and unconditionally. The simple goodness of Philemon and Baucis was re-created by Rembrandt in his famous depiction of the story. Others, including Dryden and Swift, have chosen instead to write parodies of it.

PHILEMON AND BAUCIS
Met. VIII. 616–724

obstipuere omnes nec talia dicta probarunt,
ante omnesque Lelex animo maturus et aevo,
sic ait: "inmensa est finemque potentia caeli
non habet, et quicquid superi voluere, peractum est,
620 quoque minus dubites, tiliae contermina quercus
collibus est Phrygiis modico circumdata muro;

✣ ✣ ✣

616 **obstipescō, -ere, -stipuī:** *to be amazed, astonished.* Here, the third person plural perfect active alternate form.
   omnes: this includes Theseus, the hero of Book VII, and his comrades who had taken shelter from the rains and swollen rivers in the home of the river god Achelous, where they were entertained with food and stories.
   talia: accusative plural direct object of *probarunt*. The things referred to are the words of doubt (lines 614–15) about the powers of the gods that Pirithous utters (see introduction).
   probō, -āre, -āvī, -ātum: *to authorize, sanction, approve.* Here, the syncopated third person plural perfect active: *probaverunt*.
617 **Lelex:** a participant in the hunt for the Calydonian boar, also recounted in Book VIII. With his companions, he has taken refuge from the storm in Achelous's house and it is he who will tell the story of Baucis and Philemon in order to prove that the gods possess the power of metamorphosis.
   mātūrus, -a, -um: *experienced, mature.*
   aevum, -ī (n.): *lifetime, experience, years of age.*
619 **quicquid:** variant form of *quidquid*.
   peragō, -ere, -ēgī, -actum: *to carry out, perform.*
620 **quoque:** *et quo*.
   tilia, -ae (f.): *a lime (linden) tree.* Here, a dative after *contermina*.
   conterminus, -a, -um: *nearby, adjacent.* Here, modifies *quercus*. This is the only mention of the types of trees the couple are changed into at the end of the tale.
   quercus, -ūs (f.): *an oak tree.*
621 **Phrygia, -ae (f.):** *a region in central Asia Minor.*
   modicus, -a, -um: *moderate in size.*
   circumdō, -are, -edī, -atum: (+ abl.) *to surround, encircle.*

ipse locum vidi; nam me Pelopeia Pittheus
misit in arva suo quondam regnata parenti.
haud procul hinc stagnum est, tellus habitabilis olim,
625 nunc celebres mergis fulicisque palustribus undae;
Iuppiter huc specie mortali cumque parente
venit Atlantiades positis caducifer alis.
mille domos adiere locum requiemque petentes,
mille domos clausere serae; tamen una recepit,

✣ ✣ ✣

622 **Pelopēius, -a, -um:** of or pertaining to Pelops, king of Argos, from whom the Peloponnesian peninsula gets its name.
Pittheus, -eī (m.): king of the ancient city Troezen of Argolis on the Peloponnesian peninsula. He was grandfather to Theseus and son of Pelops.
623 **arvum, -ī (n.):** *territory, country.*
parens: refers to Pittheus's father, Pelops. Here, a dative of agent with the perfect passive participle *regnata*.
624 **stagnum, -ī (n.):** *a pool, standing water.*
tellūs, -ūris (f.): *land, country.*
625 **nunc:** immediately following *olim* (624), this adverb sets up an ANTITHESIS to emphasize the change brought about by the metamorphosis.
celeber, -bris, -bre: *crowded, populous.*
mergus, -ī (m.): *a seabird, gull.*
fulica, -ae (f.): *a waterfowl, coot.*
paluster, -tris, -tre: *marshy.*
626 **parente:** refers to Jupiter, Mercury's father.
627 **venit:** this verb has two subjects, *Iuppiter* (626) and *Atlantiades*, but agrees with only one.
Atlantiadēs, -ae (m.): although this noun may refer to any offspring of Atlas, here it refers specifically to Mercury, whose mother, Maia, was a daughter of Atlas. He carries the caduceus.
positis...alis: these had to be set aside in order for the god to assume a human guise.
628 **adiere:** third person plural perfect active alternate form.
locum requiemque: HENDIADYS.
629 **mille domos:** the ANAPHORA emphasizes the rejection of the gods at all the houses in the neighborhood thereby setting off their welcome into the humble cottage of Baucis and Philemon.
sera, -ae (f.): *a crossbar for locking a door.*

630   parva quidem, stipulis et canna tecta palustri,
       sed pia Baucis anus parilique aetate Philemon
       illa sunt annis iuncti iuvenalibus, illa
       consenuere casa paupertatemque fatendo
       effecere levem nec iniqua mente ferendo;
635   nec refert, dominos illic famulosne requiras:
       tota domus duo sunt, idem parentque iubentque.

✦ ✦ ✦

630 **parva, tecta:** modify a missing *domus* or anticipate the *casa* of line 633. Ovid here stresses the simplicity and humble state of the couple's house.
  stipula, -ae (f.): *stubble*.
  canna, -ae (f.): *a small reed*.
631 **Baucis, -idis (f.):** *Baucis*, wife of Philemon.
  anus, -ūs (f.): *old woman*.
  parilis, -e: *similar, like*.
  Philēmōn, -ōnis (m.): *Philemon*, husband of Baucis.
632 **illa:** ablative of place where modifying *casa* (633), as does the final *illa* in this line. Note the slowed rhythm of this heavily SPONDAIC line, the ASSONANCE of *i* and *a*, and the balance created from the repetition of *illa*. The first occurrence refers to their youth spent in this house, the second to their old age.
  iuvenālis, -e: *youthful*.
633 **consenescō, -ere, -senuī:** *to grow old*.
  fateor, -ērī, fassus: *to profess, agree, acknowledge*.
634 **effecere:** third person plural perfect active alternate form.
  nec iniqua: LITOTES.
  inīquus, -a, -um: *discontented, resentful*.
  ferendo: its near repetition of *fatendo* in the same position in the line above graphically accentuates their humility.
635 **rēfert, -ferre, -tulit:** *it is of importance*.
  illīc (adv.): *there, in that place*.
  famulus, -ī (m.): *servant, attendant*.
  -ne: *or;* introduces the second alternative only in a double question.
  requiras: a present subjunctive in a substantive clause with *refert*. The second person address reminds us of the original setting in which this story is being told and of the audience listening.
636 **sunt:** the story now shifts into the historical present, drawing in the reader as a part of the audience too.

ergo ubi caelicolae parvos tetigere penates
summissoque humiles intrarunt vertice postes,
membra senex posito iussit relevare sedili;
640 cui superiniecit textum rude sedula Baucis
inque foco tepidum cinerem dimovit et ignes
suscitat hesternos foliisque et cortice sicco
nutrit et ad flammas anima producit anili
multifidasque faces ramaliaque arida tecto
645 detulit et minuit parvoque admovit aeno,

✧ ✧ ✧

637 **caelicola, -ae (m., f.):** *an inhabitant of heaven.*
tetigere: from *tangō*, in the alternate perfect active form.
penātēs, -ium (m. pl.): *the household gods.* Here, a METONYMY for the small cottage.

638 **summittō, -ere, -mīsī, -issum:** *to lower.* This is a GOLDEN LINE with the adjective/noun pair in INTERLOCKED WORD ORDER.
humiles: in both the literal (*submisso vertice*) sense because their humble cottage would not have been tall and in the figurative since the couple were poor and of humble origin. The line also suggests that the gods were tall in stature.
intrarunt: third person plural syncopated form of *intraverunt*.
vertex, -icis (m.): *the top of the head.*

639 **relevō, -āre, -āvī, -ātum:** *to relieve, ease.*
sedīle, -is (n.): *a seat.*

640 **superiniciō, -ere, -iniēcī, -iniectum:** *to throw over the surface.*
sēdulus, -a, -um: *attentive.*

641 **focus, -ī (m.):** *fireplace, hearth.*
cinis, -eris (m.): *ashes, embers.*
dīmoveō, -ēre, -mōvī, -mōtum: *to move about.*

642 **suscitō, -āre, -āvī, -ātum:** *to rouse, restore.*
hesternus, -a, -um: *yesterday's.*
folium, -ī (n.): *the leaf of a plant.*
cortex, -icis (m.): *the outer bark of a tree.*

643 **anima, -ae (f.):** *breath.*
anīlis, -e: *of or pertaining to an old woman.*

644 **multifidus, -a, -um:** *split, splintered.*
rāmāle, -is (n.): *branches, twigs.*

645 **parvoque:** a reminder that everything associated with this couple is small and simple.
aēnum, -ī (n.): *a pot or cauldron made of bronze.*

quodque suus coniunx riguo conlegerat horto,
truncat holus foliis; furca levat ille bicorni
sordida terga suis nigro pendentia tigno
servatoque diu resecat de tergore partem
650 exiguam sectamque domat ferventibus undis.
651 interea medias fallunt sermonibus horas
655 concutiuntque torum de molli fluminis ulva
inpositum lecto sponda pedibusque salignis.
vestibus hunc velant, quas non nisi tempore festo

✣ ✣ ✣

646 **riguus, -a, -um:** *irrigated, well-watered.*
647 **truncō, -āre, -āvī, -ātum:** *to strip off foliage.*
holus, -eris (n.): *vegetable*—probably cabbage or turnip.
furca, -ae (f.): *a length of wood with a forked end.*
ille: indicates a change of subject to Philemon.
bicornis, -e: *having two prongs.*
648 **sūs, suis (m., f.):** *pig, sow.*
tignum, -ī (n.): *timber, rafter.*
649 **resecō, -āre, -secuī, -sectum:** *to cut back, trim.*
tergus, -oris (n.): *the back of an animal.*
650 **exiguus, -a, -um:** *small, slight.*
secō, -āre, -cuī, -ctum: *to cut.* Here, the perfect participle used as an adjective.
domō, -āre, -āvī, -ātum: *to boil soft.*
fervens, -ntis: *boiling, bubbling.*
651 **fallō, -ere, fefellī, falsum:** *to while away, beguile.*
652–655a: four lines are of questionable authenticity and are omitted from this text.
655 **concutiō, -ere, -cussī, -cussum:** *to shake.*
torus, -ī (m.): *a cushion.*
ulva, -ae (f.): *rush, marsh grass.*
656 **sponda, -ae (f.):** *the frame of a bed or couch.* Here, an ablative of description.
salignus, -a, -um: *willow wood.* A simple wood to contrast with the luxurious furnishings of a wealthy Roman household. Modifies both *pedibus* and *sponda*.
657 **vēlō, -āre, -āvī, -ātum:** *to cover.*
festus, -a, -um: *suitable for a holiday, festival.*

134 ✦ OVID

      sternere consuerant, sed et haec vilisque vetusque
      vestis erat, lecto non indignanda saligno.
660 adcubuere dei. mensam succincta tremensque
      ponit anus, mensae sed erat pes tertius inpar:
      testa parem fecit; quae postquam subdita clivum
      sustulit, aequatam mentae tersere virentes.
      ponitur hic bicolor sincerae baca Minervae
665 conditaque in liquida corna autumnalia faece
      intibaque et radix et lactis massa coacti

✦ ✦ ✦

658 **sternō, -ere, strāvī, strātum:** *to strew, spread over an area, throw down.*
      consuescō, -ere, -suēvī, -suētum: *to be in the habit of, become accustomed to.*
      vilis, -e: *worthless, common, ordinary.*
659 **non indignanda:** a LITOTES stressing how noble the simple little couch is. A gerundive modifying *vestis*.
660 **adcumbō, -ere, -cubuī, -cubitum:** *to recline at table.*
      succintus, -a, -um: *to have one's clothing bound up with a girdle or belt to allow for freedom of movement.*
662 **testa, -ae (f.):** *a fragment of earthenware.*
      subditus, -a, -um: *situated beneath.*
      clīvus, -ī (m.): *slope, incline.*
663 **aequō, -āre, -āvī, -ātum:** *to make level.*
      menta, -ae (f.): *mint.*
      tergeō, -ēre, tersī, tersum: *to wipe clean.*
664 **ponitur:** this singular verb has six subjects: *baca* (664), *corna* (665), *intiba, radix, massa* (666), and *ova* (667).
      sincērus, -a, -um: *unblemished.*
      bāca, -ae (f.): *olive.*
665 **conditus, -a, -um:** *preserved.*
      liquida ... faece: CHIASTIC word order. The preserving liquid surrounds the fruits.
      cornum, -ī (n.): *the cornelian cherry.* This comes from the *cornus* tree, more commonly known as the dogwood. The fruit of certain varieties is red and edible.
      faex, faecis (f.): *the dregs or sediment of any liquid, particularly of wine; brine.*
666 **intibum, -ī (n.):** *chicory or endive.*
      rādix, -īcis (f.): *root.* Here, the radish.
      lac, lactis (n.): *milk.*
      massa, -ae (f.): *heap, lump, mass.*
      coactus, -a, -um: *curdled.*

ovaque non acri leviter versata favilla,
omnia fictilibus. post haec caelatus eodem
sistitur argento crater fabricataque fago
670 pocula, qua cava sunt, flaventibus inlita ceris;
parva mora est, epulasque foci misere calentes,
nec longae rursus referuntur vina senectae
dantque locum mensis paulum seducta secundis:
hic nux, hic mixta est rugosis carica palmis

✦ ✦ ✦

667 **non acri:** here meaning *warm*, but not burning.
favilla, -ae (f.): *ashes from a fire.*
668 **fictile, -is (n.):** *earthenware dish or pottery.* Further proof that this meal consists entirely of items found easily near the cottage. Presumably the object of a missing *in*.
caelō, -āre, -āvī, -ātum: *to engrave, emboss.*
669 **sistō, -ere, stetī, statum:** *to set, set down.*
argento: with *eodem* (668). Ovid employs comic IRONY—all the previous dishes were of earthenware, not silver.
crātēr, -ēris (m.): *a bowl used for mixing wine.*
fāgus, -ī (f.): *the beech tree.*
670 **pōculum, -ī (n.):** *a cup for drinking.*
flāvens, -entis: *yellow.*
inlinō, -ere, -lēvī, -litum: *to smear, coat.*
671 **epulae, -ārum (f.):** *feast, banquet.*
caleō, -ēre, -uī: *to be hot or warm.*
672 **referuntur:** the same wine used for the first course is here used again for the main course, a vulgarity to a wealthy Roman who varied his wine to suit the course.
673 **mensis ... secundis:** the course that followed the main course at a dinner. It usually consisted of fruits, fresh and dried, and nuts.
sēdūcō, -ere, -dūxī, -ductum: *to draw apart, move away.*
674 **hic ... palmis:** the slowed rhythm of SPONDEES helps to elaborate this course which, unlike the prior course of boiled cabbage and ham, has a greater variety to it.
nux, nucis (f.): *a nut.*
rūgōsus, -a, -um: *wrinkled.*
cāricus, -a, -um: *carian*, a type of fig.
palma, -ae (f.): *fruit of the date palm, a date.*

675 prunaque et in patulis redolentia mala canistris
et de purpureis conlectae vitibus uvae,
candidus in medio favus est; super omnia vultus
accessere boni nec iners pauperque voluntas.
   "Interea totiens haustum cratera repleri
680 sponte sua per seque vident succrescere vina:
attoniti novitate pavent manibusque supinis
concipiunt Baucisque preces timidusque Philemon
et veniam dapibus nullisque paratibus orant.
unicus anser erat, minimae custodia villae:

✧ ✧ ✧

675 **prūnum, -ī (n.):** *a plum.*
patulus, -a, -um: *broad, wide.*
redoleō, -ēre: *to give off a smell, be fragrant.*
mālum, -ī (n.): *an apple.*
canistrum, -ī (n.): *a basket.* Ovid varies the rhythm by inserting this line filled with DACTYLS.
676 **vītis, vītis (f.):** *the grapevine.*
677 **favus, -ī (m.):** *honeycomb.*
678 **accēdō, -ere, -cessī, -cessum:** *to be added.*
679 **hauriō, -īre, hausī, haustum:** *to swallow up, consume.* Here, *haustum*, a masculine accuative perfect passive participles modifies a Greek masculine singular *cratera*.
repleō, -ēre, -ēvī, -ētum: *to refill, replenish.*
680 **spons, spontis (f.):** *will, volition*; here, an idiomatic expression meaning *automatically.*
succrescō, -ere, succrēvī: *to grow up as a replacement, to be supplied anew.* Note the heavy ALLITERATION of *s* sounds.
681 **attonitus, -a, -um:** *dazed, astounded, amazed.*
novitās, -tātis (f.): *novelty, strange phenomenon.*
paveō, -ēre: *to be frightened.*
supīnus, -a, -um: *turned palm upwards.*
682 **concipiō, -ere, -cēpī, -ceptum:** *to produce, form.*
683 **venia, -ae (f.):** *justification, excuse, indulgence.*
daps, dapis (f.): *feast, meal.*
nullis: not in the strictly negative sense but rather meaning *of no significance, trifling.*
parātus, -ūs (m.): *food and utensils for the dinner table.*
684 **ūnicus, -a, -um:** *one, only one.*
anser, -eris (m.): *a goose.*

685   quem dis hospitibus domini mactare parabant;
      ille celer penna tardos aetate fatigat
      eluditque diu tandemque est visus ad ipsos
      confugisse deos: superi vetuere necari
      'di' que 'sumus, meritasque luet vicinia poenas
690   inpia' dixerunt; 'vobis inmunibus huius
      esse mali dabitur; modo vestra relinquite tecta
      ac nostros comitate gradus et in ardua montis
      ite simul!' parent ambo baculisque levati
      nituntur longo vestigia ponere clivo.
695   tantum aberant summo, quantum semel ire sagitta
      missa potest: flexere oculos et mersa palude

✢ ✢ ✢

685 **dis:** variant form of *deīs*.
    domini: i.e., *dominus et domina*, Philemon and Baucis.
    mactō, -āre, -āvī, -ātum: *to kill, slay, sacrifice*.
686 **penna, -ae (f.):** *feather, wing*. This line has a nice balance to it—the subject and verb embrace an adjective and noun pair. The SPONDEES slow the line, reflecting the meaning.
687 **ēlūdō, -ere, -sī, -sum:** *to elude, avoid capture*.
688 **confugiō, -ere, -fūgī:** *to flee to (someone) for safety*.
689 **luō, -ere, -ī:** *to pay (as a penalty)*.
690 **inpia:** piety was at the very heart of Roman religion and society. It was manifested in the close observance of the rites required for proper balance and relations with the gods. Adherence to these duties promoted cohesion among families and obedience to the state. Conversely, impiety incurred the wrath of the gods and social instability.
    inmūnis, -e: *free from, exempt*.
692 **comitō, -āre, -āvī, -ātum:** *to follow*.
    arduum, -ī (n.): *high elevation*.
694 **nītor, -tī, -sus:** *to strive, move with difficulty, exert oneself*. The heavily SPONDAIC line mimics the plodding exertion of the old couple as they climb the mountain.
    vestīgium, -ī (n.): *footprint, footstep*.
    clīvus, -ī (m.): *slope, incline*.
695 **tantum ... quantum:** *just so far ... as*.
696 **mergō, -ere, mersī, mersum:** *to flood, inundate*; here, the perfect passive participle as an adjective.
    palūs, -ūdis (f.): *a swamp*.

cetera prospiciunt, tantum sua tecta manere,
dumque ea mirantur, dum deflent fata suorum,
illa vetus dominis etiam casa parva duobus
700 vertitur in templum: furcas subiere columnae,
stramina flavescunt aurataque tecta videntur
caelataeque fores adopertaque marmore tellus.
talia tum placido Saturnius edidit ore:
'dicite, iuste senex et femina coniuge iusto
705 digna, quid optetis.' cum Baucide pauca locutus
iudicium superis aperit commune Philemon:
'esse sacerdotes delubraque vestra tueri
poscimus, et quoniam concordes egimus annos,
auferat hora duos eadem, nec coniugis umquam

+ + +

698 **suorum:** modifies a missing noun; probably refers to their people, i.e., their friends and neighbors.
699 **dominis:** dative with *parva*.
700 **subeō, -īre, -īvī, -itum:** *to replace.*
701 **strāmen, -inis (n.):** *straw thatch.*
flāvescō, -ere: *to become golden.*
702 **foris, foris (f.):** *door, double door.*
adoperiō, -īre, -uī, -tum: *to cover over.*
marmor, -oris (n.): *marble.*
703 **talia:** *the following.*
Sāturnius, -a, -um: a patronymic for Jupiter.
ēdō, -ere, ēdidī, ēditum: *to utter, to deliver a message.* In spite of the harsh punishment he has just levied on the region, Jupiter speaks to the old couple in a calm voice befitting his divine presence.
705 **locutus:** perfect participle of a deponent verb, which will have an active meaning in English.
706 **aperiō, -īre, -uī, -tum:** *to reveal, disclose.*
707 **dēlūbrum, -ī (n.):** *temple, shrine.* Here, a poetic plural referring to their former cottage.
tueor, -ērī, tuitus: *to observe, watch over, guard.*
709 **auferat:** the first of three jussive subjunctives embodying their request. The others are *videam* and *sim tumulandus* (710).

710   busta meae videam, neu sim tumulandus ab illa.'
        vota fides sequitur: templi tutela fuere,
        donec vita data est; annis aevoque soluti
        ante gradus sacros cum starent forte locique
        narrarent casus, frondere Philemona Baucis,
715   Baucida conspexit senior frondere Philemon.
        iamque super geminos crescente cacumine vultus
        mutua, dum licuit, reddebant dicta 'vale' que
        'o coniunx' dixere simul, simul abdita texit
        ora frutex: ostendit adhuc Thyneius illic
720   incola de gemino vicinos corpore truncos.
        haec mihi non vani (neque erat, cur fallere vellent)

✦ ✦ ✦

710 **bustum, -ī (n.):** *tomb.*
     tumulō, -āre, -āvī, -ātum: *to entomb.* Here, a passive periphrastic denoting necessity or obligation.
711 **vota ... sequitur:** i.e., their request is fulfilled.
     tūtēla, -ae (f.): *guardian, protection.*
712 **solūtus, -a, -um:** *weak.*
714 **frondeō, -ēre:** *to grow foliage.*
     Philemona: a Greek accusative singular ending.
715 **Baucida:** a Greek accusative singular ending.
716 **cacūmen, -inis (n.):** *the tip or top of a tree.* With *crescente* creates a strong ALLITERATION.
718 **simul, simul:** the immediate repetition of this word emphasizes the extraordinarily close relationship of the elderly couple.
     abditus, -a, -um: *hidden, concealed.*
719 **frutex, -icis (f.):** *green growth.*
     ostendit: with this present tense verb Ovid abruptly brings the reader back to present time and to the banquet scene at Lelex's house where the story is being recounted.
     adhuc: with this adverb Ovid establishes the *aition* (origin) for this passage: to this day the inhabitants of the region still point to the twin trees growing side by side.
     Thȳnēius, -a, -um: the inhabitants of Bithynia, a region in northwestern Asia Minor stretching to the southern coast of the Black Sea. Here, it modifies *incola* (720).
720 **geminō ... truncos:** the INTERLOCKED WORD ORDER here mimics the intertwined tree trunks.
     truncus, -ī (m.): *the trunk of a man or tree.*
721 **neque ... vellent:** read *neque erat* [causa] *cur* [me] *fallere vellent.*

narravere senes; equidem pendentia vidi
serta super ramos ponensque recentia dixi
'cura deum di sint, et, qui coluere, colantur.'"

+ + +

722 **vidi:** Ovid has brought us full circle, back to the banquet hall and to Lelex's own first words of lines 620–622.
723 **serta, -ōrum (n.):** *garlands, wreaths.*
724 **cūra, -ae (f.):** *object of concern, beloved person.* Here, a singular noun with plural intent.
  deum di ... coluere, colantur: In a double use of POLYPTOTON, Ovid is typically playful here, filling this last line of the tale with variations of these two pairs of words, so essential to the message of the story.
  colō, -ere, -uī, cultum: *worship*

Orpheus and Eurydice

ORPHEUS AND EURYDICE
Book X. 1–85

Ovid begins Book X of the *Metamorphoses* by telling the story of the wedding day of Orpheus and Eurydice and of her death by snakebite on that very day. Because of the skill and beauty of his singing, Orpheus is able to persuade Persephone and Hades to allow him to bring his bride back to the upper world, but when he looks back to be sure she is following him, Eurydice vanishes back into the lower world. At the beginning of Book XI, lines 1–84, Ovid portrays Orpheus's violent death at the hands of a raging band of Maenads who tear him to pieces, angry because of Orpheus's ultimate rejection of women. It is only in the underworld that Orpheus will be reunited with and enjoy his bride. In the entire fifteen books of the *Metamorphoses*, there are few happy and successful marriages; for this poet, it is the world of disorder, of violence and violation, that is emphasized.

It is no accident that the poet places this story where he does. Book IX ends with the story of Iphis, whose mother disguised her in infancy as a boy so that her father would not kill her. When she, disguised as a boy, is affianced to a beautiful young girl, the story might have ended in disaster, but with the help of the goddess Isis, Iphis becomes in the end a real boy, and a happy and fruitful marriage begins, for the poet writes:

> Venus, Juno, and Hymen joined to bless
> The wedding rite; their love was sanctified.
> And Iphis gained Ianthe, groom and bride.

In contrast, Book X begins with the arrival of Hymen for the wedding of Orpheus and Eurydice, but Hymen's ominous sputtering torch foretells the tragic outcome that follows immediately after the ceremony.

Much has been written about Ovid's debt to Vergil's *Georgics*, where Vergil tells the first known version of the story (many of the details Ovid includes can be found in *Georgics* IV. 452–527). Significantly different from the Vergilian passage is the voice given to Eurydice, who there rebukes Orpheus for looking back and causing her return to the underworld; Ovid, however, revises Eurydice's reaction with these simple words:

> *iamque iterum moriens non est de coniuge quicquam*
> *questa suo (quid enim nisi se quereretur amatam?)*
> *supremumque 'vale,' quod iam vix auribus ille*
> *acciperet, dixit revolutaque rursus eodem est.*

> Dying she does not complain about her husband
> (for how could she complain about being loved?)
> He heard her final 'farewell,' which barely reached
> his ears, and having spoken it, she turned back again.

Ovid also moves the tale of Orpheus and Eurydice away from the sexual paradigm that Vergil offers, a romantic heterosexual union, to end his own version with a passage on homosexual love in typical Ovidian defiance of what is traditional and even legally accepted in the Augustan world. Losing Eurydice, Orpheus henceforth rejects the love of women. Having established the theme of antipathy to women, it is not surprising that Ovid narrates the story of Pygmalion in the middle of Book X, where a male is so disgusted by female behavior that he can only love a woman that he himself creates, a statue of his ideal.

It is the aftermath of the death of Eurydice that more interests Ovid, for after a period of fasting and mourning and abstention of all intercourse with women, Orpheus turns to stories of the love of young boys, and sings, surrounded by an audience of trees who have gathered round him, of Cyparissus, a youth loved by Apollo, of Ganymede, cupbearer of the gods and the object of Jupiter's love, and of Hyacinth, another favorite of Apollo. All these mortal youths died. In his own version of the marriage and tragic death of Eurydice, Ovid stresses as well the magic of Orpheus's song (see lines 17–53), and Orpheus's emotional and physical reaction to the second loss of his beloved (lines 64–85). It is the power of the poet to charm the dead and to halt temporarily their eternal punishments, and to captivate the stern and forbidding rulers of the underworld, as well as Orpheus's ultimate rejection of women that interest Ovid in his retelling of this story.

ORPHEUS AND EURYDICE
Met. X. 1–85

> Inde per inmensum croceo velatus amictu
> aethera digreditur Ciconumque Hymenaeus ad oras
> tendit et Orphea nequiquam voce vocatur.
> adfuit ille quidem, sed nec sollemnia verba
> 5 nec laetos vultus nec felix attulit omen.
> fax quoque, quam tenuit, lacrimoso stridula fumo
> usque fuit nullosque invenit motibus ignes.

✦ ✦ ✦

1   **inde:** Hymen is coming from the wedding of Iphis and Ianthe, recounted at the end of Book IX, directly to the wedding of Orpheus and Eurydice. He provides the link between these two stories in typically random, Ovidian fashion.

  immensum . . . aethera: this CHIASTIC word order surrounding the adjective *velatus* provides a double enclosure (both the *aether* and the cloak) for the subject *Hymenaeus* in line 2.

  croceus, -a, -um: *saffron-colored, yellow*—the color of brides' veils.

2   **aethera:** here, the Greek accusative singular ending, modified by *immensum,* line 1.

  dīgredior, -gredī, -gressus: *to depart, go away.*

  Cicones, -um (m. pl.): *the Cicones,* a people of southern Thrace whose women will violently murder Orpheus in Book XI. Here, a genitive dependent on *oras.*

  Hymenaeus, -ī (m.): *Hymen,* the personified god representing weddings and marriages.

3   **tendō, -ere, tetendī, -tum/sum:** *to proceed.*

  Orphēus, -a, -um: *of or relating to Orpheus,* a Thracian bard and husband of Eurydice. The phrase *Orphea nequiquam* provides three spondaic feet in the line. In slowing down the rhythm here, Ovid emphasizes the futility of Orpheus's summoning Hymen to his wedding service, an ill-boding omen.

  voce vocatur: This ALLITERATION points out graphically Orpheus's best known quality, his voice, which will play a greater role later in the story.

4   **nec:** introduces the first element in a TRICOLON.

  sollemnis, -is, -e: *solemn, ceremonial.*

6   **lacrimōsus, -a, -um:** *tearful.* Not only does the smoke cause tears but the ill-fated marriage will soon be cause for tears as well.

  strīdulus, -a, -um: *making a shrill sound.*

7   **mōtus, -ūs (m.):** *motion, action, movement.*

exitus auspicio gravior: nam nupta per herbas
dum nova naiadum turba comitata vagatur,
10   occidit in talum serpentis dente recepto.
quam satis ad superas postquam Rhodopeius auras
deflevit vates, ne non temptaret et umbras,
ad Styga Taenaria est ausus descendere porta
perque leves populos simulacraque functa sepulcro

✣ ✣ ✣

8   **exitus, -ūs (m.):** *outcome, result, fate.*
    auspicium, -ī (n.): *portent, fortune, luck.*
9   **vagor, -ārī, -ātus:** *to wander, roam.* This abrupt change to the present tense makes the image, although occurring in the past, more vivid.
    Nāis, -idis (f.): *a nymph, river nymph, naiad.*
10 **occidō, -ere, -idī, -āsum:** *to be struck down, to die.* With this direct, unemotional pronouncement, Ovid removes Eurydice from the story entirely.
    tālus, -ī (m.): *ankle.*
    dens, dentis (f.): *tooth.*
11 **quam:** antecedent is *nupta* of line 8.
    superus, -a, -um: *upper, above, heavenly.*
    Rhodopeius, -a, -um: *of Mount Rhodope,* a mountain range in Thrace.
    aura, -ae (f.): *breeze, air.*
12 **dēfleō, -ēre, -ēvī, -ētum:** *to lament, sorrow, weep for.*
    vātēs, -is (m.): *poet, prophet, bard.* Orpheus is here introduced as one of the great bards.
    ne: introduces a double negative purpose clause with its verb, *temptaret,* in the imperfect subjunctive. The seriousness of what Orpheus is about to attempt (descent into the underworld) is highlighted by SPONDEES.
13 **Styx, Stygis (f.):** *the Styx,* the principal river of the underworld and by METONYMY, the underworld itself. Here, a Greek accusative object of *ad*.
    Taenarius, -a, -um: *of or relating to Taenarus,* the southernmost point of the Peloponnesus, thought to be an entrance to the underworld. Along with *umbras* and *Styga,* this is the third reference to the underworld in two lines.
14 **simulācrum, -ī (n.):** *image, statue, shades.*
    fungor, -ī, functus: *to perform, observe, suffer, experience.* Here, with an ablative object.

148 ♦ OVID

15   Persephonen adiit inamoenaque regna tenentem
     umbrarum dominum pulsisque ad carmina nervis
     sic ait: 'o positi sub terra numina mundi,
     in quem reccidimus, quicquid mortale creamur,
     si licet et falsi positis ambagibus oris
20   vera loqui sinitis, non huc, ut opaca viderem
     Tartara, descendi, nec uti villosa colubris
     terna Medusaei vincirem guttura monstri:

✦ ✦ ✦

15   **Persephonē, -ēs (f.):** *Persephone,* the daughter of Demeter and Zeus, and wife of Pluto. A Greek accusative object of *adiit.*
     inamoenus, -a, -um: *unpleasant, unlovely.* Often in Ovid's stories, he describes a *locus amoenus,* a place of rest, shade, water, greenery, and coolness. The underworld is completely opposite.
16   **dominum:** a second object of *adiit.*
     pellō, -ere, pepulī, pulsum: *to strike, beat.*
     nervus, -ī (m.): *string of a musical instrument or bow.*
17   **nūmen, -inis (n.):** *divine power, divinity.* Here, a vocative.
     mundus, -ī (m.): *the universe, the world, the earth.*
18   **recidō, -ere, -cidī:** *to fall back, sink.*
     quisquis, quidquid (quicquid): *anyone who, anything that.* Introduces a relative clause of characteristic.
19   **ambāgēs, -um (f.):** *long-winded, digressive speech, circumlocution.*
20   **sinitis:** a second verb in the *si* clause. Supply a missing *me* as its object.
     non: to be taken with *descendi.*
     ut: introduces a purpose clause dependent on *descendi.*
     opācus, -a, -um: *shady, dark.*
21   **Tartara, -ōrum (n. pl.):** *the infernal regions, the underworld.*
     villōsus, -a, -um: *hairy, shaggy.*
     coluber, -brī (m.): *snake, serpent.* Here, an ablative dependent on *villosa.*
22   **ternī, -ae, -a:** *three apiece.*
     Medusaeus, -a, -um: *of or relating to Medusa,* one of the Gorgons. Both she and Cerberus have snakes for hair.
     vinciō, -īre, vīcī, victum: *to fasten, bind, tie up.* This central verb in the line surrounded by two adjective/noun pairs in CHIASTIC word order creates a GOLDEN LINE.
     guttur, -uris (n.): *throat.* Here, the accusative object of *vincirem.*
     monstrum, -ī (n.): *a monstrous or horrible creature.*

causa viae est coniunx, in quam calcata venenum
vipera diffudit crescentesque abstulit annos.
25 posse pati volui nec me temptasse negabo:
vicit Amor. supera deus hic bene notus in ora est;
an sit et hic, dubito: sed et hic tamen auguror esse,
famaque si veteris non est mentita rapinae,
vos quoque iunxit Amor. per ego haec loca plena timoris,
30 per Chaos hoc ingens vastique silentia regni,
Eurydices, oro, properata retexite fata.
omnia debemur vobis, paulumque morati

✦ ✦ ✦

23 **coniunx:** Ovid has yet to name Orpheus's wife.
    calcō, -āre, -āvī, -ātum: *to tread or trample on.*
24 **vipera, -ae (f.):** *a viper or poisonous snake.*
    diffundō, -ere, -ūdī, -ūsum: *to spread, diffuse.*
    crescō, -ere, crēvī, crētum: *to grow, increase; arise.*
25 **nec … negabo:** a LITOTES.
26 **deus:** Amor.
27 **an:** introduces an indirect question dependent on *dubito*.
    hic: the two instances of *hic* in this line are adverbial but recall the adjective *hic* of line 26.
    auguror, -ārī, -ātus: *to foretell, predict.*
    esse: supply a missing *Amor* as subject of this infinitive.
28 **fama:** Ovid refers here to the story of the kidnapping and rape of Persephone, a story he recounts in Book V of the *Metamorphoses*.
    mentior, -īrī, -ītus: *to tell a falsehood, to lie.*
    rapīna, -ae (f.): *kidnapping, the forcible carrying off of a person.*
29 **vos:** Orpheus appeals directly to Proserpina and Pluto here.
    ego: the placement of this subject pronoun so early in the clause, and in a phrase where it has no syntactical purpose, creates suspense and intensifies the action of the verb when it is encountered two lines further on. The term for this sort of anticipation is PROLEPSIS.
30 **vastus, -a, -um:** *desolate, dreary, endless.*
31 **Eurydicē, -ēs (f.):** *Eurydice*, wife of Orpheus. This is the first time she is named.
    retexō, -ere, -xuī, -textum: *to undo, cancel, retract.* Imperative plural here, calling on the *vos*, Pluto and Proserpina, of line 29.
32 **omnia:** a rather awkward use of the neuter accusative to encompass all humans. Ovid adds weight to the seriousness of the content here by using three SPONDEES.

serius aut citius sedem properamus ad unam.
tendimus huc omnes, haec est domus ultima, vosque
humani generis longissima regna tenetis.
haec quoque, cum iustos matura peregerit annos,
iuris erit vestri: pro munere poscimus usum;
quodsi fata negant veniam pro coniuge, certum est
nolle redire mihi: leto gaudete duorum.'
40   Talia dicentem nervosque ad verba moventem
exsangues flebant animae; nec Tantalus undam
captavit refugam, stupuitque Ixionis orbis,

✤ ✤ ✤

33   **sēdēs, -is (f.):** *house, dwelling.* Here used metaphorically to refer to the underworld, death.
34   **tendō, -ere, tetendī, tentum:** *to proceed, progress.*
36   **haec:** taken with *matura*, refers to Eurydice.
     peragō, -ere, -ēgī, -actum: *to carry out, perform.*
37   **iūs, iūris (n.):** *authority, jurisdiction, power, right.* Along with *usum*, this is language of the legal world. Orpheus is pleading a legal case here, *ususfructus.*
     poscimus: a poetic plural.
38   **venia, -ae (f.):** *justification, excuse, indulgence.*
39   **redire:** to the upper world.
     mihi: a dative case as the subject of an infinitive with an impersonal verb.
     letum, -ī (n.): *death.*
40   **dicentem, moventem:** participles modifying an assumed accusative Orpheus.
41   **exsanguis, -is, -e:** *pale, bloodless, exhausted.*
     Tantalus, -ī (m.): *Tantalus,* an immortal who, having abused the advantages granted to him by the gods and unable to be killed, had to endure everlasting punishment in the underworld for his offence. He remains continually hungry and thirsty, water and food always just beyond his grasp.
42   **stupeō, -ēre, -uī:** *to be amazed, gape, become paralyzed.*
     Ixīōn, -onis (m.): *Ixion,* the father of the Centaurs who was bound to a perpetually revolving wheel in the underworld for his attempt to seduce Juno.

nec carpsere iecur volucres, urnisque vacarunt
Belides, inque tuo sedisti, Sisyphe, saxo. — *Abl. of cause*
45 tunc primum lacrimis victarum carmine fama est   *Indirect statement*
    Abl of means Eumenidum maduisse genas, nec regia coniunx
sustinet oranti nec, qui regit ima, negare,
Eurydicenque vocant: umbras erat illa recentes
inter et incessit passu de vulnere tardo.

✢ ✢ ✢

43   **carpō, -ere, -sī, -tum**: *to pass over, pursue one's way; gather, pluck, pick.*
     iecur, -oris (n.): *the liver.* This is a reference to Tityus. For attempting to seduce Latona he was banished to the lower regions where he was spread over nine acres and vultures daily ate away at his liver, which was restored nightly.
     volucris, -cris (f.): *bird, vulture.*
     urnisque: an ablative with *vacarunt*
44   **Bēlis, -idos (f.)**: also known as the Danaides, these 50 daughters of Danaus were forced to marry their cousins, the 50 sons of Aegyptus. With one exception, they all killed their husbands on their wedding night and for this suffered in the underworld. Their punishment was to fill urns with large holes in their bottoms.
     Sīsyphus, -ī (m.): *Sisyphus,* renowned for his cunning and deception, his eternal punishment in the underworld is to roll a rock up a hill that is destined to roll back down again. This is the fifth punishment Ovid mentions in three and a half lines and he ends these depictions with a vivid ALLITERATION—*sedisti, Sisyphe, saxo.*
     saxum, -ī (n.): *rock, boulder.*
46   **Eumenis, -idos (f.)**: *one of the Eumenides,* the furies. Modified by *victarum,* 45. A HYPERBATON.
     madeō, -ēre, -uī: *to grow wet.*
     gena, -ae (f.): *cheek.*
     rēgius, -a, -um: *royal, regal.*
47   **sustineō, -ēre, -uī**: *to endure, tolerate.* Both *regia coniunx* and *qui regit ima* govern this singular verb.
     oranti: dative case after *negare.*
     imus, -a, -um: *lowest, bottommost.*
49   **incēdō, -ere, -ssī**: *to step, walk.*
     passus, -ūs (m.): *pace, stride.* The SPONDEES here mimic Eurydice's halting pace.

152 ✦ OVID

50   hanc simul et legem Rhodopeius accipit heros,
    ne flectat retro sua lumina, donec Avernas
    exierit valles; aut inrita dona futura.
    carpitur adclivis per muta silentia trames,
    arduus, obscurus, caligine densus opaca,
55   nec procul afuerunt telluris margine summae:
    hic, ne deficeret, metuens avidusque videndi
    flexit amans oculos, et protinus illa relapsa est,
    bracchiaque intendens prendique et prendere certans
    nil nisi cedentes infelix arripit auras.
60   iamque iterum moriens non est de coniuge quicquam
    questa suo (quid enim nisi se quereretur amatam?)

✦ ✦ ✦

50   **hanc:** Eurydice. Along with *legem* these two objects create a ZEUGMA with emphasis on the law he must abide by rather than on the return of his wife.
51   **lumen, -inis (n.):** *light, brilliance; eye.*
    Avernus, -a, -um: *of or relating to Lake Avernas,* the entrance to the underworld and by extension the underworld itself.
52   **inritus, -a, -um:** *to no effect, in vain.*
53   **adclīvis, -is, -e:** *upwards sloping, inclined.*
    muta silentia: a stunning PLEONASM.
    trāmes, -itis (m.): *a footpath, track, path.*
54   **cālīgō, -inis (f.):** *murkiness, mistiness, darkness.*
55   **tellūs, -ūris (f.):** *land, country.*
56   **dēficiō, -ere, -ēcī, -ectum:** *to fade, fail, falter.* Here, an imperfect subjunctive in a clause of fearing having Eurydice as its subject and dependent on *metuens,* modifying Orpheus.
    avidus, -a, -um: *eager, greedy, ardent.*
57   **relābor, -bī, -psus:** *to slip back, slide back, recede.*
58   **brācchium, -ī (n.):** *arm.*
    intendō, -ere, -dī, -tum: *to stretch, spread out.*
    prendō, -ere, -dī, -sum: *to take hold of, grasp, seize.*
    certō, -āre, -āvī, -ātum: *to contend, dispute, struggle.*
59   **arripiō, -ere, arripuī, arreptus:** *to grab hold of, seize.*
    aura, -ae (f.): *breeze, air.*
60   **quicquam (adv.):** *in any respect, at all.*
61   **quid:** here, a direct object of *quereretur.* After several heavily spondaic lines, the five DACTYLS here move the line quickly just as Eurydice herself quickly fades.

ORPHEUS AND EURYDICE ✦ 153

supremumque 'vale,' quod iam vix auribus ille
acciperet, dixit revolutaque rursus eodem est.
Non aliter stupuit gemina nece coniugis Orpheus,
65 quam tria qui timidus, medio portante catenas,
colla canis vidit, quem non pavor ante reliquit,
quam natura prior saxo per corpus oborto,
quique in se crimen traxit voluitque videri
Olenos esse nocens, tuque, o confisa figurae,
70 infelix Lethaea, tuae, iunctissima quondam
pectora, nunc lapides, quos umida sustinet Ide.
orantem frustraque iterum transire volentem
portitor arcuerat: septem tamen ille diebus

✦ ✦ ✦

62 **supremus, -a, -um:** *last, final.* Here modifying *vale* as though a neuter noun.
   auris, auris (f.): *ear.*
63 **eōdem (adv.):** *to the same place.*
64 **Non aliter ... quam:** a classic introduction to a SIMILE. However, the SIMILE follows the main clause *stupuit ... Orpheus.*
   nex, necis (f.): *death.* Here, an ablative of cause.
65 **tria:** modifies *colla*, line 66. An example of HYPERBATON.
   qui: a reference to an unknown man who was turned to stone after seeing Hercules leading Cerberus on a chain.
   mediō portante: an unusual application of the ablative absolute modifying a direct object.
   catēna, -ae (f.): *chain, fetters.* Here, the object of *portante.*
66 **pavor, -ōris (m.):** *fear, terror, fright.*
   ante: to be taken with *quam* (67).
67 **natura prior:** another subject for the verb *reliquit.*
   oborior, -īrī, -tus: *to rise up, spring up.*
69 **Olenos:** subject of both *traxit* and *voluit*, line 68. His shame was to be turned into stone like his wife although he was innocent of any wrongdoing.
   tuque, confisa figurae, infelix Lethaea: a vocative case TRICOLON.
   cōnfīdō, -ere, cōnfīsus sum (+ dat.): *to give trust to, to trust.*
70 **Lethaea:** wife of Olenos, who was turned to stone due to her pride.
   quondam (adv.): *once, formerly.*
71 **quos:** antecedents are *Olenos* (69), and *Lethaea* (70).
   ūmidus, -a, -um: *wet, moist, watery.*
   Īda (Idē), -ae (-ēs) (f.): a mountain, either near Troy or on Crete.
72 **orantem:** modifies a missing *Orpheus,* as does *volentem.*
   transire: the river Styx back into the underworld.
73 **portitor, -ōris (m.):** *ferryman, carrier.*
   arceō, -ere, -uī: *to prevent from approaching, repulse, drive away.*

        squalidus in ripa Cereris sine munere sedit;
75   cura dolorque animi lacrimaeque alimenta fuere.
        esse deos Erebi crudeles questus, in altam
        se recipit Rhodopen pulsumque aquilonibus Haemum.
            Tertius aequoreis inclusum Piscibus annum
        finierat Titan, omnemque refugerat Orpheus
80   femineam Venerem, seu quod male cesserat illi,
        sive fidem dederat; multas tamen ardor habebat
        iungere se vati, multae doluere repulsae.
        ille etiam Thracum populis fuit auctor amorem
        in teneros transferre mares citraque iuventam
85   aetatis breve ver et primos carpere flores.

Marginalia: "Happening in March" (next to lines 78–79); "Doluerunt" (next to line 82)

✦ ✦ ✦

74   **ripa, -ae (f.):** *riverbank.*
       Cereris ... munere: a METONYMY for the gift of Ceres—bread.
76   **Erebus, -ī (m.):** the god of darkness and by extension refers to the
       underworld regions.
77   **pulsō, -āre, -āvī, -ātum:** *to beat, strike repeatedly.*
       Haemus, -ī (m.): a mountain range in northern Thrace.
78   **inclūsus, -a, -um:** *enclosed.*
79   **Tītān, -nos (m.):** *Titan,* the sun god.
80   **Venerem:** here through METONYMY *Venerem* refers not to the goddess
       herself but rather to what she stands for—love, especially passionate,
       sexual love for a woman.
       seu: alternate form of *sīve*—whether.
       cēdō, -ere, cessī, cessum: *to yield, give way, to be inferior to.*
81   **multās:** modifies unspecified women.
       ardor, -ōris (m.): *passion, ardor.*
83   **Thrax, -ācis (m.):** *Thracian,* a native of Thrace.
       populis: a dative with *auctor.*
       auctor, -ōris (m.): *founder, author, originator.*
84   **tener, -era, -erum:** *tender, sensitive; fragile.*
       mās, maris (m.): *the male of the species.*
       citrā (prep. + acc.): *before, sooner than.*
       iuventa, -ae (f.): *the period of youth.* Orpheus is the first man to shun the
       love of women and instead to love boys.
85   **aetatis:** an objective genitive to be taken with both *ver* and *flores.*
       vēr, -ris (n.): *the season of spring, the springtime of life, youth.*

Pygmalion

PYGMALION
Met. X. 238–97

Ovid's Pygmalion is one of the stories told by the singer/poet Orpheus in an effort to assuage his grief over the loss of his bride Eurydice. The story follows an account of the Propoetides who had denied the divinity of Venus. The goddess punished this group of girls by forcing them into prostitution and later turning them into stone. Pygmalion, an artist, is so disgusted by the foul activities of these girls that he avoids all real women. Instead, he creates for himself the ideal woman out of ivory, a statue of such exquisite beauty that he falls in love with its perfection. A misogynist, he abhors real, flesh-and-blood women, and can love only a lifeless image. At a festival honoring Venus, whom he genuinely reveres, he wishes silently that his statue come to life. When he returns home and caresses the ivory, it softens and turns to flesh beneath his hands. Pygmalion gains an ideal wife, and Venus sanctifies his union with her, a union which produces a child named Paphos.

An earlier source of a story about a king called Pygmalion described an arrogant man who defiled a statue of Venus by attempting to make love to it. Ovid's Pygmalion, however, is depicted as a moral man, who, revolted by the immoral Propoetides, is rewarded by the goddess. But at the same time, when the poet also emphasizes Pygmalion's erotic attraction for his beautiful statue, he suggests that Pygmalion may not be quite as pure as he appears.

This tale has through the ages inspired plays, poems, ballets, operas, and paintings. Although in the Middle Ages the Pygmalion story was linked to idolatry, narcissism, and madness, many recent critics perceive in it the transforming power of art in the hands of a great creative artist. Shakespeare in *The Winter's Tale* was fascinated by the idea of changing a woman's identity. George Bernard Shaw, in his play called *Pygmalion*, which is set in nineteenth-century London, and Lerner and Lowe, creators of *My Fair Lady*, a musical based on Shaw's play, turn their modern Pygmalion, Professor Henry Higgins, into a type of arrogant male superiority, who changes a humble seller of flowers into an upper-class lady as a kind of scientific experiment.

Obscenus, a, um - polluted, foul
Numen, numinis, n. - Divine power, divinity
Vulgo (1) - to prostitute
Cedo, cedere, cessi, cessus - to yield, give away, be inferior
Sanguis, sanguinis m. - blood, bloodline
Induresco, Indurescere, Indurui - to harden
Discrimen, Discriminis, n. - difference, distinction
Silex, silicis, m. - rock, stone
Caelebs, caelibus - unmarried
Thalemus, i, m - bedroom
Vitium, i, n - vice
Ebur, eburis, n - Ivory

PYGMALION
Met. X. 238–297

"Sunt tamen obscenae Venerem Propoetides ausae
esse negare deam; pro quo sua numinis ira
240   corpora cum fama primae vulgasse feruntur,
utque pudor cessit, sanguisque induruit oris,
in rigidum parvo silicem discrimine versae.

"Quas quia Pygmalion aevum per crimen agentis
viderat, offensus vitiis, quae plurima menti
245   femineae natura dedit, sine coniuge caelebs
vivebat thalamique diu consorte carebat.
interea niveum mira feliciter arte

✦ ✦ ✦

238   **Prōpoetides, -um (f. pl.):** These were young women from Amathus, a city in Cyprus sacred to Venus.
239   **quō:** probably a neuter pronoun referring to their foul deed.
240   **vulgō, -āre, -āvī, -ātum:** *to prostitute.*
241   **indūrescō, -esere, -uī:** *to harden, become hard.*
242   **discrīmen, -inis (n.):** *difference, distinction.*
243   **quas:** refers to the Propoetides.
      Pygmaliōn, -ōnis (m.): a legendary king of Cyprus although Ovid never refers to him as a king. Here, the nominative singular.
244   **offensus, -a, -um:** *offended, displeased.*
      vitium, -ī (n.): *vice, moral failing.*
      quae ... dedit: this clause represents an egregious instance of a generalization based on the behavior of the Propoetides.
      plurima: neuter accusative plural referring back to *vitiis.*
245   **caelebs, -libis:** *unmarried (male), bachelor.* The juxtaposition of this adjective with *coniuge* graphically sets forth the dilemma of this story. Pygmalion, a hater of women, wants and needs a woman.
246   **thalamus, -ī (m.):** *bedroom, marriage chamber.*
      consors, -rtis (f.): *partner.*
247   **niveus, -a, -um:** *white, snowy-white.* This adjective connotes a cold white, emblematic of the lifeless beauty Pygmalion has created. The HYPERBATON here helps to create suspense.
      mira ... arte: like Daedalus, Pygmalion crafts a metamorphosis of his own.
      fēlīciter (adv.): *successfully.*

sculpsit ebur formamque dedit, qua femina nasci
nulla potest, operisque sui concepit amorem.
250 virginis est verae facies, quam vivere credas,
et, si non obstet reverentia, velle moveri:
ars adeo latet arte sua, miratur et haurit
pectore Pygmalion simulati corporis ignes.
saepe manus operi temptantes admovet, an sit
255 corpus an illud ebur, nec adhuc ebur esse fatetur,
oscula dat reddique putat loquiturque tenetque
et credit tactis digitos insidere membris
et metuit, pressos veniat ne livor in artus,
et modo blanditias adhibet, modo grata puellis

✦ ✦ ✦

248 **sculpō, -ere, -psī, -ptum:** *to carve.*
     ebur, -oris (n.): *ivory.*
     qua: an unusual ablative; translate *with which.*
249 **concipiō, -ere, -cēpī, -ceptum:** *to conceive, to fall (in love).*
250 **credas:** a potential subjunctive; the poet's address to the reader makes the story more vivid.
251 **obstō, -āre, -stitī, -stātum:** *to stand in the way, block the path.*
     reverentia, -ae (f.): *awe, shyness, modesty.* This refers to the feelings of the statue, as if it were alive.
252 **ars adeo latet arte sua:** ASSONANCE; this phrase, an ANTITHESIS, is applicable to Ovid's own work. It has become proverbial of art which is so skillful it makes its products appear to be works of nature.
     hauriō, -īre, hausī, haustum: *to consume, drink.*
253 **ignes:** in poetry this word often refers to the fire of love.
254 **an . . . an:** *whether . . . or.*
257 **insīdō, -ere, -sēdī, -sessum:** *to sink in, become embedded.*
258 **līvor, -ōris (m.):** *bluish coloring, bruise.*
259 **blanditia, -ae (f.):** *flattery, compliment, endearing comment.*
     adhibeō, -ēre, -uī, -itum: *to apply.*
     modo, modo: the ANAPHORA here creates a sense of immediacy and makes the activity more vivid.

260   munera fert illi conchas teretesque lapillos
       et parvas volucres et flores mille colorum
       liliaque pictasque pilas et ab arbore lapsas
       Heliadum lacrimas; ornat quoque vestibus artus,
       dat digitis gemmas, dat longa monilia collo,
265   aure leves bacae, redimicula pectore pendent:
       cuncta decent; nec nuda minus formosa videtur.
       conlocat hanc stratis concha Sidonide tinctis

✦ ✦ ✦

decent—fitting, suitable

260 **munera:** it was a standard practice of the elegiac lover to present his *puella* with gifts of this same sort.
   concha, -ae (f.): *shell*. This noun stands in apposition to *munera* as do the next six accusative nouns: *lapillos* (260) *volucres* (261) *flores* (261) *liliaque* (262) *pilas* (262) and *lacrimas* (263).
   teres, -etis: *smooth, rounded*. The POLYSYNDETON here and throughout this description isolates each element, drawing attention to the different items, and helps to move the lines along.
   lapillus, -ī (m.): *small stone*.
261 **volucris, -cris (f.):** *a bird*.
262 **līlium, -ī (n.):** *a lily*. Note that DIASTOLE lengthens the *-que* and emphasizes the POLYSYNDETON.
   pīla, -ae (f.): *ball, sphere*.
   lābor, -ī, lāpsus: *to drip*.
263 **Hēliades, -um (f. pl.):** daughters of the sun god, Helios and Clymene, sisters of Phaethon. They were changed into poplar trees and their tears of mourning for the loss of their brother became amber.
264 **gemma, -ae (f.):** *jewel, gem*.
   monīle, -is (n.): *a necklace*.
265 **bāca, -ae (f.):** *a pearl*.
   redimīculum, -ī (n.): *a band, wreath, garland*.
266 **cunctus, -a, -um:** *all, every*.
   nec ... videtur: LITOTES.
267 **strātum, -ī (n.):** *coverlet, throw*.
   concha Sidonide: refers to a shellfish indigenous to the waters off Sidon, a Phoenician city, from which came a rare purple dye. Sidon was synonomous with the production of dye hence the *concha Sidonide* came to stand for the color purple—rare and regal. This whole phrase, *stratis ... tinctis*, forms a CHIASMUS.
   tingō, -ere, -nxī, -nctum: *to dye, stain*.

162 ✦ OVID

adpellatque tori sociam adclinataque colla
mollibus in plumis, tamquam sensura, reponit.
270 "Festa dies Veneris tota celeberrima Cypro
venerat, et pandis inductae cornibus aurum
conciderant ictae nivea cervice iuvencae,
turaque fumabant, cum munere functus ad aras
constitit et timide 'si, di, dare cuncta potestis,
275 sit coniunx, opto,' non ausus 'eburnea virgo'
dicere Pygmalion 'similis mea' dixit 'eburnae.'
sensit, ut ipsa suis aderat Venus aurea festis,

✦ ✦ ✦

268 **adclīnō, -āre, -āvī, -ātum:** *to lean or rest on.*
     colla: Ovid frequently uses the plural for singular parts of the body.
269 **repōnō, -ere, -posuī, -positum:** *to lay to rest.*
270 **dies:** although most commonly masculine (especially in prose), here, and frequently in poetry, feminine.
     Cyprus, -ī (f.): an island in the eastern Mediterranean Sea known for its worship of Venus.
271 **pandus, -a, -um:** *curved, bent, bowed*
     indūcō, -ere, -dūxī, -ductum: *to cover, spread on or over.*
     aurum: a Greek accusative with the passive participle *inductae* to describe the material used for the gilding.
272 **concidō, -ere, -ī:** *to fall, collapse.*
     īciō, -ere, īcī, ictum: *to strike, beat.*
     nivea: another use of the color of cold snow associated with purity as in line 247.
     cervix, -vīcis (f.): *the neck, back of the neck.*
     iuvenca, -ae (f.): *a cow, heifer.*
273 **tūs, tūris (n.):** *incense.*
     fūmō, -āre, -āvī, -ātum: *to give off smoke.*
     mūnus, -eris (n.): *ritual duty.*
274 **constō, -āre, -stitī:** *to take up a position; to stand up.*
275 **eburneus, -a, -um:** *of ivory.*
276 **similis:** HYPERBATON; the exaggerated separation of *mea* from *coniunx* graphically represents Pygmalion's hesitation in expressing his true wish.
     eburnus, -a, -um: *of ivory.*
277 **sensit:** the subject here is the same as that in the next clause—*Venus.*

vota quid illa velint et, amici numinis omen,
flamma ter accensa est apicemque per aera duxit.
280 ut rediit, simulacra suae petit ille puellae
incumbensque toro dedit oscula: visa tepere est;
admovet os iterum, manibus quoque pectora temptat:
temptatum mollescit ebur positoque rigore
subsidit digitis ceditque, ut Hymettia sole
285 cera remollescit tractataque pollice multas
flectitur in facies ipsoque fit utilis usu.
dum stupet et dubie gaudet fallique veretur,
rursus amans rursusque manu sua vota retractat.

✦ ✦ ✦

278 **vōtum, -ī (n.)**: *prayer, vow, oath.*
velint: subjunctive in an indirect question dependent on *sensit* (277) and *quid* (278).
279 **ter (adv.)**: *three times.* The number three is always significant and often implies divine intervention. Here, since Venus is present at her own festival, it signifies her direct response.
apex, apicis (m.): *a tip of a flame.* Here, *apicemque duxit* is best translated "and the flame lept up."
āēr, āeris (m.): *the air.*
280 **simulācrum, -ī (n.)**: *an image, statue.*
simulacra suae ... puellae: the reference to the statue as well as the girl anticipates the transformation.
petit: the abrupt shift to the present tense makes the following description of the miracle more vivid.
281 **incumbō, -ere, -cubuī**: *to lie on.*
tepeō, -ēre: *to be warm, tepid.* Often used of the passion of love.
283 **mollescō, -ere**: *to become soft.*
rigor, -ōris (m.): *stiffness, rigidity.*
284 **subsīdō, -ere, -sēdī**: *to give way.*
ut: introduces a SIMILE comparing the softening statue to beeswax.
Hymettia: modifies *cera*, 285. This is the adjectival form of *Hymettus*, a mountain near Athens that was known for its honey.
285 **tractō, -āre, -āvī, -ātum**: *to handle, manage.*
pollex, -icis (m.): *the thumb.*
286 **faciēs, -eī (f.)**: *shape.*
288 **amans**: here, the noun, not the participle.
sua vota: refers to those things he had wished for and prayed for, i.e., that his statue become a wife.
retractō, -āre, -āvī, -ātum: *to handle, feel for a second time.*

corpus erat! saliunt temptatae pollice venae.
290 tum vero Paphius plenissima concipit heros
verba, quibus Veneri grates agat, oraque tandem
ore suo non falsa premit dataque oscula virgo
sensit et erubuit timidumque ad lumina lumen
attollens pariter cum caelo vidit amantem.
295 coniugio, quod fecit, adest dea, iamque coactis
cornibus in plenum noviens lunaribus orbem
illa Paphon genuit, de qua tenet insula nomen."

✦ ✦ ✦

289 **temptatae pollice:** nearly the same phrase as used in the SIMILE in line 285.
saliō, -īre, -uī, -tum: *to leap*, i.e., *to pulse*.
vēna, -ae (f.): *blood vessel, vein*.
290 **Paphius, -a, -um:** *of or pertaining to the city of Paphos on the island of Cyprus*.
concipiō, -ere, -cēpī, -ceptum: *to form, produce, conceive*.
hērōs, -ōos (m.): *a hero*.
291 **grātēs, -ium (f. pl.):** *thanks*; a variation of the more common *gratias agere* meaning *to give thanks*.
292 **non falsa:** *genuine*; LITOTES for emphasis.
293 **ērubēscō, -ere, -buī:** *to blush with shame or modesty*. Pygmalion's statue, full of modesty, blushes, unlike the Propoetides who, because of their vileness, lost the ability to blush in line 241. This reference to modesty at the end of the story is reminiscent of the statue's *reverentia* in line 251.
lumen: here meaning *eye*.
294 **attollō, -ere:** *to lift up, raise*.
295 **coniugium, -ī (n.):** *marriage*.
296 **cornibus:** with *coactis* describes the phases of the moon.
lūnāris, -e: *of or pertaining to the moon*.
297 **illa:** refers to the ivory statue which is now a woman.
Paphos, -ī (m., f.): *the child of Pygmalion*. By tradition a son who became the founder of the Cyprian city of Paphos which was sacred to Venus. Ovid ends his tale with an aition (origin) of how the city got its name.
gignō, -ere, genuī, genitum: *to give birth to*.
qua: the gender of this relative pronoun is problematic as it should refer to the masculine Paphos. Some texts prefer *quo*.

METRICAL TERMS

Caesura—a natural break in the hexameter line where a word end occurs within a metrical foot. In Ovid, this is often in the third foot in a hexameter line. Some hexameter lines contain double caesurae, one in the second and one in the fourth foot. Caesurae usually correspond to pauses or breaks in the meaning. Caesurae are traditionally indicated by two vertical lines: ‖.

Third foot caesura:

Met. I. 527:   – ⏑ ⏑ | – ⏑ ⏑ | – ‖
                Tum quoque visa decens: ‖

                –| – – | – ⏑ ⏑ | – –
                nudabant corpora venti

Second and fourth foot caesurae:

Met. I. 505:   – ⏑ ⏑ | – ‖ –| – ⏑ ⏑ | – ‖
                nympha, mane! ‖ *Sic agna lupum,* ‖

                – | – ⏑ ⏑ | – –
                sic cerva leonem

Dactyl—a long syllable, followed by two short syllables – ⏑ ⏑.

Diaeresis—coincidence of word end and the end of a metrical foot. It may occur in any foot of a hexameter line; it is the regular break in a pentameter line.

                – ⏑ ⏑ | – ⏑ ⏑ –‖ – ⏑ ⏑ | – ⏑ ⏑ | –
Amores I. 1.2:   *edere, materia* ‖ *conveniente modis.*

Diastole—the lengthening of a syllable regularly short.

Elegiac couplet—the meter of Latin love elegy and of all of Ovid's *Amores*. It consists of a dactylic hexameter line followed by a pentameter line.

Elision—the suppression or dropping of a final vowel, dipthong, or vowel plus *m* before a word beginning with an initial vowel or *h*:

Amores I. 1.4: – ⏑ ⏑ | – – | – ‖ – ⏑ ⏑|– ⏑ ⏑| –
dicitur atque unum surripuisse pedem.

Hexameter—a metrical line of six feet (dactyls and spondees are interchangeable, except for the fifth foot, which is usually a dactyl and the sixth foot which is always a spondee).

Ictus—metrical stress which falls on the first syllable in the foot. When this corresponds with the natural stress (accent) of a word, the syllable receives greater emphasis.

Pentameter—a metrical line of five feet divided into two halves. The first half consists of two feet, which may be either dactyls or spondees, followed by a half foot that is always a single long syllable (two-and-a-half feet). The caesura between the two halves coincides with a diaeresis. The second half of the line always contains two dactyls followed by a single long syllable (two-and-a-half feet).

$$- \cup \cup\ |\ - \cup \cup\ |\ - \|\ - \cup \cup\ |\ - \cup \cup\ |\ -$$
$$\updownarrow \qquad \updownarrow$$
$$-\ -\ \ |\ -\ -\ \ |\ -\ \|\ -\cup\cup\ |\ -\cup\cup\ |\ -$$

Spondee—a metrical foot with two long syllables (either by nature or by position); indicated as – –.

Syncope—loss of a short vowel or a syllable within a word.

Amores I. 3.6: *accipe, qui pura **norit** amare fide!*

Systole—the shortening of a syllable regularly long.

FIGURES OF SPEECH

Allegory—an extended narrative that suggests an implied meaning in addition to the one stated on the surface; for example, the story of Daedalus and Icarus might be viewed as an illustrative story about excessive mortal pride.

Alliteration—repetition of initial sounds in two or more words.

Met. VIII. 716: *iamque super geminos crescente cacumine vultus*

Anaphora—repetition of a word at the beginning of phrases or clauses.

Amores I. 3.5–6: ***Accipe**, per longos tibi qui deserviat annos;*
 ***accipe**, qui pura norit amare fide!*

Antithesis—an opposition of ideas in a balanced grammatical structure.

Met. I. 469: . . . ***fugat hoc, facit illud*** *amorem*

Apostrophe—addressing a person or abstraction as if present.

Met. I. 488–89: *ille quidem obsequitur, sed **te** decor iste quod **optas** esse vetat, votoque **tuo tua** forma repugnat:*

Assonance—juxtaposition of similar sounds (usually vowels) in a series of words.

Amores I. 3.14: ***nuda**que simplicitas **purpureus**que **pudor**.*

Asyndeton—the omission of a conjunction.

Met. I. 512–14: . . . *non incola montis, (et)*
 non ego sum pastor, (et) non hic armenta gregesque
 horridus observo.

Chiasmus—an arrangement of words in an ABBA pattern.

Met. VIII. 187: ***omnia possideat**, non **possidet aera** Minos.*
  A   B   B   A

Ellipsis—the omission of a word or words necessary for the sense.

Amores I. 9.20: . . . *hic portas frangit, at ille* (***frangit***) *fores.*

Enjambment—a line which continues into the next without a grammatical break.

Met. I. 517–18: . . . *per me, quod eritque **fuitque estque**, patet; per me concordant carmina nervis.*

Golden Line—a line with a verb in the center and two pairs of words in interlocked word order on each side of the verb.

Met. VIII. 638: ***summissoque humiles** intrarunt **vertice postes***
　　　　　　　　　　A　　　　　B　　　　　　　A　　　　B

Hendiadys—using **two** nouns connected by a conjunction to express **one** idea:

Amores I. 9.42: *mollierant animos **lectus** et **umbra** meos*

Hyperbaton—a significant distortion of normal word order.

Met. VIII. 229–30: *oraque caerulea patrium clamantia nomen excipiuntur aqua, . . .*

Hyperbole—exaggeration for rhetorical effect.

Met. I. 460: *stravimus **innumeris** tumidum Pythona **sagittis**.*

Hysteron Proteron—a reversal of the natural order of ideas.

Met. VIII. 696–97: . . . *flexere oculos et **mersa** palude **cetera** prospiciunt, tantum sua **tecta** manere,*

Interlocked Word Order (Synchesis)—the arrangement of a group of words to form an ABAB pattern (often used to emphasize the closeness of the words to one another).

Amores I. 12.24: *quas **aliquis duro cognitor ore** legat*
　　　　　　　　　　　　A　　　　B　　　A　　　B

Irony—purposeful discrepancy for rhetorical effect between an assertion and intended or understood meaning.

Met. VIII. 668–70: . . . *post haec caelatus* ***eodem***
sistitur ***argento*** *crater fabricatque fago pocula*, . . .

Litotes—affirming something by stating its opposite with a negative.

Met. IV. 122: ***non aliter quam*** *cum vitiato fistula plumbo*

Metaphor—an implied comparison suggesting a likeness between two things.

Amores I. 9.1: ***militat*** *omnis* ***amans****, et habet sua* ***castra*** *Cupido*

Metonymy—use of one noun for another that is closely related.

Met. I. 483: *illa velut crimen* ***taedas*** *exosa* ***iugales***

Onomatopoeia—use of sounds that reflect meaning.

Met. IV. 70: ***murmure*** *blanditiae* ***minimo*** *transire solebant.*

Oxymoron—the use of seemingly contradictory words in the same phrase.

Met. X. 287: *dum stupet et* ***dubie gaudet*** *fallique veretur,*

Personification—treating something inanimate as if human.

Amores III. 15.19–20: ***imbelles elegi****, genialis Musa,* ***valete****,*
post mea mansurum fata superstes opus.

Pleonasm—use of unnecessary and additional words to express an idea.

Met. X. 283–84: *temptatum* ***mollescit*** *ebur positoque rigore*

Polyptoton—the use of the same word in different inflexional forms in the same sentence.

Met. VIII. 724: *cura* ***deum di*** *sint, et, qui,* ***coluere, colantur***

Polysyndeton—use of more conjunctions than are necessary.

Met. VIII. 665–66: *condita**que** in liquida corna autumnalia faece intiba**que** **et** radix **et** lactis massa coacti*

Prolepsis—introduction of a word before it is naturally appropriate.

Met. VIII. 197–98: *ore renidenti modo, **quas** vaga moverat aura, captabat **plumas***

Simile—a comparison between two similar things; introduced by *velut, ut,* or *sic.*

Met. VIII. 213: *ante volat comitique timet, **velut ales**, ab alto*

Synchesis—see **Interlocked Word Order**.

Synechdoche—use of the part of something to represent the whole of it.

Met. IV. 86: *cumque domo exierint, urbis quoque **tecta** relinquant,*

Transferred Epithet—an adjective used to characterize one thing or person applied to another that is closely associated with it for emphasis.

Met. VIII. 676: *et de **purpureis** conlectae **vitibus** uvae,*

Tricolon Crescendo—three examples in an ascending order of size or importance.

Amores I. 11.9–10: ***nec** silicum venae **nec** durum in pectore ferrum **nec** tibi simplicitas ordine maior adest.*

Zeugma—the linking of two words by a single verb thereby creating a paradoxical clash because one subject or object is literal and the other abstract or figurative.

Met. IV. 129: *illa redit iuvenemque **oculis animoque requirit**,*

HIGH-FREQUENCY WORD LIST

The following list contains words that occur five or more times in the selected Ovid passages.

ā, ab - (+ abl.) from
accipiō, -ere, -cēpī, -ceptum - to receive, accept
ad - (+ acc.) to, at; by the light of
adhūc (adv.) - already; yet, as yet, still
āēr, āeris (m.) - air
aes, aeris (n.) - money, pay
āiō - to say, assert; reply
alter ... alter - the one ... the other
altus, -a, -um - high; deep
amans, -ntis (m., f.) - lover
amō, -āre, -āvī, -ātum - to love; to fall in love
amor, -ōris (m.) - love, love affair
an (conj.) - or, or rather; whether
annus, -ī (m.) - year
ante (adv.) - previously, once; in front, ahead (prep. + acc.) before, in front of
aqua, -ae (f.) - water, sea
arbor, -oris (f.) - tree
arma, -ōrum (n. pl.) - arms, weapons; fighting, war
ars, -tis (f.) - skill, art
at (conj.) - at least, but, yet; while, whereas
atque (conj.) - and in fact, and what is more, and indeed, and even
aura, -ae (f.) - breeze, air
aut (conj.) - or
aut ... aut - either ... or

bellum, -ī (n.) - war

caelum, -ī (n.) - sky, heaven
campus, -ī (m.) - field
carmen, -minis (n.) - poetry, song
carpō, -ere, -sī, -tum - to pass over, pursue one's way
causa, -ae (f.) - cause, reason, inspiration
cēdō, -ere, cessī, cessum - to yield, give way; to be inferior
cēra, -ae (f.) - wax, beeswax
certus, -a, -um - accurate, precise, sure
color, -ōris (m.) - color
coniunx, -iugis (f., m.) - wife, bride; husband
corpus, -oris (n.) - body
cum (conj.) - when; (prep. + abl.) with, along with
cūra, -ae (f.) - care, anxiety, worry; object of concern, beloved person

dē - (+ abl.) from
deus, -ī (m.) - god, deity
dīcō, -ere, dīxī, dictum - to say; to appoint, fix
digitus, -ī (m.) - finger; toe
dō, dare, dedī, datum - to give; to allow; to cause to go
dominus, -ī (m.) - master, owner
domus, -ī (f.) - house, home, household

dum (conj.) - while
duo, -ae, -o - two
dux, -cis (m.) - general, leader

ē, ex - (+ abl.) from
ebur, -oris (n.) - ivory
ego - I
eō, īre, i(v)ī, itum - to go
eōdem (adv.) - to the same place
et (conj.) - and; also; even
et ... et - both ... and; also

faciō, -ere, fēcī, factum - to make, do; bring about, inspire; to act; to reveal; to see that
fallō, -ere, fefellī, falsum - to deceive, trick; to fail; to while away, beguile
ferō, ferre, tulī, lātum - to tell, relate; to carry, bear, bring
ferus, -a, -um - fierce, wild
fidēs, -ēī (f.) - good faith, honesty, honor
flectō, -ere, flexī, flectum - to bend
forma, -ae (f.) - appearance; good looks, beauty
fugiō, -ere, -ī, -itum - to flee

gaudeō, -ēre, gāvīsus - to rejoice; to be pleased
geminus, -a, -um - double; pair of, twin
gravis, grave - heavy, weighty; important; hard to capture

habeō, -ēre, -uī, -itum - to have, possess; to hold
hic, haec, hoc - this, the latter
hostis, -is (m.) - enemy

iaceō, -ēre, -uī, -tum - to lie down, lie; to be overthrown
iam (adv.) - now
ignis, -is (m.) - fire, star
ille, illa, illud - that, the former; he, she
illīc (adv.) - there, in that place
in - (+ acc.) over, affecting; for, towards; into; among; (+ abl.) in, on
infēlix, -icis - unhappy, ill-fated, unlucky
inquam, inquit - to say
inter - (+ acc.) among; between
ipse, -a, -um - oneself, itself
iterum (adv.) - again, another time
iubeō, -ēre, iussī, iussum - to order, bid, command
iungō, -ere, -xī, -ctum - to join (in marriage)

lacertus, -ī (m.) - upper arm
lacrima, -ae (f.) - tear
legō, -ere, lēgī, lectum - to choose, select, pick out; to read
levis, -e - light, not ponderous
licet, -ēre, -uī, -itum - it is permitted, one may; (conj.) although
locus, -ī (m.) - place; open land
longus, -a, -um - long, tall
loquor, -quī, -cūtus - to speak

magnus, -a, -um - great, large
maneō, -ēre, -sī, -sum - to remain, stay
manus, -ūs (f.) - hand; armed force, band
medius, -a, -um - middle, middle of; between; in half, half; medium, moderate
membrum, -ī (n.) - part of the body; limb of tree or body
mens, -tis (f.) - mind; inclination

meus, -a, -um - my
mīles, -itis (m.) - soldier
miser, -era, -erum - wretched, miserable
modo (adv.) - just now, recently, lately; just, only
mollis, -e - gentle, smooth; soft
moveō -ēre, mōvī, mōtum - to move, strike; rouse
multus, -a, -um - much
mundus, -ī (m.) - heavens, universe, world, earth

nam (conj.) - for, to be sure
nascor, -ī, nātus - to be born
nātūra, -ae (f.) - nature, natural world
nātus, -ī (m.) - son
nē (conj.) - lest, in order that . . . not; do not
nec - and . . . not; not even
negō, -āre, -āvī, -ātum - to say not; to deny
nervus, -ī (m.) - string of a musical instrument or bow
nimium (adv.) - excessively, extremely, very much
nisi (conj.) - if not
nōmen, -minis (n.) - name, family name, fame, reputation
nōn (adv.) - not
noster, -tra, -trum - our
novus, -a, -um - new, unfamiliar
nox, -ctis (f.) - night
nūdus, -a, -um - bare, pure, open, simple; naked, unclothed
nullus, -a, -um - no one, nobody, nothing; no; insignificant, trifling
nunc (adv.) - now, at this time

oculus, -ī (m.) - eye
omnis, -e - each, every, all

opus, -eris (n.) - task, undertaking, work, job; need
orbis, -is (m.) - globe, world
ordō, -dinis (m.) - order; class, rank; a linear arrangement
ōrō, -āre, -āvī, -ātum - to pray, beseech, beg
ōs, ōris (n.) - face; mouth
osculum, -ī (n.) - mouth, lips; kiss

pārens, -entis (m., f.) - ancestor, parent
pars, -tis (f.) - part, portion; side
pater, -tris (m.) - father
pectus, -oris (n.) - chest, breast
pendeō, -ēre, pependī - to hang, hang down, fall
penna, -ae (f.) - wing, feather
per - (+ acc.) through, throughout
perdō, -ere, -idī, -itum - to waste one's effort or time; to destroy
pēs, pedis (m.) - foot, metrical foot
petō, -ere, -īvī, -ītum - to seek, look for; to seek the hand of in marriage, to court
placeō, -ēre, -uī, -itum - (+ dat.) to be pleasing or acceptable
pondus, -eris (n.) - weight
pōnō, -ere, posuī, positum - to put, place, arrange; to lay aside, abandon
possum, posse, potuī - to be able
postquam (conj.) - after, when
premō, -ere, -ssī, -ssum - to press on, push; to cover
prō - (+ abl.) on account of, because of
puella, -ae (f.) - girl, young woman
puer, -ī (m.) - boy

queror, -rī, questus - to complain
quī, quae, quod - who, which
quis, quid - who? what?
quisque, quaeque, quidque - each, each one, each thing
quod (conj.) - because; that, the fact that
quoque (adv.) - also, too

rāmus, -ī (m.) - branch
redeō, -īre, -iī, -itum - to return
regnum, -ī (n.) - kingdom, domain
relinquō, -ere, -liquī, -lictum - to leave behind

saepe (adv.) - often
sed (conj.) - but
semper (adv.) - always
sentiō, -īre, sēnsī, sēnsum - to feel, sense
sī (conj.) - if
sīc (adv.) - thus, in this way, in like manner
sine - (+ abl.) without
spectō, -āre, -āvī, -ātum - to look at, observe
sub - (+ abl.) under, underneath; at the base of; (+ acc.) at the base of, just at
sum, esse, fuī, futūrus - to be
summus, -a, -um - greatest; highest
super - (+ acc.) over
suus, -a, -um - his, her, its, their

tabella, -ae (f.) - writing tablet
tamen (adv.) - nevertheless
tangō, -ere, tetigī, tāctum - to touch, come in contact with
tegō, -ere, texī, tēctum - to cover, conceal
tellūs, -ūris (f.) - land, country

temptō, -āre, -āvī, -ātum - to try, attempt; to handle, touch, feel
teneō, -ēre, -uī, -tum - to hold, have; to catch
terra, -ae (f.) - earth, ground
timidus, -a, -um - fearful, apprehensive, timid
tōtus, -a, -um - the whole of
trahō, -ere, trāxī, tractum - to drag, draw; to influence
trānseō, -īre, -īvī, -itum - to cross, pass through
tū - you (sing.)
tum (adv.) - then, at that moment
tuus, -a, -um - your (sing.)

ubi (adv.) - where, when
umbra, -ae (f.) - shade, darkness, shadow
unda, -ae (f.) - body of flowing water, river; water
ūnus, -a, -um - one; alone
ut (conj.) - just as, like; when; in order that; since
uterque, utraque, utrumque - each, each . . . of the two

vacuus, -a, -um - empty, unattached, free, unoccupied
valē, valēte - farewell! good-bye!
vātēs, -is (m.) - poet, prophet
vel (conj.) - either . . . or; at any rate
veniō, -īre, vēnī, ventum - to come
Venus, -eris (f.) - Venus, goddess sacred to love and lovers
verbum, -ī (n.) - word
vestis, -is (f.) - clothing; cloth
vetus, -eris - old, of a former time, ancient
videō, -ēre, vīsī, vīsum - to see, observe, gaze upon; to consider
virgō, -inis (f.) - maiden

vix (adv.) - hardly, scarcely
vocō, -āre, -āvī, -ātum - to call
volō, velle, voluī - to wish for; to wish
vōs - you (pl.)
vulnus, -eris (n.) - wound, injury
vultus, -ūs (m.) - facial expression; face

GLOSSARY

Words marked with a ~ are also listed in the High-Frequency Word List.

A
ā (interj.) - ah!
~ā, ab - (+ abl.) from
abditus, -a, -um - hidden, concealed
abdūco, -dūcere, -dūxī, -ductum - to carry off
abeō, -īre, -iī, -itum - to change, be transformed into
abscīdō, -dere, -dī, -sum - to separate, cut off
absum, -esse, āfuī, āfutūrus - to be missing; to be away from
absūmō, -ere, -sumpsī, -sumptum - to use up, squander, spend
ac (conj.) - and
accēdō, -ere, -cessī, -cessum - to follow in accordance; to be added
accendō, -ere, -dī, -censum - to light, ignite; (pass.) to flare up
accingō, -ere, -cinxī, -cinctum - to gird, equip
~accipiō, -ere, -cēpī, -ceptum - to receive, accept
accommodō, -āre, -āvī, -ātum - to fasten on, fit
acer, -eris (n.) - maple wood
ācer, ācris, ācre - vigorous, energetic
acervus, -ī (m.) - a disordered mass, chaos

Achillēs, -is (m.) - Achilles, Greek hero of the Trojan War
acūtus, -a, -um - pointed, sharp
~ad - (+ acc.) to, at; by the light of
adclīnō, -āre, -āvī, -ātum - to lean or rest on
adclīvis, -is, -e - upwards sloping, inclined
adcumbō, -ere, -cubuī, -cubitum - to recline at table
addō, -ere, -idī, -itum - to add, attach
addūco, -ere, -dūxī, -ductum - to pull taut
adeō, -īre, -iī, -itum - to approach
adeō (adv.) - especially, extremely, to such a degree
adflō, -āre, -āvī, -ātum - to breathe onto, blow onto
adhibeō, -ēre, -uī, -itum - to apply
~adhūc (adv.) - already; yet, as yet, still
adimō, -ere, -ēmī, -emptum - to take away
adiuvō, -āre, -iūvī, -iūtum - to help, assist
admittō, -ere, -mīsī, -missum - to give loose rein to, release, let go
admoveō, -ēre, -mōvī, -mōtum - to move or place near to
adnuō, -ere, -uī, -ūtum - to nod; to nod in approval

177

adoleō, -ēre, -uī, adultum - to burn
adoperiō, -īre, -uī, -tum - to cover over
adpellō, -āre, -āvī, -ātum - to call, address, name
adserō, -ere, -uī, -tum - to lay claim to
adsiduus, -a, -um - constantly present, persistent
adspergō, -ginis (f.) - sprinkling, splashing, scattering
adspiciō, -ere, -spexī, -spectum - to observe, behold, catch sight of
adsum, -esse, -fuī, -fūtūrus - to be present
adulter, -erī (m.) - adulterer
adūrō, -ere, -ussī, -ustum - to burn, scorch
adversus, -a, -um - opposing, obstructing, standing in the way
aedēs, -is (f.) - temple, sanctuary
aemula, -ae (f.) - a female imitator
aēnum, -ī (n.) - a pot or cauldron made of bronze
aequalis, -is, -e - symmetrical, even
aequō, -āre, -āvī, -ātum - to make level
aequor, -oris (n.) - calm, flat surface of the sea
aequus, -a, -um - like, equal; **ex aequō** - equally
~**āēr, āeris (m.)** - air
~**aes, aeris (n.)** - money, pay
aestus, -ūs (m.) - heat
aestuō, -āre, -āvī, -ātum - to seethe; to blaze
aetās, -ātis (f.) - age
aethēr, -eris (m.) - air, sky
aevum, -ī (n.) - lifetime, experience, years of age

affectō, -āre, -āvī, -ātum - to aspire to, attempt
agilis, -e - active, busy
agitābilis, -is, -e - mobile
agitō, -āre, -āvī, -ātum - to shake, brandish
agmen, -minis (n.) - army
agna, -ae (f.) - ewe lamb
agō, -ere, ēgī, actum - to lead, drive; to deliver, give; spend (time); **quid agam** - how am I?
~**āiō** - to say, assert, reply
āla, -ae (f.) - wing
albus, -a, -um - white, clear, colorless
āles, -itis (m.) - large bird
alimentum, -ī (n.) - food, nourishment
aliquis, aliquid - someone, something
aliter (adv.) - otherwise, differently
alius, alia, aliud - another
alligō, -āre, -āvī, -ātum - to tie, fasten
altē (adv.) - at a great height
~**alter . . . alter** - the one . . . the other
~**altus, -a, -um** - high; deep
alumnus, -ī (m.) - a "son" in the sense of a product of a particular environment
alveus, -ī (m.) - a hollowed-out vessel, dish
~**amans, -ntis (m., f.)** - lover
Amathusius, -a, -um - of or pertaining to a town on Cyprus, sacred to Venus
ambāgēs, -um (f.) - long-winded, digressive speech, circumlocution
ambiguum, -ī (n.) - uncertainty, doubt

GLOSSARY ✦ 179

ambiō, -īre, -uī, -ītum - to surround, encircle
ambitiōsus, -a, -um - vain, ambitious, conceited
ambō, -ae, -ō - both, the two
amīca, -ae (f.) - mistress
amictus, -ūs (m.) - cloak
amīcus, -a, -um - friendly, loving
~amō, -āre, -āvī, -ātum - to love, fall in love
~amor, -ōris (m.) - love, love affair
Amphitrītē, -ēs (f.) - the wife of Neptune and so, by extension, a personification of the sea
amplector, -ī, -plexus - to embrace
~an (conj.) - or, or rather; whether
an . . . an - whether . . . or
ancilla, -ae (f.) - female slave
Andromachē, -ēs (f.) - Andromache, wife of Hector
anhēlitus, -ūs (m.) - gasp, panting
anīlis, -e - of or pertaining to an old woman
anima, -ae (f.) - soul, life; breath
animal, -ālis (n.) - animal
animus, -ī (m.) - courage, spirit, morale; mind, soul
~annus, -ī (m.) - year
ansa, -ae (f.) - a handle
anser, -eris (m.) - goose
~ante (adv.) - previously, once; in front, ahead; (prep. + acc.) before, in front of
antrum, -ī (n.) - cave
anus, -ūs (f.) - an old woman
anxius, -a, -um - anxious, worried, troubled
Āonius, -a, -um - of Aonia, Boeotian; of or connected with the Muses, poetic
aperiō, -īre, -uī, -tum - to reveal, disclose

apex, apicis (m.) - a tip of a flame
apis, -is (f.) - bee
Apollineus, -a, -um - of or pertaining to Apollo
aptō, -āre, -āvī, -ātum - to fit, put into position
aptus, -a, -um - (+ dat.) appropriate, fitting, suited
~aqua, -ae (f.) - water, sea
aquila, -ae (f.) - eagle
aquilō, -onis (m.) - the north wind
aquōsus, -a, -um - watery, wet
āra, -ae (f.) - altar
arātor, -ōris (m.) - ploughman
aratrum, -ī (n.) - plow
~arbor, -oris (f.) - tree
arboreus, -a, -um - of or pertaining to trees, arboreal
arceō, -ere, -uī - to prevent from approaching, repulse, drive
arcus, -ūs (m.) - bow
ardens, -ntis - burning, blazing, hot
ardeō, -ēre, arsī, arsum - to burn, be inflamed
ardor, -ōris (m.) - passion, ardor
arduum, -ī (n.) - high elevation
arduus, -a, -um - tall, lofty
ārea, -ae (f.) - open space out-of-doors
argentum, -ī (n.) - silver
Argēus, -a, -um - Greek
āridus, -a, -um - dry
arista, -ae (f.) - harvest
~arma, -ōrum (n. pl.) - arms, weapons; fighting, war
armātus, -a, -um - armed
armentum, -ī (n.) - herd
arripiō, -ere, arripuī, arreptus - to grab hold of, seize
~ars, -tis (f.) - skill, art
artus, -ūs (m.) - limb of a tree or body; a joint of the body

arvum, -ī (n.) - field, ploughed land; territory, country
arx, -cis (f.) - summit, peak
asper, -era, -erum - wild, rough, harsh
aspiciō, -ere, -spexī, -spectum - to look at, gaze upon, observe
astrum, -ī (n.) - star, heavenly body
~**at** (conj.) - at least, but, yet; while, whereas
āter, ātra, ātrum - black, dark-colored, stained
Atlantiadēs, -ae (m.) - Mercury, a grandson of Atlas
~**atque** (conj.) - and in fact, and what is more, and indeed, and even
Atrīdēs, -ae (m.) - a male descendant of Atreus, king of Argos and Mycenae; usually used of Agamemnon
attenuō, -āre, -āvī, -ātum - to enfeeble, lessen, weaken
Atticus, -ī (m.) - Atticus
attollō, -ere - to lift up, raise
attonitus, -a, -um - dazed, astounded
auctor, -ōris (m.) - founder, author, originator
auctus, -a, -um - increased in intensity
audax, -ācis - bold, confident
audeō, -ēre, ausus - to go so far as to, dare, have the courage
audiō, -īre, -īvī, -ītum - to hear
auferō, -ferre, abstulī, ablātum - to carry away, carry off
augeō, -ēre, auxī, auctum - to increase, augment, strengthen
auguror, -ārī, -ātus - to foretell, predict
Augustus, -ī (m.) - Caesar Augustus, emperor

Augustus, -a, -um - of or pertaining to the emperor Augustus
~**aura, -ae (f.)** - breeze, air
aurātus, -a, -um - golden
aureus, -a, -um - golden
auris, -is (f.) - ear
Aurōra, -ae (f.) - Aurora, goddess of the dawn
aurum, -ī (n.) - gold
auspicium, -ī (n.) - portent, fortune, luck
Auster, -trī (m.) - the south wind, the south
~**aut** (conj.) - or
~**aut ... aut** - either ... or
autumnālis, -e - autumnal
avārus, -a, -um - greedy, avaricious, miserly
avēna, -ae (f.) - stem, stalk
Avernus, -a, -um - of or relating to Lake Avernas, the entrance to the underworld and by extension the underworld itself
āversor, -ārī, -ātus - to turn away from in disgust, reject
avidus, -a, -um - eager, greedy, ardent
avis, avis (f.) - bird
āvius, -a, -um - distant, remote

B

Babylōnius, -a, -um - Babylonian
bāca, -ae (f.) - olive; pearl
baculum, -ī (n.) - walking stick, staff
Baucis, -idis (f.) - Baucis, wife of Philemon
Bēlis, -idos (f.) - also known as the Danaides, these 50 daughters of Danaus were forced to marry their cousins, the 50 sons of Aegyptus
~**bellum, -ī (n.)** - war

bellus, -a, -um - pretty, beautiful
bene (adv.) - well
bicolor, -ōris - having two colors
bicornis, -e - having two prongs
blanditia, -ae (f.) - flattery, compliment, endearing comment
blandus, -a, -um - charming, seductive, caressing
bonus, -a, -um - good, worthy, reliable
Boōtēs, -ae (m.) - Bootes, a constellation
Boreās, -ae (m.) - the north wind, the north
bōs, bovis (m., f.) - bull, cow
brācchium, -ī (n.) - arm
brevis, -e - short
Brīsēis, -idos (f.) - Briseis, Achilles's slave and concubine
būbō, -ōnis (m.) - the horned owl
bustum, -ī (n.) - tomb
buxus, -ī (f.) - boxwood

C

cacūmen, -cūminis (n.) - the tip or top of a tree
cadō, -ere, cecidī, cāsum - to fall down
cādūcifer, -erī (m.) - Mercury, the bearer of the caduceus
caecus, -a, -um - blind
caedēs, -is (f.) - slaughter, killing
caedō, -ere, cecīdī, caesum - to kill, murder, slaughter
caelebs, -libis - unmarried male, bachelor
caelestis, -is, -e - heavenly, divine, celestial
caelicola, -ae (m., f.) - an inhabitant of heaven
caelō, -āre, -āvī, -ātum - to engrave, emboss
~caelum, -ī (n.) - sky, heaven
caeruleus, -a, -um - blue, greenish blue
calcō, -āre, -āvī, -ātum - to tread or trample on
caleō, -ēre, -uī - to be hot or warm
calidus, -a, -um - warm
cālīgō, -inis (f.) - murkiness, mistiness, darkness
callidus, -a, -um - clever, resourceful
Calymnē, -ēs (f.) - an island off the coast of Asia Minor
~campus, -ī (m.) - field
candidus, -a, -um - glistening
canis, canis (m.) - dog, hound
canistrum, -ī (n.) - a basket
canna, -ae (f.) - a small reed
canō, -ere, cecinī, cantum - to sing, tell of, relate
cantō, -āre, -āvī, -ātum - to sing, celebrate in song
capax, -ācis - capable
capillus, -ī (m.) - hair
capiō, -ere, cēpī, captum - to capture, contain
Capitōlium, -ī (n.) - the Capitoline Hill
captīvus, -a, -um - captured, hunted
captō, -āre, -āvī, -ātum - to seek out; try to catch
captus, -a, -um - captured
caput, -itis (n.) - head
cardō, -inis (m.) - hinge
careō, -ēre, -uī, -itum - (+ abl.) to be lacking
cāricus, -a, -um - carian, a type of fig
cariōsus, -a, -um - decayed, withered
~carmen, -minis (n.) - poetry, song

carnifex, -ficis (m.) - executioner
~carpō, -ere, -sī, -tum - to pass over, pursue one's way
cārus, -a, -um - beloved, dear
casa, -ae (f.) - cottage
castra, -ōrum (n. pl.) - camp
cāsus, -ūs (m.) - misfortune, event
catēna, -ae (f.) - chain, fetters
caterva, -ae (f.) - band, squadron, troop
Catullus, -ī (m.) - Catullus
~causa, -ae (f.) - cause, reason, inspiration
causor, -ārī, -ātus - to plead as an excuse or reason
cautus, -a, -um - cautious
cavus, -a, -um - hollow, concave
~cēdō, -ere, cessī, cessum - to yield, give way; to be inferior
celeber, -bris, -bre - crowded, populous, festive
celer, -eris, -ere - swift
celsus, -a, -um - high, lofty
~cēra, -ae (f.) - wax, beeswax
Cerēs, -eris (f.) - Ceres, goddess of open fields and agriculture
certē (adv.) - at any rate, at least; certainly, without a doubt
certō, -āre, -āvī, -ātum - to contend, dispute, struggle
~certus, -a, -um - accurate, precise, sure
cerva, -ae (f.) - deer
cervix, -īcis (f.) - neck
cēterus, -a, -um - the rest of, remaining
chaos, -ī (n.) - a formless state
Cicones, -um (m. pl.) - the Cicones, a people of southern Thrace
cicūta, -ae (f.) - poisonous hemlock (*Conium maculatum*)
cingō, -ere, cinxī, cinctum - to gird, encircle, surround, bind

cinis, -eris (m.) - ashes, embers
circumdō, -are, -edī, -atum - (+ abl.) to surround, encircle
circumfluus, -a, -um - that flows around
circumfundō, -fundere, -fūdī, -fūsum - to surround, spread round, envelop
cithara, -ae (f.) - lyre
citrā (prep. + acc.) - before, sooner than
citus, -a, -um - rapid, speedy
clāmō, -āre, -āvī, -ātum - to shout
Claros, -ī (f.) - Claros, a small town, sacred to Apollo, on the central coast of Asia Minor
clārus, -a, -um - loud, shrill
claudō, -ere, -sī, -sum - to close, shut
clāvus, -ī (m.) - nail
clīvus, -ī (m.) - slope, incline
coactus, -a, -um - curdled
coctilis, -e - of baked bricks
coeō, -īre, -iī, -itum - to come together, unite
coepī, coepisse, coeptum - to begin
coerceō, -ēre, -uī, -itum - to restrain, restrict, control, bind up
cognātus, -a, -um - related by birth, kindred
cognitor, -ōris (m.) - attorney
cognitus, -a, -um - known to be
cognoscō, -ere, -nōvī, -nitum - to recognize
cōgō, -ere, coēgī, coactum - to force, compel; to bring together
colligō, -ere, -lēgī, -lectum - to gather together, collect
collis, -is (m.) - hill, mountain
collum, -ī (n.) - neck

colō, -ere, -uī, cultum - to till, cultivate; to worship
~color, -ōris (m.) - color
coluber, -brī (m.) - snake, serpent
columba, -ae (f.) - dove
columna, -ae (f.) - column, pillar
coma, -ae (f.) - hair
comes, -itis (m., f.) - companion
comitō, -āre, -āvī, -ātum - to follow
commendō, -āre, -āvī, -ātum - to recommend, make agreeable or attractive
committō, -ere, -mīsī, -missum - to entrust
commūnis, -e - shared, common
cōmō, -ere, -psī, -ptum - to adorn, arrange
complector, -ī, -plexus - to embrace
complexus, -ūs (m.) - embrace
compōnō, -ere, -posuī, -positum - to compose, put together
comprimō, -ere, -pressī, -pressum - to pack closely or densely, squeeze
comptus, -a, -um - adorned
concha, -ae (f.) - shell
concidō, -ere, -ī - to fall, collapse
concipiō, -ere, -cēpī, -ceptum - to produce, form; to conceive
concordō, -āre, -āvī, -ātum - to agree, harmonize
concors, -cordis - agreeing, harmonious
concutiō, -ere, -cussī, -cussum - to shake
conditus, -a, -um - preserved
condō, -ere, -idī, -itum - to inter, lay to rest
cōnfīdō, -ere, cōnfīsus - to give trust, to trust (+ dat.)

confugiō, -ere, -fūgī - to flee to for safety
congeriēs, -ēī (f.) - heap, pile, mass
congestus, -a, -um - piled up
coniugium, -ī (n.) - marriage
~coniunx, -iugis (f., m.) - wife, bride; husband
conligō, -ere, -lēgī, -lectum - to gather together, collect
conlocō, -āre, -āvī, -ātum - to place, position, arrange
conpescō, -ere, -uī - to quench
conplector, -ī, -plexus - to embrace
conpōnō, -ere, -posuī, -positum - to place together
conprendō, -ere, -dī, -sum - to seize, catch hold of
conscius, -ī (m.) - accomplice, conspirator
consenescō, -ere, -senuī - to grow old
consistō, -ere, -stitī - to settle, stand
consors, -rtis (f.) - partner
conspiciō, -ere, -spexī, -spectum - to see, witness
constō, -āre, -stitī - to take up a position; to stand up
consuescō, -ere, -suēvī, -suētum - to be in the habit of, become accustomed to
consūmō, -ere, -psī, -ptum - to consume, devour
contentus, -a, -um - content, satisfied
conterminus, -a, -um - nearby, adjacent
contiguus, -a, -um - adjacent, neighboring
contingō, -ere, -tigī, -tactum - to come about, happen

continuō (adv.) - forthwith, immediately, without delay
contrā - (+ acc.) on the opposite side; (adv.) to the opposite side
contrarius, -a, -um - opposing
cōnūbium, -ī (n.) - the rite of marriage
conveniens, -entis - (+ dat.) fitting, appropriate, consistent
conveniō, -īre, -vēnī, -ventum - to be suitable or adapted for; to come together, meet
conversus, -a, -um - turned, changed
convexus, -a, -um - hollowed, arching, convex
convincō, -ere, -vīcī, -victum - to prove, demonstrate
Corinna, -ae (f.) - Corinna
corniger, -era, -erum - having horns
cornū, -ūs (n.) - horn, bow
cornum, -ī (n.) - a cornelian cherry
~corpus, -oris (n.) - body
Corsicus, -a, -um - of or belonging to the island of Corsica off the western coast of Italy
cortex, -icis (m.) - outer bark of a tree
crātēr, -ēris (m.) - a mixing bowl for wine
crēdibilis, -e - capable of being believed, credible, likely
crēdō, -ere, -idī, -itum - to believe, trust
creō, -āre, -āvī, -ātum - to create, appoint
crescō, -ere, crēvī, crētum - to grow, increase; arise
Crētē, -ēs (f.) - the island of Crete

crīmen, -minis (n.) - reproach, blame; evil thing
crīnis, crīnis (m.) - hair, tresses
croceus, -a, -um - saffron-colored, yellow
crūdēlis, -is, -e - cruel
cruentō, -āre, -āvī, -ātum - to stain with blood
cruentus, -a, -um - bloody
cruor, -ōris (m.) - blood; bloodshed; gore
crūs, crūris (n.) - lower leg, shin
crux, crucis (f.) - wooden frame or cross on which criminals were hanged or impaled
cultus, -a, -um - refined, sophisticated, elegant, revered
~cum - (conj.) when; (prep. + abl.) with, along with
cunctus, -a, -um - all; every
cupīdō, -dinis (f.) - desire, longing
Cupīdō, -dinis (m.) - Cupid
cupiō, -ere, -īvī, -ītum - to desire
cur (adv.) - why?
~cūra, -ae (f.) - care, anxiety, worry; object of concern, beloved person
cūrō, -āre, -āvī, -ātum - to bother with, care about
currō, -ere, cucurrī, cursum - to run, fly quickly
cursus, -ūs (m.) - running, rushing
curvāmen, -minis (n.) - curvature, arc
cuspis, -pidis (f.) - spear, lance; sharp point, tip
custōdia, -ae (f.) - defence, guard
custōs, -ōdis (m., f.) - watchman, doorkeeper
Cyprus, -ī (f.) - the island of Cyprus
Cytherēa, -ae (f.) - Venus

D

Daedalus, -ī (m.) - Daedalus, builder of the labyrinth in Crete and father of Icarus
damnōsus, -a, -um - ruinous, destructive
Daphnē, -ēs (f.) - Daphne, daughter of the river god Peneus; loved by Apollo and changed into a laurel tree
daps, dapis (f.) - feast, meal
~dē - (+ abl.) from
dea, -ae (f.) - goddess
debeō, -ēre, -uī, -itum - to owe, be indebted to
decens, -entis - graceful, attractive
decet, -ēre, -uit - to be right, fitting, proper; to be becoming or appropriate
dēclīvis, -is, -e - sloping, falling, declining
decor, -ōris (m.) - beauty, good looks
dēdecet, -ēre, -uit - to disgrace, dishonor
dēdicō, -āre, -āvī, -ātum - to dedicate
dēferō, -ferre, -tulī, -lātum - to bring down, carry down
dēficiō, -ere, -ēcī, -ectum - to fade, fail, falter
dēfleō, -ēre, -ēvī, -ētum - to lament, feel sorrow
dēlicia, -ae (f.) - pleasure, delight
Dēlius, -iī (m.) - Apollo
Dēlos, -ī (f.) - Delos, an island in the Aegean
Delphicus, -a, -um - of or connected to Delphi
dēlūbrum, -ī (n.) - temple, shrine
dēmissus, -a, -um - low, close to the ground
dēmittō, -ere, -mīsī, -missum - to thrust, drive
dēmō, -ere, -psī, -ptum - to remove, take away
dens, dentis (f.) - tooth
densus, -a, -um - thick, dense
dēpōnō, -ere, -posuī, -positum - to lay aside, get rid of; to allay
dēprendō, -ere, -ī, -prensum - to catch, discover
dēscendō, -ere, -scendī, -scēnsūrus - to come down, go down, climb down, descend
dēserō, -ere, -uī, -tum - to withdraw, desert, abandon
dēserviō, -īre - to serve zealously, devote oneself
dēsīdia, -ae (f.) - idleness, inactivity, leisure
dēsidiōsus, -a, -um - idle, lazy
dēsinō, -ere, -si(v)ī, -situm - to cease, stop, desist
dēsultor, -ōris (m.) - a circus rider who leaps from horse to horse
dēsum, -esse, -fuī - to be lacking, wanting
~deus, -ī (m.) - god, deity
dēvoveō, -ēre, -vōvī, -vōtum - to curse
dexter, -tra, -trum - right, righthand
Diāna, -ae (f.) - Diana, twin sister to Apollo, virgin goddess of woodlands
~dīcō, -ere, dīxī, dictum - to say; to appoint, fix
diēs, -ēī (f.) - day
difficilis, -e - troublesome
diffundō, -undere, -ūdī, -ūssum - to spread out, diffuse
~digitus, -ī (m.) - finger; toe
dignus, -a, -um - worthy

dīgredior, -gredī, -gressus - to depart, go away
dīmittō, -ere, -mīsī, -missum - to direct oneself to; to let go
dīmoveō, -ēre, -mōvī, -mōtum - to move about
dirimō, -imere, -ēmī, -emptum - to separate, break up
dīrus, -a, -um - dreadful, awful
discēdō, -ere, -cessī, -cessum - to depart, go away
discinctus, -a, -um - easygoing, undisciplined
discordia, -ae (f.) - disagreement, discord
discrīmen, -inis (n.) - difference, distinction
dispār, -ris - unequal, dissimilar
dispōnō, -ōnere, -osuī, -ositum - to distribute, place here and there
dissaepiō, -īre, -psī, -ptum - to separate off
dissociō, -āre, -āvī, -ātum - to separte, break apart
distinguō, -ere, -nxī, -nctum - to divide up, mark off, separate
diū (adv.) - for a long time
dīvellō, -ere, -vulsī, -vulsum - to tear apart, tear open, tear in two
dīversus, -a, -um - differing, distinct
dīvīnus, -a, -um - pertaining to the gods, divine
~dō, dare, dedī, datum - to give; to allow, cause to go
doctus, -a, -um - expert, skilled
dolens, -entis - grieving, sorrowing
doleō, -ēre, -uī, -itūrus - to be sorry, sad, to be in pain, hurt
dolor, -ōris (m.) - pain, grief
domina, -ae (f.) - mistress
dominor, -ārī, -ātum - to rule, be master
~dominus, -ī (m.) - master, owner
domō, -āre, -āvī, -ātum - to boil soft
~domus, -ī (f.) - house, home, household
dōnec (conj.) - as long as
dōnō, -āre, -āvī, -ātum - to give as a gift, grant
dōnum, -ī (n.) - gift
dubitō, -āre, -āvī, -ātum - to hesitate; to doubt
dubius, -a, -um - uncertain
dūcō, -ere, dūxī, ductum - to lead; to shape, develop, mold
~dum (conj.) - while
~duo, -ae, -o - two
duplex, -plicis - twofold, deceitful, duplicitous
duplicō, -āre, -āvī, -ātum - to double in size or amount
dūrus, -a, -um - stubborn, hard; unsympathetic, uncaring, dull
~dux, -cis (m.) - general, leader

E
~ē, ex - (+ abl.) from
~ebur, -oris (n.) - ivory
eburneus, -a, -um - of ivory
eburnus, -a, -um - of ivory
ecce (interj.) - behold! look!
ēdō, -ere, -idī, -itum - to publish; produce, put forth; to deliver a message, utter
effervescō, -ere, efferuī - to become violently agitated, seethe
efficiō, -ere, -fēcī, -fectum - to cause to be, become
effigiēs, -ēī (f.) - likeness, shape
effūsus, -a, -um - loose, flowing
egeō, -ēre, -uī - to be without, lack

~ego - I
ēgredior, -ī, -gressus - to go out, leave
ei (interj.) - oh!
ēiaculor, -ārī, -ātus - to shoot forth
elegī, -ōrum (m. pl.) - elegiac verses
elementum, -ī (n.) - one of the four basic substances of the universe (earth, air, water, fire), an element
ēlīdō, -ere, -līsī, -līsum - to expel, force out, drive out
ēlūdō, -ere, -lūsī, -lūsum - to elude, avoid capture
ēmicō, -āre, -āvī, -ātum - to spurt, shoot forth
ēmodulor, -ārī, -ātum - to sing in rhythm
enim (conj.) - indeed, truly
ensis, -is (m.) - sword
~eō, īre, i(v)ī, itum - to go
~eōdem (adv.) - to the same place
ephēmeris, -idos (f.) - a record book, daybook, diary
epulae, -ārum (f. pl.) - feast, banquet
eques, -itis (m.) - a member of the equestrian order
equidem (adv.) - truly, indeed
equus, -ī (m.) - horse
Erebus, -ī (m.) - the underworld
ergo (adv.) - therefore, for that reason
ērigō, -ere, -rexī, -rectum - to raise oneself
eripiō, -ere, -ripuī, -reptum - to snatch, pluck
errō, -āre, -āvī, -ātum - to wander about
ērubescō, -ere, -buī - to blush with shame or modesty

ērudiō, -īre, -īvī, -ītum - to teach, instruct
~et (conj.) - and; also; even
~et ... et - both ... and
etiam (adv.) - even; likewise; indeed
etsī (conj.) - even if, although
Eumenis, -idos (f.) - one of the Eumenides, the furies
Eurus, -ī (m.) - Eurus, the east wind
evolvō, -ere, -vī, -utum - to free, release
exaudiō, -īre, -īvī, -ītum - to hear, listen
excēdō, -ere, -cessī, -cessum - to go away, pass out of, depart
excipiō, -ere, -cēpī, -ceptum - to accept, receive
exeō, -īre, -iī, -itum - to go out; emerge
exhorreō, -ēre - to shudder
exiguus, -a, -um - small, slight
exilium, -ī (n.) - exile
eximō, -ere, -ēmī, -emptum - to take away, banish
exitium, -ī (n.) - destruction, ruin
exitus, -ūs (m.) - outcome, result, fate
exōsus, -a, -um - hating, despising
expallescō, -ere, -paluī - to turn pale
experiens, -ntis - active
expers, -pertis - (+ gen.) lacking experience or knowledge, free from
exsanguis, -is, -e - pale, bloodless, exhausted
extendō, -ere, -dī, -tum - to stretch out, thrust out
exterō, -ere, -trīvī, -trītum - to wear down, trample on

exterreō, -ēre, -uī, -itum - to terrify, frighten
extinguō, -ere, -tinxī, -tinctum - to die, perish
extrēmus, -a, -um - farthest, outermost
exuviae, -ārum (f. pl.) - spoils

F

fabricator, -ōris (m.) - maker, fashioner
fabricō, -āre, -āvī, -ātum - to work, fashion, shape
fabrīlis, -e - of or belonging to a metalworker, skilled; fabricated
fābula, -ae (f.) - gossip, scandal, myth, story
faciēs, -iēī (f.) - appearance, looks, shape; beauty
~faciō, -ere, fēcī, factum - to make, do; to bring about, inspire; to act; to reveal, to see that
faex, -cis (f.) - the dregs or sediment of any liquid, particularly of wine; brine
fāgineus, -a, -um - of the beech tree
fāgus, -ī (f.) - beech tree
~fallō, -ere, fefellī, falsum - to deceive, trick; to fail; to while away, beguile
falsus, -a, -um - false, not genuine
fama, -ae (f.) - reputation
famulus, -ī (m.) - servant, attendant
fateor, -ērī, fassus - to profess, agree; acknowledge
fatīgō, -āre, -āvī, -ātum - to exhaust, tire out
fātum, -ī (n.) - destiny, death, end
favilla, -ae (f.) - ashes of a fire
favus, -ī (m.) - honeycomb

fax, facis (f.) - torch, firebrand
fēcundus, -a, -um - fertile, fruitful
fēlīciter (adv.) - successfully
fēlix, -īcis - fruitful, fertile
fēmina, -ae (f.) - woman
fēmineus, -a, -um - female, feminine, womanly
fera, -ae (f.) - wild animal
~ferō, ferre, tulī, lātum - to tell, relate; to carry, bear, bring
ferreus, -a, -um - iron-like, hard-hearted, unfeeling
ferrum, -ī (n.) - iron, steel; blade, sword
~ferus, -a, -um - fierce, wild
fervens, -ntis - hot, fresh; boiling, bubbling
festum, -ī (n.) - holiday, festival
festus, -a, -um - (+ *diēs*) holiday
fētus, -ūs (m.) - fruit or product of a plant
fictilis, -e - earthenware, pottery
~fidēs, -ēī (f.) - good faith, honesty, honor
fīdus, -a, -um - faithful, loyal
fīgō, -ere, -xī, -xum - to pierce, run through; to fix, fasten, lodge
figūra, -ae (f.) - shape, appearance
fīlia, -ae (f.) - daughter
fīlius, -ī (m.) - son
fīlum, -ī (n.) - yarn, thread
findō, -ere, fidī, fissum - to split
fingō, -ere, finxī, fictus - to invent, feign
fīniō, -īre, -īvī, -ītum - to finish, end
fīnis, fīnis (m.) - boundary, remotest limit
fīō, fierī - to become, be made
fistula, -ae (f.) - pipe, tube; pan-pipe
flāmen, -minis (n.) - wind, breeze
flamma, -ae (f.) - flame

flāvens, -entis - yellow, golden
flāvescō, -ere - to become golden
flāvus, -a, -um - fair-haired, blonde; yellow
~flectō, -ere, flexī, flectum - to bend
fleō, -ēre, -ēvī, -ētum - to weep, weep for
flētus, -ūs (m.) - weeping, tears
flōs, -ōris (m.) - flower, blossom
flūmen, -minis (n.) - river
flūmineus, -a, -um - of or associated with a river
focus, -ī (m.) - hearth, fireplace
folium, -ī (n.) - leaf of a plant
fons, -ntis (m.) - spring of water
forāmen, -minis (n.) - hole, aperture
forās (adv.) - out-of-doors
foris, foris (f.) - door, double door
~forma, -ae (f.) - appearance; good looks, beauty
formōsus, -a, -um - beautiful
fors, -tis (f.) - chance, luck
forte (adv.) - by chance, accidentally
fortis, -e - strong, courageous, brave, powerful
fortiter (adv.) - vigorously, powerfully, with great force
foveō, -ēre, fōvī, fōtum - to make warm
frangō, -ere, frēgī, fractum - to break, smash
frater, -tris (m.) - brother
fretum, -ī (n.) - strait, sea
frigidus, -a, -um - cool, cold
frīgus, -oris (n.) - cold, chill
frondeō, -ēre - to grow foliage
frons, -dis (f.) - foliage, leafy boughs
frons, -tis (f.) - forehead, brow
fruor, -ī, -ctus - to enjoy
frustrā (adv.) - to no purpose, in vain
frutex, -icis (f.) - green growth
fuga, -ae (f.) - flight, fleeing
fugax, -ācis - running away, fleeing
~fugiō, -ere, -ī, -itum - to flee
fugō, -āre, -āvī, -ātum - to cause to flee, drive away, repel
fulgeō, -ēre, fulsī - to glisten, gleam
fulgor, -ōris (m.) - lightning, flame, flashing
fulica, -ae (f.) - waterfowl, coot
fulmen, -inis (n.) - thunderbolt
fūmō, -āre, -āvī, -ātum - to give off smoke
fūmus, -ī (m.) - smoke
funēbris, -e - deadly, funereal
fungor, -ī, functus - to perform, observe
furca, -ae (f.) - a length of wood with a forked end
furtīvus, -a, -um - clandestine, secret

G
galea, -ae (f.) - helmet
Gallicus, -a, -um - of Gaul
garrulus, -a, -um - loquacious, talkative, wordy
~gaudeō, -ēre, gāvīsus - to rejoice; to be pleased
gelidus, -a, -um - icy cold
~geminus, -a, -um - double; pair of, twin
gemma, -ae (f.) - jewel, gem
gena, -ae (f.) - cheek
gener, -erī (m.) - son-in-law
geniālis, -e - creative, festive
genitor, -ōris (m.) - father; ancestor
gens, -tis (f.) - race, group of people

genu, -ūs (n.) - knee
genus, -eris (n.) - race, nation
gerō, -ere, gessī, gestum - to wage; to bear, carry
gestāmen, -minis (n.) - load, burden
gestiō, -īre, -īvī - to desire eagerly, want, be anxious to
gignō, -ere, genuī, genitum - to give birth to
glomerō, -āre, -āvī, -ātum - to form or gather into a ball
gloria, -ae (f.) - glory
gradus, -ūs (m.) - step
grandis, -is, -e - large, massive
graphium, -ī (n.) - stylus
grātēs, -ium (f. pl.) - thanks
grātus, -a, -um - welcome; pleasant, attractive
~gravis, grave - heavy, weighty; important; hard to capture
gravitās, -ātis (f.) - weight, heaviness
gravō, -āre, -āvī, -ātum - to make heavy, weigh down
grex, gregis (m.) - flock
guttur, -uris (n.) - throat

H

~habeō, -ēre, -uī, -itum - to have, possess; to hold
habilis, -e - suitable, fit
habitābilis, -e - inhabitable
habitō, -āre, -āvī, -ātum - to live, dwell
hāc (adv.) - on this side; **hāc faciō** - to be on a side
Haemus, -ī (m.) - a mountain range in northern Thrace
haereō, -ēre, haesī, haesum - to cling; to be brought to a standstill; to be perplexed, hesitate

harundō, -dinis (f.) - reed; shaft of an arrow, arrow
haud (adv.) - not
hauriō, -īre, hausī, haustum - to swallow up, consume; to drink in, draw in
haustus, -ūs (m.) - a drawn quantity of liquid, drink
Hector, -oris (m.) - Hector, son of Priam, prince of Troy
Hēliades, -um (f. pl.) - daughters of the sun god Helios
Helicē, -ēs (f.) - the constellation Ursa Major
Helicōnius, -a, -um - of Helicon
herba, -ae (f.) - plant, herb
hērēs, -ēdis (m.) - heir, successor
hērōs, -ōos (m.) - hero
hesternus, -a, -um - yesterday's
heu (interj.) - alas
~hic, haec, hoc - this, the latter
hīc (adv.) - here, in this place
hinc (adv.) - from this place; on this side
hodiē (adv.) - today
holus, -eris (n.) - vegetable (i.e., cabbage, turnip)
homō, -inis (m.) - a human being, the human race
honestus, -a, -um - honorable
honor, -ōris (m.) - honor, mark of esteem, glory
hōra, -ae (f.) - hour, time
horridus, -a, -um - rough in manners, rude, uncouth; hairy
horrifer, -era, -erum - dreadful, freezing
hortor, -ārī, -ātus - to encourage
hortus, -ī (m.) - garden
hospes, -itis (m.) - visitor, stranger, guest; (adj.) of or pertaining to a guest
~hostis, -is (m.) - enemy

hūc (adv.) - here, to this place
hūmānus, -a, -um - pertaining to human beings, human
humilis, -e - humble, lowly
humus, -ī (f.) - earth, ground
Hymēn (m.) - the god of marriage, wedding
Hymenaeus, -ī (m.) - Hymen, the personified god representing weddings and marriages
Hymettius, -a, -um - of or pertaining to Mt. Hymettus near Athens, famous for its honey

I

~iaceō, -ēre, -uī, -tum - to lie down, lie; to be overthrown
~iam (adv.) - now
Iapetus, -ī (m.) - one of the Titans, father of Prometheus
ibi (adv.) - there, in that place
Īcarus, -ī (m.) - Daedalus's son
iciō, -ere, īcī, ictum - to strike, beat
ictus, -ūs (m.) - blow, stroke, thrust
Īda (Idē), -ae (-ēs) (f.) - a mountain, either near Troy or on Crete
īdem, eadem, idem - the same
ideō (adv.) - for that reason
iecur, -oris (n.) - the liver
ignārus, -a, -um - unaware, ignorant, unfamiliar, unknown, blind
ignāvus, -a, -um - lazy, sluggish
igneus, -a, -um - fiery, burning
~ignis, -is (m.) - fire, star
ignōtus, -a, -um - unfamiliar, unknown
īlia, -ium (n. pl.) - the gut, groin
illāc (adv.) - by that way

~ille, illa, illud - that, the former; he, she
~illīc (adv.) - there, in that place
illinc (adv.) - on the other side
imāgō, -inis (f.) - likeness, image
imbellis, -e - not suited to warfare, unwarlike
imber, -bris (m.) - rain
imitor, -ārī, -ātus - to imitate, resemble
inmensum, -ī (n.) - infinite space, immeasurable expanse
immundus, -a, -um - unclean, foul, impure
impediō, -īre, -īvī, -ītum - to hinder, impede
impellō, -ere, -pulī, -pulsum - to push forward, urge on
īmus, -a, -um - the lowest, bottommost
~in - (+ acc.) over, affecting; for, towards; into; among; (+ abl.) in, on
inamoenus, -a, -um - unpleasant, unlovely
incēdō, -ere, -ssī - to step, walk
incertus, -a, -um - disarranged, not fixed; not sure, uncertain
inclūsus, -a, -um - shut in on all sides, enclosed
incola, -ae (m., f.) - inhabitant
increpō, -āre, -uī, -itum - to make a loud rattle, clang, noise
incubō, -āre, -uī, -itum - to throw oneself upon
incumbō, -ere, -cubuī - to lean over or on; to lie on
inde (adv.) - therefore, and so
indigestus, -a, -um - disorderly, confused
indignor, -ārī, -ātum - to consider as unworthy or improper

indignus, -a, -um - not deserving, unworthy
indūcō, -ere, -dūxī, -ductum - to cover, spread on or over
induō, -ere, -uī, -ūtus - to put on, clothe oneself
indūrescō, -escere, -uī - to harden, become hard
inermis, -e - unarmed, defenseless
iners, -rtis - lazy, feeble
infāmis, -e - infamous, disgraced
~infēlix, -icis - unhappy, ill-fated, unlucky
inferior, -ius - lower, bottom, second
infestus, -a, -um - hostile
ingeniōsus, -a, -um - clever
ingenium, -ī (n.) - character, spirit, nature
ingens, ingentis - huge
ingrātus, -a, -um - ungrateful, thankless
inhaereō, -ēre, -haesī, -haesum - to stick, cling, attach, grasp
inhibeō, -ēre, -uī, -itum - to restrain, check, stop
inīquus, -a, -um - resentful, discontented
inlinō, -ere, -lēvī, -litum - to smear, coat
inmensus, -a, -um - boundless, immense, huge
inmineō, -ēre - to be poised over
inmūnis, -e - (+ gen.) free from, exempt
innabilis, -e - not able to be swum in, unswimmable
innītor, -ī, -nixus - to lean on, rest on
innumerus, -a, -um - countless, innumerable
innuptus, -a, -um - unmarried

inornātus, -a, -um - not adorned, disheveled, unarranged
inpār, -ris - unequal
inpatiens, -ntis - impatient
inpediō, -īre, -īvī, -ītum - to hinder, impede
inpellō, -ere, -pulī, -pulsum - to push, drive, set in motion
inperfectus, -a, -um - unfinished, incomplete
inpiger, -gra, -grum - quick, energetic, tireless
inpius, -a, -um - impious, irreverent, undutiful
inpleō, -ēre, -ēvī, -ētum - to fill up
inpōnō, -ere, -posuī, -positum - to place on
inpulsus, -ūs (m.) - thrust, blow
~inquam, inquit - to say
inquīrō, -ere, -quisīvī, -sītus - to inquire, ask
inrītō, -āre, -āvī, -ātum - to provoke, arouse
inritus, -a, -um - to no effect, in vain
insānus, -a, -um - frenzied, mad, insane
insequor, -sequī, -secūtus - to pursue
insīdō, -ere, -sēdī, -sessum - to sink in, become embedded
insignis, -e - outstanding, remarkable, distinguished
instabilis, -e - not able to be stood upon
instar (n.) - (+ gen.) according to, like
instruō, -ere, -xī, -ctum - to instruct, equip, outfit
insula, -ae (f.) - island
intendō, -ere, -dī, -tum - to stretch, spread out
~inter - (+ acc.) among; between

intereā (adv.) - meanwhile
intibum, -ī (n.) - chicory or endive
intōnsus, -a, -um - unshorn, uncut
intrō, -āre, -āvī, -ātum - to go into, enter
inūtilis, -e - useless
invādō, -ere, -vāsī, -vāsum - to attack, set on
inveniō, -īre, -ī, -tum - to discover
inventum, -ī (n.) - discovery, invention
invideō, -ēre, -vīdī, -vīsum - to refuse, be unwilling
invidus, -a, -um - envious, malevolent
Īō (f.) - Io
~ipse, -a, -um - oneself, itself
īra, -ae (f.) - anger, rage, wrath
īrātus, -a, -um - angry, furious
is, ea, id - he, she, it; this, that
iste, -a, -ud - that of yours
ita (adv.) - thus, in this way
iter, -ineris (n.) - journey, passage
~iterum (adv.) - again, another time
~iubeō, -ēre, iussī, iussum - to order, bid, command
iūdicium, -ī (n.) - decision, pronouncement
iugālis, -e - nuptial, matrimonial
iūgerum, -ī (n.) - a measurement of land equal approximately to two-thirds of an acre
iugōsus, -a, -um - hilly, mountainous
iugum, -ī (n.) - mountain heights
~iungō, -ere, -xī, -ctum - to join (in marriage)
Iūnōnius, -a, -um - of or pertaining to Juno
Iuppiter, Iovis (m.) - Jupiter
iūs, iūris (n.) - authority, jurisdiction, power, right

iustus, -a, -um - just, fair
iuvenālis, -e - youthful
iuvenca, -ae (f.) - heifer, cow
iuvencus, -ī (m.) - young bull
iuvenis, -e - young
iuventa, -ae (f.) - the period of youth
Ixīōn, -onis (m.) - Ixion

L
lābor, -ī, lāpsus - to slip, slide; to drip
labor, -ōris (m.) - labor, toil, hardship, task
labōrō, -āre, -āvī, -ātum - to be anxious, worried, distressed
lac, -ctis (n.) - milk
~lacertus, -ī (m.) - upper arm
~lacrima, -ae (f.) - tear
lacrimōsus, -a, -um - tearful
lacus, -ūs (m.) - a lake, pond, or pool
laedō, -ere, laesī, laesum - to harm, injure
laetus, -a, -um - joyful
laevus, -a, -um - left, left hand
laniō, -āre, -āvī, -ātum - to tear, mangle
lapidōsus, -a, -um - stony, gritty
lapis, lapidis (m.) - stone, pebble
lapillus, -ī (m.) - small stone, gem
lascīvus, -a, -um - naughty, unrestrained, mischievous
lassō, -āre, -āvī, -ātum - to tire, exhaust
lātē (adv.) - over a large area, widely
latebra, -ae (f.) - hiding place
lateō, -ēre, -uī - to hide; to take refuge; to be concealed, lie hidden
Latius, -a, -um - Roman
lātus, -a, -um - broad, wide

laudō, -āre, -āvī, -ātum - to praise
laurea, -ae (f.) - the laurel/bay tree
laurus, -ī (f.) - foliage of the laurel (bay) tree; the laurel tree
laus, -dis (f.) - praise, glory
lea, -ae (f.) - lioness
leaena, -ae (f.) - lioness
Lebinthos, -ī (f.) - an island off the east coast of Greece
lectus, -ī (m.) - bed, couch
~legō, -ere, lēgī, lectum - to choose, select, pick out; to read
leō, -ōnis (m.) - lion
lepus, -oris (m.) - hare
Lethaea, -ae (f.) - wife of Olenos who was turned to stone due to her pride
lētum, -ī (n.) - death
~levis, -e - light, not ponderous
levitās, -tātis (f.) - lightness (of weight)
leviter (adv.) - lightly
levō, -āre, -āvī, -ātum - to lift off, remove; to relieve, support
lex, lēgis (f.) - law, rule; **sine lege** - in disorder, unruly
līber, lībera, līberum - free, unrestrained
liber, -brī (m.) - inner bark of a tree
lībertās, -tātis (f.) - liberty
lībrō, -āre, -āvī, -ātum - to level, balance
~licet, -ēre, -uī, -itum - it is permitted, one may; (conj.) although
lignum, -ī (n.) - wood, firewood
ligō, -āre, -āvī, -ātum - to bind, join together
līlium, -ī (n.) - lily
līmen, -minis (n.) - threshold, doorstep
līmes, -mitis (m.) - path, track

līnum, -ī (n.) - thread, string
liquidus, -a, -um - liquid, fluid
līs, lītis (f.) - quarrel, dispute, disagreement
lītoreus, -a, -um - of the seashore
littera, -ae (f.) - letter
lītus, lītoris (n.) - the shore
līvor, -ōris (m.) - bluish coloring, bruise
locō, -āre, -āvī, -ātum - to place
~locus, -ī (m., n. pl.) - place, open land
~longus, -a, -um - long, tall
~loquor, -quī, -cūtus - to speak
luctus, -ūs (m.) - grief, mourning
lūdō, -ere, lūsī, lūsum - to trick, deceive
lūmen, -minis (n.) - light, brilliance; eye
lūna, -ae (f.) - moon
lūnāris, -e - of or pertaining to the moon
lūnō, -āre, -āvī, -ātum - to curve, bend
luō, -ere, -ī - to pay as a penalty, amend for
lupus, -ī (m.) - wolf
lustrō, -āre, -āvī, -ātum - to move through or around, roam
lūsus, -ūs (m.) - playing, sporting
lux, lūcis (f.) - light of day, **sub luce** - at dawn
Lyaeus, -ī (m.) - Bacchus
lyra, -ae (f.) - lyre, lute

M

mactō, -āre, -āvī, -ātum - to kill, slay, sacrifice
madefaciō, -ere, -fēcī, -factum - to soak, drench
madeō, -ēre, -uī - to grow wet
madescō, -ere, -uī - to become wet or soaking

Maenas, -adis (f.) - female worshipper of Bacchus, Bacchante, Maenad
magis (adv.) - more
~magnus, -a, -um - great, large
maior, -ius - greater, larger
male (adv.) - unpleasantly, badly
malum, -ī (n.) - evil, wickedness
mālum, -ī (n.) - an apple
malus, -a, -um - wicked
mandō, -āre, -āvī, -ātum - to order, command
māne (adv.) - early in the day, morning
~maneō, -ēre, -sī, -sum - to remain, stay
Mantua, -ae (f.) - the city of Mantua in the north of Italy
~manus, -ūs (f.) - hand; armed force, band
mās, maris (m.) - the male of the species
margō, -inis (m.) - margin
marītus, -ī (m.) - husband
marmor, -oris (n.) - marble
Mars, -tis (m.) - Mars, god of war
massa, -ae (f.) - heap, lump, mass
māter, -tris (f.) - mother
māteria, -ae (f.) - material, subject matter
māteriēs, -iēī (f.) - material, subject matter
mātūrus, -a, -um - mature, experienced,
mātūtīnus, -a, -um - of the early morning, eastern
medicīna, -ae (f.) - medicine
medicō, -āre, -āvī, -ātum - to dye
medium, -ī (n.) - a neutral or undecided state
~medius, -a, -um - middle, middle of; between; in half, half, medium, moderate

medulla, -ae (f.) - marrow
Medusaeus, -a, -um - of or relating to Medusa
mel, mellis (n.) - honey
melior, -ius - better, finer, superior
melius (adv.) - better, more fittingly
~membrum, -ī (n.) - part of the body; limb of tree or body
meminī, -isse - to remember
~mens, -tis (f.) - mind; inclination
mensa, -ae (f.) - table
menta, -ae (f.) - mint
mentior, -īrī, -ītus - to tell a falsehood, to lie
mereō, -ēre, -uī, -itum - to earn
mergō, -ere, -rsī, -rsum - to flood, inundate
mergus, -ī (m.) - sea bird, gull
meritus, -a, -um - deserving, just
mēta, -ae (f.) - turning post, goal
metuō, -ere, -uī -ūtum - to fear, be afraid
metus, -ūs (m.) - fear
~meus, -a, -um - my
micō, -āre, -āvī - to flash, glitter, glisten
~mīles, -itis (m.) - soldier
mīlitia, -ae (f.) - military service
mīlitō, -āre, -āvī, -ātum - to serve as a soldier, be a soldier
mille (n.) - (indecl.) a thousand
Minerva, -ae (f.) - Minerva, the goddess associated with handicrafts (particularly spinning) and war
minimus, -a, -um - smallest, very small, least
ministerium, -ī (n.) - duty, office, work
ministra, -ae (f.) - an assistant
minium, -ī (n.) - bright red dye, cinnabar
minor, -us - smaller

Mīnōs, -ōis (m.) - Minos, king of Crete
minuō, -ere, -uī, -ūtum - to make smaller
minus (adv.) - less, to a smaller degree
mīrābilis, -e - wondrous, extraordinary
mīror, -ārī, -ātus - to wonder at, be surprised
mīrus, -a, -um - remarkable, extraordinary, wondrous
misceō, -ēre, -uī, mixtum - to mix together, blend
~miser, -era, -erum - wretched, miserable
miserābilis, -e - pitiable
miserandus, -a, -um - wretched, pitiable
mittō, -ere, mīsī, missum - to let go, set free; send, shoot
mixtus, -a, -um - mixed
moderātē (adv.) - gently, in a restrained manner
moderor, -ārī, -ātum - to control, manipulate
modicus, -a, -um - moderate in size
~modo (adv.) - just now, recently, lately; just, only
modus, -ī (m.) - measure, meter, rhythm
moenia, -ium (n. pl.) - defensive walls encircling a town
mōlēs, -is (f.) - a large mass, crowd, throng
mollescō, -ere - to become soft
molliō, -īre, -īvī, -ītum - to soften, weaken
~mollis, -e - gentle, smooth; soft
moneō, -ēre, -uī, -itum - to advise, recommend
monīle, -is (n.) - necklace
monimentum, -ī (n.) - memorial
monitus, -ūs (m.) - warning, advising
mons, -tis (m.) - mountain, mountainous country
monstrum, -ī (n.) - a monstrous or horrible creature
mora, -ae (f.) - delay
morior, -ī, mortuus - to die
moror, -ārī, -ātus - to delay, wait; to hold back
mors, -tis (f.) - death
morsus, -ūs (m.) - bite
mortālis, -e - mortal, human
mōrum, -ī (n.) - the fruit of the mulberry tree
mōrus, -ī (f.) - mulberry tree
mōs, mōris (m.) - character, morals, behavior
mōtus, -ūs (m.) - motion, action, movement
~moveō, -ēre, mōvī, mōtum - to move, strike; rouse
mox (adv.) - soon
mucrō, -ōnis (m.) - tip or point of a sword
multifidus, -a, -um - split, splintered
multum (adv.) - very, greatly
~multus, -a, -um - much
~mundus, -ī (m.) - the universe, the world, the earth
mūnus, -eris (n.) - gift, present; ritual duty
murmur, -is (n.) - mutter, whisper
mūrus, -ī (m.) - wall, city wall
Mūsa, -ae (f.) - Muse
mūtō, -āre, -āvī, -ātum - to change, replace
mūtus, -ī (m.) - silent
mūtuus, -a, -um - mutual, reciprocal
myrtus, -ī (f.) - foliage of the myrtle tree

N

Nabataeus, -a, -um - a people of northern Arabia
Nāid, -idis (f.) - a nymph, river nymph, naiad
~**nam** (conj.) - for, to be sure
Napē, -ēs (f.) - Nape
narrō, -āre, -āvī, -ātum - to tell, relate
~**nascor, -ī, nātus** - to be born
Nāsō, -ōnis (m.) - Naso, Ovid's cognomen
nāta, -ae (f.) - daughter
nātālis, -e - of or belonging to birth
~**nātūra, -ae (f.)** - nature, natural world
~**nātus, -ī (m.)** - son
~**nē** (conj.) - lest, in order that . . . not; do not
nebula, -ae (f.) - mist, fog
~**nec** - and . . . not; not even
necō, -āre, -āvī, -ātum - to kill, put to death
~**negō, -āre, -āvī, -ātum** - to say not; to deny
nempe (conj.) - to be sure, no doubt, certainly
nemus, -oris (n.) - wood, sacred grove
nepōs, -ōtis (m., f.) - grandson, granddaughter
neque (conj.) - and . . . not
nēquīquam (adv.) - in vain
~**nervus, -ī (m.)** - string of a musical instrument or bow
nesciō, -īre, -īvī, -ītum - not to know, to be unfamiliar with; **nescio quis** - some, little, insignificant
neu (conj.) - nor
nēve (conj.) - and that . . . not
nex, necis (f.) - death

nīdus, -ī (m.) - nest
niger, -gra, -grum - black, dark-colored
nīl/nihilum, -ī (n.) - not anything, nothing
nimbus, -ī (m.) - cloudburst, rainstorm
nimis (adv.) - too much, excessively, too
~**nimium** (adv.) - excessively, extremely, very much
nimius, -a, -um - too much, too great
Ninus, -ī (m.) - Ninus, king of Assyria and second husband to Semiramis
~**nisi** (conj.) - if not
nitidus, -a, -um - bright, radiant, shining
nītor, -tī, -sus - to strive, move with difficulty, exert oneself
nitor, -ōris (m.) - brilliance, brightness, splendor, elegance
niveus, -a, -um - white, snowy-white
nix, nivis (f.) - snow
nocens, -ntis - guilty
nocturnus, -a, -um - nightly, of the night
nolō, nolle, noluī - not to want or wish
~**nōmen, -minis (n.)** - name, family name, fame, reputation
nōminō, -āre, -avī, -ātum - to name, call by name
~**nōn** (adv.) - not
nōndum (adv.) - not yet
nōs - we
noscō, -ere, nōvī, nōtum - to learn
~**noster, -tra, -trum** - our
nota, -ae (f.) - note, mark
nōtitia, -ae (f.) - acquaintance

notō, -āre, -āvī, -ātum - to mark, inscribe, scratch; to notice
nōtus, -a, -um - famous, well-known
novem - (indecl.) nine
noviens (adv.) - nine times
novissimus, -a, -um - last, final
novitās, -tātis (f.) - novelty, strange phenomenon
novō, -āre, -āvī, -ātum - to make or devise as new
~**novus, -a, -um** - new, unfamiliar
~**nox, -ctis (f.)** - night
nūbēs, nūbis (f.) - cloud
nūdō, -āre, -āvī, -ātum - to make naked, expose
~**nūdus, -a, -um** - bare, pure, open, simple; naked, unclothed
~**nullus, -a, -um** - no one, nobody, nothing; no; insignificant, trifling
nūmen, -minis (n.) - divine power, divinity
numerus, -ī (m.) - number, rhythm, measure, meter
~**nunc** (adv.) - now, at this time
nūper (adv.) - recently
nupta, -ae (f.) - bride
nūtriō, -īre, -īvī, -ītum - to encourage, foster
nūtus, -ūs (m.) - nod
nux, -cis (f.) - nut
nympha, -ae (f.) - demi-goddess spirit of nature, nymph; unmarried girl

O

oblinō, -ere, -lēvī, -litum - to besmear, make dirty
oblīquus, -a, -um - slanting
oborior, -īrī, -tus - to rise up, spring up
obscūrus, -a, -um - dim, dark
obscēnus, -a, -um - polluted, foul, ill-omened
obsequor, -sequī, -secūtus - to comply, gratify, humor
observō, -āre, -āvī, -ātum - to watch over, guard
obsideō, -ēre, -sēdī, -sessum - to occupy, beseige
obsistō, -ere, -stitī, -stitum - to stand in the way of, block, impede
obstipescō, -ere, -stipuī - to be amazed, astonished
obstō, -āre, -stitī, -stātum - to stand in the way, block the path
obstruō, -ere, -xī, -ctum - to block, obstruct
obtūsus, -a, -um - blunt, dull
obvius, -a, -um - opposing, confronting
occidō, -ere, -idī, -āsus - to be struck down, to die
occiduus, -a, -um - setting, going down, western
occupō, -āre, -āvī, -ātum - to seize, occupy
ōcior, ōcius - swifter, faster
~**oculus, -ī (m.)** - eye
ōdī, odisse, ōsum - to hate, dislike
odōrātus, -a, -um - sweet-smelling, fragrant
offensus, -a, -um - offended, displeased
officium, -ī (n.) - duty
Ōlēnus, -ī (m.) - Olenus
ōlim (adv.) - a long time ago
ōmen, -minis (n.) - omen
~**omnis, -e** - each, every, all
onerōsus, -a, -um - heavy, weighty
onus, -eris (n.) - burden
opācus, -a, -um - shady, dark
opifer, -era, -erum - aid-bringing, helper

opifex, -ficis (m.) - craftsman, artisan
ops, opis (f.) - (sing.) aid, help, military strength; (pl.) wealth
optō, -āre, -āvī, -ātum - to desire, wish for
~opus, -eris (n.) - task, undertaking, work, job; need
ōra, -ae (f.) - shore; region, district
ōrāculum, -ī (n.) - oracular power, divine utterance
~orbis, -is (m.) - globe, world
orbus, -a, -um - bereft, deprived, destitute
~ordō, -dinis (m.) - order; class, rank; a linear arrangement
Oriens, -ntis (m.) - the East
origō, -inis (f.) - rise, beginnings
Ōrīōn, -onis (m.) - the constellation Orion
ornō, -āre, -āvī, -ātum - to adorn, decorate, attire
~ōrō, -āre, -āvī, -ātum - to pray, beseech, beg
Orpheus, -eī (m.) - Orpheus, a Thracian bard and husband of Eurydice
~ōs, ōris (n.) - face; mouth
os, ossis (n.) - bone
~osculum, -ī (n.) - mouth, lips; kiss
ostendō, -ere, -tendī, -tentum - to show, point out
ōtium, -ī (n.) - leisure
ōvum, -ī (n.) - egg

P
paciscor, -ī, pactus - to agree upon
pactum, -ī (n.) - agreement
Paeān, -nis (m.) - Apollo, as healer; a hymn or praise addressed to Apollo
Paelignus, -a, -um - of the Paelignian region in central Italy
pāgina, -ae (f.) - page
pallidus, -a, -um - pale, lacking color
palma, -ae (f.) - fruit of the palm, a date
palūs, -ūdis (f.) - swamp, floodwater
paluster, -tris, -tre - marshy
pandus, -a, -um - curved, bent, bowed
Paphius, -a, -um - of or pertaining to the city of Paphos on Cyprus
Paphos, -ī (m.) - the child of Pygmalion
pār, paris - equal
parātus, -ūs (m.) - preparation
parcus, -a, -um - thrifty, frugal
~pārens, -entis (m., f.) - ancestor, parent
pāreō, -ēre, -uī, -itum - to obey
pariēs, -etis (m.) - wall
parilis, -e - similar, like
pariter (adv.) - in the same manner, likewise; at the same time, simultaneously
Parnāsus, -ī (m.) - Parnasus, a mountain in Greece at the base of which is Delphi, sacred to both Apollo and the Muses
parō, -āre, -āvī, -ātum - to prepare
Paros, -ī (f.) - Paros, an island in the Aegean Sea
~pars, -tis (f.) - part, portion; side
partim (adv.) - in part, partly
parvus, -a, -um - small
passim (adv.) - here and there, scattered about
passus, -ūs (m.) - pace, stride
pastor, -ōris (m.) - shepherd
Patarēus, -a, -um - of or related to Patara, a coastal city in southern Asia Minor with an oracle of Apollo

pateō, -ēre, -uī - to be visible or revealed; to be open
~pater, -tris (m.) - father
patior, -tī, passus - to allow, permit
patrius, -a, -um - of or pertaining to a father
patulus, -a, -um - broad
paucus, -a, -um - few
paulātim (adv.) - little by little, by degrees
paulum (adv.) - a little bit, to a small extent
pauper, -eris - poor, scanty
paupertās, -tātis (f.) - poverty
paveō, -ēre - to be frightened
pavor, -ōris (m.) - fear, terror, fright
pāx, pācis (f.) - peace
~pectus, -oris (n.) - chest, breast, heart
pelagus, -ī (n.) - open sea
pellō, -ere, pepulī, pulsum - to fend off, drive away, repel; to strike, beat
Pelopēius, -a, -um - of or pertaining to the Peloponnesian peninsula
penātēs, -ium (n. pl.) - the household gods
~pendeō, -ēre, pependī - to hang, hang down, fall
Pēnēis, -idos - descended from the river god Peneus
Pēnēius, -a, -um - of or connected with the river god Peneus
penitus (adv.) - thoroughly, completely
~penna, -ae (f.) - wing, feather
~per - (+ acc.) through, throughout
peragō, -ere, -ēgī, -actum - to carry out, perform

perārō, -āre, -āvī, -ātum - to plow through, inscribe
percipiō, -ere, -cēpī, -ceptum - to catch hold of
percutiō, -ere, -cussī, -cussum - to strike, beat
~perdō, -ere, -idī, -itum - to waste one's effort or time; to destroy
peremō, -ere, -ī, -ptum - to kill
perennis, -e - lasting, enduring
perferō, -ferre, -tulī, -lātum - to suffer, endure, undergo; carry, convey
perīclum - see **periculum**
perīculum, -ī (n.) - danger
perlegō, -ere, -lēgī, -lectum - to read over, read through
permātūrescō, -ere, -tūruī - to become fully ripe
permittō, -ere, -īsī, -issum - to permit, allow, sanction
perōdī, -disse, -sum - to despise, loathe
perpetuus, -a, -um - eternal, everlasting
Persephonē, -ēs (f.) - Persephone, the daughter of Demeter and Zeus, and wife of Pluto
persequor, -sequī, -secūtus - to follow all the way, accompany
Persidis, -is - Persian
perveniō, -īre, -vēnī, -ventum - to penetrate, extend, reach; to arrive
pervigilō, -āre, -āvī, -ātum - to keep watch all night
~pēs, pedis (m.) - foot; metrical foot
pestifer, -era, -erum - deadly, pernicious, pestilential
~petō, -ere, -īvī, -ītum - to seek, look for; to seek the hand of in marriage, to court

GLOSSARY ✦ 201

pharetra, -ae (f.) - quiver
pharetrātus, -a, -um - wearing a quiver
Philēmōn, -onis (m.) - Philemon, husband of Baucis
Phoebē, -ēs (f.) - Diana, twin sister to Apollo
Phoebus, -ī (m.) - Apollo
Phrygia, -ae (f.) - Phrygia, a region in central Asia Minor
pictus, -a, -um - painted
Pīerides, -um (f. pl.) - the Muses, daughters of Pierus
piger, -gra, -grum - sluggish, inactive
pīla, -ae (f.) - ball, sphere
piscis, -is (m.) - fish
Pittheus, -eī (m.) - Pittheus, son of Pelops and grandfather to Theseus
pius, -a, -um - dutiful, conscientious, pious
~placeō, -ēre, -uī, -itum - (+ dat.) to be pleasing or acceptable
placidus, -a, -um - agreeable, kindly
plaga, -ae (f.) - territory, region, expanse
plangor, -ōris (m.) - beating, lamentation
plēnus, -a, -um - full
plūma, -ae (f.) - feather
plumbum, -ī (n.) - lead
plūrimus, -a, -um - most plentifully supplied, greatest in amount
plūs, plūris (n.) - more
plūs (adv.) - more
pluvia, -ae (f.) - rain
pluviālis, -is, -e - rainy
pōculum, -ī (n.) - a drinking cup
poena, -ae (f.) - penalty, punishment
poēta, -ae (m.) - poet
pollex, -icis (m.) - thumb
pompa, -ae (f.) - ceremonial procession
pōmum, -ī (n.) - fruit
~pondus, -eris (n.) - weight
~pōnō, -ere, posuī, positum - to put, place, arrange; to lay aside, abandon
pontus, -ī (m.) - sea
populus, -ī (m.) - people
porrigō, -igere, -exī, -ectum - to stretch out, extend
porta, -ae (f.) - gate, entryway
portitor, -ōris (m.) - ferryman, carrier
portō, -āre, -āvī, -ātum - to carry
poscō, -ere, poposcī - to demand, ask for insistently
possideō, -ēre, -sēdī, -sessum - to control
~possum, posse, potuī - to be able
post - (+ acc.) after
posterus, -a, -um - next, following
postis, -is (m.) - door jamb, door, lintel
~postquam (conj.) - after, when
potens, -tis - powerful, mighty, influential
potentia, -ae (f.) - power, influence
praebeō, -ēre, -uī, -itum - to offer, provide
praeceptum, -ī (n.) - teaching, piece of advice
praecipitō, -āre, -āvī, -ātum - to plunge down, sink
praecordia, -ōrum (n. pl.) - heart, chest, breast
praeda, -ae (f.) - prey
praedor, -ārī, -ātus - to take as prey, catch

praeferō, -ferre, -tulī, -lātum - (+ dat.) to prefer, esteem more
praeripiō, -ere, -ripuī, -reptum - to seize, snatch away
praetereō, -īre, -iī, -itum - to pass by
precor, -ārī, -ātus - to pray for, implore, beg, beseech
~**premō, -ere, -ssī, -ssum** - to press on, push; to cover
prendō, -ere, -dī, -sum - to take hold of, grasp, seize
prex, precis (f.) - prayer
Priamēis, -idos (f.) - Cassandra, daughter of Priam
prīmum (adv.) - first, for the first time
prīmus, -a, -um - first
principiō (adv.) - in the beginning, to start with
prior, -us - first, earlier
prius (adv.) - first
~**prō** - (+ abl.) on account of, because of
proavus, -ī (m.) - forefather
probō, -āre, -āvī, -ātum - to authorize, sanction, approve
procul (adv.) - far off, at a great distance
prōdūcō, -ere, -dūxī, -ductum - to bring forth, lead forth
prohibeō, -ēre, -uī, -itum - to prevent; to refuse
prōiciō, -ere, -iēcī, -iectum - to throw down
prōlēs, -is (f.) - offspring
prōmō, -ere, -psī, -ptum - to bring forth, draw forth, produce
prōnus, -a, -um - lying on the face or stomach, headlong
properō, -āre, -āvī, -ātum - to hasten
Prōpoetides, -um (f. pl.) - young women from Cyprus

prospiciō, -ere, -spexī, -spectum - to see before one, have a view
prōsum, prōdesse, prōfuī, prōfutūrus - to benefit, be helpful or useful to
prōtinus (adv.) - forthwith, at once, immediately, suddenly
prōveniō, -īre, -vēnī, -ventum - to come into being, arise
proximus, -a, -um - next
pruīnōsus, -a, -um - frosty
prūnum, -ī (n.) - a plum
pudor, -ōris (m.) - modesty
~**puella, -ae (f.)** - girl, young woman
~**puer, -ī (m.)** - boy
pugnō, -āre, -āvī, -ātum - to fight, contend with
pulcher, -ra, -um - beautiful
pullus, -a, -um - dingy, somber
pulsō, -āre, -āvī, -ātum - to beat, strike repeatedly
pulvis, -eris (m.) - dust
purpureus, -a, -um - radiant, glowing, blushing; purple, crimson
pūrus, -a, -um - pure, unsoiled
putō, -āre, -āvī, -ātum - to think, consider; to imagine
Pygmaliōn, -ōnis (m.) - Pygmalion, king of Cyprus
Pyramus, -ī (m.) - Pyramus
Pythōn, -ōnis (m.) - a serpent slain by Apollo

Q

quā (adv.) - where, in which direction
quam - (rel. adv.) than
quaerō, -ere, quaesīvī, -sītum - to require, demand; to seek
quantō ... tantō (adv.) - by however much ... by just so much

quantuluscumque, -acumque, -umcumque - however small
quantus, -a, -um - how great
quatiō, -ere, quassum - to shake
-que - and; **-que . . . -que** - both . . . and . . .
quercus, -ūs (f.) - oak tree; oak garland
~**queror, -rī, questus** - to complain
~**quī, quae, quod** - who, which
quia (conj.) - because, since
quīcumque, quaecumque, quodcumque - the person who, whoever, whatever
quid (adv.) - why? for what reason?
quidem (adv.) - certainly, indeed, it is true
quīn (adv.) - why not?
quīn (conj.) - so as to prevent, so that . . . not
quinque - five
quintus, -a, -um - fifth
~**quis, quid** - who? what?
quisquam, quicquam - anyone, anything
~**quisque, quaeque, quidque** - each, each one, each thing
quisquis, quidquid - anyone who, whoever
quō (adv.) - for that reason; in order that; by which degree, by how much
~**quod (conj.)** - because; that, the fact that
quondam (adv.) - once, formerly
quoniam (conj.) - since
~**quoque (adv.)** - also, too

R
radius, -ī (m.) - ray of light
rādix, -īcis (f.) - root; radish
rādō, -ere, rāsī, -sum - to rub clean, erase; to graze, scrape, scratch
rāmāle, -is (n.) - branches, twigs
~**rāmus, -ī (m.)** - branch
rapidus, -a, -um - swift-moving
rapina, -ae (f.) - pillage; prey
raucus, -a, -um - harsh-sounding, raucous
recēdō, -ere, -ssī, -ssum - to withdraw, retire
recens, -ntis - recent, fresh
recidō, -ere, -cidī - to fall back, sink
recipiō, -ere, -cēpī, -ceptum - to receive, make welcome
recondō, -ere, -idī, -itum - to close again
reddō, -ere, -idī, -itum - to deliver; to give back, return
~**redeō, -īre, -iī, -itum** - to return
redimīculum, -ī (n.) - band, wreath, garland
redimiō, -īre, -iī, -ītum - to wreathe, encircle
redoleō, -ēre - to give off a smell, be fragrant
referō, -ferre, rettulī, relātum - to bring back, bring out
rēfert, -ferre, -tulīt - it is of importance
refertus, -a, -um - crammed full
refugiō, -ere, -fūgī - to shrink from, recoil from
rēgia, -ae (f.) - royal palace, court
regiō, -ōnis (f.) - direction
rēgius, -a, -um - royal, regal
regnō, -āre, -āvī, -ātum - to reign, govern, hold sway
~**regnum, -ī (n.)** - kingdom, domain
regō, -ere, -xī, -ctum - to govern, control, rule
relābor, -bī, -psus - to slip back, slide back, recede
relevō, -āre, -āvī, -ātum - to relieve, ease

~relinquō, -ere, -liquī, -lictum - to leave behind
remaneō, -ēre, -sī, -sum - to remain, stay put
rēmigium, -ī (n.) - oars, wings
remollescō, -ere - to grow soft again, melt
remoror, -ārī, -ātus - to linger, delay
removeō, -ēre, -mōvī, -mōtum - to remove
renīdeō, -ēre - to smile with pleasure, beam
renovō, -āre, -āvī, -ātum - to renew
reparō, -āre, -āvī, -ātum - to renew, revive, restore
repellō, -ere, reppulī, repulsus - to drive off, drive back
reperiō, -īre, repperī, repertum - to find, discover
repertor, -ōris (m.) - originator, discoverer
repetō, -ere, -īvī, -ītum - to repeat
repleō, -ēre, -ēvī, -ētum - to refill, replenish
repōnō, -ere, -posuī, -positum - to lay to rest
repugnō, -āre, -āvī, -ātum - to resist, fight against
requiēs, -ētis (f.) - (requiem, acc.) rest, relaxation
requiescō, -ere, -quēvī, -quētum - to rest, lie at rest
requīrō, -ere, -quīsīvī, -quīsītum - to ask, inquire about; to seek out, look for
rēs, -eī (f.) - matter, thing
rescrībō, -ere, -scrīpsī, -scrīptum - to write back in response
resecō, -āre, -secuī, -sectum - to cut back, trim

resīdō, -ere, -sēdī, -sessum - to fall back, subside
resistō, -ere, -stitī - to halt, pause
respiciō, -ere, -spexī, -spectum - to look back, look around
respondeō, -ēre, -dī, -sum - to answer, reply
restō, -āre, -itī - to linger, remain; to stand firm; to stop
resupīnus, -a, -um - lying on one's back
resurgō, -ere, -surrexī, -surrectum - to rise up again
retexō, -ere, -xuī, -textum - to undo, cancel, retract
retineō, -ēre, -uī, -tentum - to hold, grasp, cling
retractō, -āre, -āvī, -ātum - to handle or feel a second time
retrō (adv.) - backwards
revellō, -ere, -vellī, -vulsum - to remove, tear away
reverentia, -ae (f.) - shyness, awe, modesty
revocō, -āre, -āvī, -ātum - to summon back
revolvō, -ere, -ī, -ūtum - to cause to return, to go back to
Rhēsus, -ī (m.) - Rhesus, a Thracian
Rhodopē, -ēs (f.) - a mountain range in western Thrace
Rhodopeius, -a, -um - of Mount Rhodope
rictus, -ūs (m.) - open jaws
rīdeō, -ēre, rīsī, rīsum - to laugh
rigidus, -a, -um - rigid, stiff
rigor, -ōris (m.) - stiffness, rigidity
riguus, -a, -um - irrigated, well-watered
rīma, -ae (f.) - crack
rīpa, -ae (f.) - riverbank
rīvalis, -is (m.) - rival

rōdō, -ere, rōsī, -sum - to eat away, erode
rogō, -āre, -āvī, -ātum - to beg, implore
rogus, -ī (m.) - funeral pyre
Rōma, -ae (f.) - Rome
rostrum, -ī (n.) - snout, muzzle
rota, -ae (f.) - wheel
rubeō, -ēre - to turn red
rubor, -ōris (m.) - redness
rudis, -e - crude, rough
rūgōsus, -a, -um - wrinkled
rumpō, -ere, rūpī, ruptum - to burst, break through
rūpēs, -is (f.) - rocky cliff
rursus (adv.) - in addition, besides
rūs, rūris (n.) - countryside
rusticus, -a, -um - rustic, crude, unrefined

S
sacer, -cra, -crum - sacred, holy
sacerdōs, -ōtis (m., f.) - priest, priestess
saeculum, -ī (n.) - generation
~saepe (adv.) - often
saepēs, -is (f.) - hedge
saevus, -a, -um - wild, savage, untamed
sagitta, -ae (f.) - arrow
sagittifer, -era, -erum - loaded with arrows, arrow-bearing
salignus, -a, -um - willow wood
saliō, -īre, -uī, -tum - to jump, leap
salūs, -ūtis (f.) - safety
Samos, -ī (f.) - an island in the eastern Mediterranean Sea
sānābilis, -e - curable
sanctus, -a, -um - sacrosanct, holy, sacred, pure
sanguis, -guinis (m.) - blood, bloodline

sanguinulentus, -a, -um - blood red
satis (adv.) - enough
Sāturnius, -a, -um - of Saturn, i.e., Jupiter
satus, -a, -um - sprung (from a parent)
saxum, -ī (n.) - rock, boulder
scelerātus, -a, -um - wicked, accursed, impious
scindō, -ere, scicidī, scissum - to split, rend, tear apart
sciō, -īre, -īvī, -ītum - to know
scrībō, -ere, -psī, -ptum - to write
sculpō, -ere, -psī, -ptum - to carve
Scythia, -ae (f.) - Scythia, a region north and east of the Black Sea
secō, -āre, -cuī, -ctum - to cut
secernō, -ernere, -rēvī, -rētum - to isolate, cut off
secundus, -a, -um - second
~sed (conj.) - but
sedeō, -ēre, sēdī, sessum - to sit
sēdēs, -is (f.) - house, dwelling
sedīle, -is (n.) - seat
sēducō, -ere, -dūxī, -ductum - to move away, draw apart
sēdulus, -a, -um - attentive, persistent, zealous
segnis, -e - inactive, sluggish
semel (adv.) - once, a single time
semen, -inis (n.) - seed
Semīramis, -idis (f.) - Semiramis, a Syrian queen
~semper (adv.) - always
senecta, -ae (f.) - old age
senectūs, -ūtis (f.) - old age
senex, senis - old
senīlis, -e - old, aged
senior, -ius - older
~sentiō, -īre, sensī, sensum - to feel, sense
sentis, -is (m.) - bramble, briar

sepeliō, -īre, -īvī, sepultum - to bury, entomb
septem (indecl.) - seven
sepulcrum, -ī (n.) - tomb, grave
sequor, -quī, -cūtus - to follow; to come next in order
sera, -ae (f.) - a crossbar for locking a door
sermō, -ōnis (m.) - talk, conversation
serpens, -entis (f., m.) - snake, serpent
serta, -ōrum (n. pl.) - garlands, wreaths
sērus, -a, -um - late, after the expected time
servō, -āre, -āvī, -ātum - to guard; save, keep
serviō, -īre, -īvī, -ītum - to be devoted or subject to; to serve
sex - six
~sī (conj.) - if
~sīc (adv.) - thus, in this way, in like manner
siccō, -āre, -āvī, -ātum - to dry, dry up
siccus, -a, -um - dry
Sīdonis, -idis - of or pertaining to Sidon, a town on the Phoenician coast known for its purple dyeing process
sīdus, -eris (n.) - constellation, star
signum, -ī (n.) - signal, sign for action; military standard
silens, -entis - silent
silentium, -ī (n.) - silence
silex, -icis (m.) - hard rock or stone; flint
silva, -ae (f.) - forest, woodland
similis, -e - like, similar
simplicitās, -tātis (f.) - lack of sophistication, frankness
simul (adv.) - together, with one another; at the same time
simulācrum, -ī (n.) - image, statue
simulō, -āre, -āvī, -ātum - to pretend, simulate
sincērus, -a, -um - unblemished
~sine - (+ abl.) without
sinister, -tra, -trum - left, lefthand
sinō, -ere, sīvī, situm - to permit, allow to take place
sinuōsus, -a, -um - having a bowed form, curved
sistō, -ere, stetī, statum - to set, set down
Sīsyphus, -ī (m.) - Sisyphus
sitis, -is (f.) - thirst
situs, -ūs (m.) - neglect, disuse
sive (conj.) - whether, or if
sōbrius, -a, -um - sober, not intoxicated
socius, -a, -um - of or pertaining to a partner, kindred, companionable, fellow
sōl, sōlis (m.) - sun
soleō, -ēre, -itus - to be accustomed to
solidus, -a, -um - solid, firm
solitus, -a, -um - usual, accustomed
sollemnis, -is, -e - solemn, ceremonial
solum, -ī (n.) - earth, soil
sōlus, -a, -um - alone, only
solūtus, -a, -um - loose, unfastened, undone; weak
somnus, -ī (m.) - sleep, sleepiness
sōpītus, -a, -um - sleepy
sopōrō, -āre, -āvī, -ātum - to put to sleep
sorbeō, -ēre, -uī, -itum - to drink up, absorb
sordidus, -a, -um - grimy, dirty, unwashed
soror, -ōris (f.) - sister

spargō, -ere, sparsī, sparsum - to scatter, strew
spatior, -ārī, -ātus - to walk about
speciēs, -iēī (f.) - appearance, impression
~spectō, -āre, -āvī, -ātum - to look at, observe
speculātor, -ōris (m.) - scout, spy
sperō, -āre, -āvī, -ātum - to hope for, look forward to; to expect
spēs, -eī (f.) - hope, expectation
spīculum, -ī (n.) - tip, point; arrow
spissus, -a, -um - thick, dense
splendidus, -a, -um - bright, shining
sponda, -ae (f.) - the frame of a bed or couch
spons, -ntis (f.) - will, volition
spūmō, -āre, -āvī, -ātum - to foam, froth
squālidus, -a, -um - coated with dirt, filthy
stāgnum, -ī (n.) - pool
statuō, -ere, -uī, -ūtum - to make up one's mind, decide
sterilis, -e - futile
sternō, -ere, strāvī, strātum - to strew, lay low, spread over an area, throw down
stīpes, -itis (m.) - tree trunk; woody branch
stipula, -ae (f.) - stubble
stīva, -ae (f.) - the shaft of a plow handle
stō, stāre, stetī, stātum - to stand
strāmen, -inis (n.) - straw thatch
strātum, -ī (n.) - coverlet, throw
strēnuus, -a, -um - restless, keen
strīdō, -ere, -ī - to make a high-pitched sound; to whistle, shriek, hiss
strīdulus, -a, -um - making a shrill sound

stringō, -ere, -nxī, strictum - to touch lightly, graze; to unsheathe
strix, -igis (f.) - a screech owl
stupeō, -ēre, -uī - to be amazed, stunned, dazed
Styx, Stygis (f.) - the Styx, the principal river of the underworld, the underworld itself
~sub - (+ abl.) under, underneath; at the base of; (+ acc.) at the base of, just at
subditus, -a, -um - situated beneath
subeō, -īre, -īvī, -itum - to spread upwards; to replace
sūbiciō, -ere, -iēcī, -iectum - to harness, put under the control of
sublimis, -is, -e - lofty, directed upwards
subscrībō, -ere, -scripsī, -scriptum - to write below
subsīdō, -ere, -sēdī - to give way
succintus, -a, -um - having one's clothes bound up with a girdle or belt
succrescō, -ere, -ēvī - to grow up as a replacement, to be supplied anew
sufferō, -ferre, sustulī, sublātum - to hold up, sustain weight
suffundō, -ere, -fūdī, -fūsum - to pour into, overspread; to color, redden, blush
sui - himself, herself, itself, themselves
Sulmō, -ōnis (m.) - Sulmo, in the province of Paelignia; the town of Ovid's birth
~sum, esse, fuī, futūrus - to be
summittō, -ere, -mīsī, -missum - to lower
~summus, -a, -um - greatest; highest

sumptus, -ūs (m.) - expenditure
~super - (+ acc.) over
superbus, -a, -um - haughty, proud, arrogant
superī, -ōrum (m. pl.) - those inhabiting the heavens, the heavenly deities
superiniciō, -ere, -iniēcī, -iniectum - to throw over a surface
superstes, -itis - surviving after death
supersum, -esse, -fuī, -futūrus - to remain, be left over
superus, -a, -um - upper, above, heavenly
supīnus, -a, -um - turned palm upwards
suppleō, -ēre, -ēvī, -ētum - to fill up
supremus, -a, -um - last, final
surgō, -ere, surrexī, surrectum - to rise up
surrigō, -ere, surrexī, surrectum - to rise up
surripiō, -ere, -rripuī, -rreptum - to steal
sūs, suis (m., f.) - pig, sow
suscitō, -āre, -āvī, -ātum - to rouse, restore
suspendium, -ī (n.) - hanging
suspendō, -ere, -ī, -pensum - to hang, suspend
sustineō, -ēre, -uī - to endure, tolerate
~suus, -a, -um - his, her, its, their

T
~tabella, -ae (f.) - writing tablet
tābescō, -ere, tābuī - to melt gradually
tabula, -ae (f.) - account book
tacitus, -a, -um - silent, quiet

taeda, -ae (f.) - torch made of pine wood
Taenarius, -a, -um - of or relating to Taenarus
tālis, -e - such
tālus, -ī (m.) - ankle
tam (adv.) - so, so very
~tamen (adv.) - nevertheless
tamquam (conj.) - as if
tandem (adv.) - at last, finally
~tangō, -ere, tetigī, tactum - to touch, come in contact with
Tantalus, -ī (m.) - Tantalus
tantum (adv.) - only, merely, just;
tantum ... quantum - just so far ... as
tantus, -a, -um - so great, such a great
tardē (adv.) - slowly
tardus, -a, -um - slow-moving
Tartara, -ōrum - the infernal regions, the underworld
tectum, -ī (n.) - roof, ceiling; house
tectus, -a, -um - covered with a roof, roofed
~tegō, -ere, texī, tectum - to cover, conceal
~tellūs, -ūris (f.) - land, country
telum, -ī (n.) - weapon, shaft
temerārius, -a, -um - reckless, thoughtless, rash
Tempē (n. pl.) - (indecl.) a valley known for its pastoral beauty at the foot of Mt. Olympus
temperō, -āre, -āvī, -ātum - to moderate, regulate
templum, -ī (n.) - temple
temperiēs, -ēī (f.) - mild climate, moderation
~temptō, -āre, -āvī, -ātum - to try, attempt; to handle, touch, feel

tempus, -oris (n.) - time; temple of the forehead
tendō, -ere, tetendī, -tum/sum - to proceed
tenebrae, -ārum (f. pl.) - darkness
Tenedos, -ī (f.) - an island sacred to Apollo in the Aegean Sea
~teneō, -ēre, -uī, -tum - to have, hold, preserve; to catch
tener, -era, -erum - tender, sensitive; fragile
tenuis, -e - fine, thin, tender
tepeō, -ēre - to be warm, tepid
tepescō, -ere, -uī - to grow warm
tepidus, -a, -um - warm
ter (adv.) - three times
teres, -etis - smooth, rounded
tergeō, -ēre, tersī, tersum - to wipe clean
tergum, -ī (n.) - back
tergus, -oris (n.) - back of an animal
ternī, -ae, -a - three apiece
~terra, -ae (f.) - earth, ground
terrēnus, -a, -um - belonging to the ground, earthly
tertius, -a, -um - third
testa, -ae (f.) - a fragment of earthenware
textum, -ī (n.) - woven fabric, cloth
thalamus, -ī (m.) - bedroom, marriage chamber
Thisbē, -ēs (f.) - Thisbe
Thrax, -ācis (m.) - Thracian
Thrēicius, -a, -um - Thracian
Thÿnēius - of or pertaining to the region of Bithynia
thyrsus, -ī (m.) - a wand, usually covered with vine leaves, and carried by worshippers of Bacchus
tignum, -ī (n.) - timber, rafter

tilia, -ae (f.) - the lime (linden) tree
timeō, -ēre, -uī - to fear, be afraid
~timidus, -a, -um - fearful, apprehensive, timid
timor, -ōris (m.) - fear, dread
tingō (tinguō), -ere, -nxī, -nctum - to wet, soak; to dye, stain
Tītān, -nos (m.) - Titan, the sun-god
tollō, -ere, sustulī, sublātum - to pick up; to raise up
tonitrus, -ūs (m.) -ua (n.) - thunder
torpor, -ōris (m.) - numbness, heaviness
torus, -ī (m.) - cushion, bed
tot - (indecl.) so many
totidem - as many, the same number of
totiens (adv.) - so often
~tōtus, -a, -um - the whole of
tractō, -āre, -āvī, -ātum - to handle, manage
trādō, -ere, -idī, -itum - to deliver, hand over
~trahō, -ere, traxī, tractum - to drag, draw; to influence
trāiciō, -ere, -iēcī, -iectum - to transfix, pierce
trāmes, -itis (m.) - a footpath, track, path
~transeō, -īre, -īvī, -itum - to cross, pass through
transferō, -ferre, -tulī, -latum - to transfer
transitus, -ūs (m.) - passage
tremebundus, -a, -um - trembling, quivering
tremō, -ere, -uī - to tremble
tremulus, -a, -um - quivering, shaking
trepidō, -āre, -āvī, -ātum - to tremble, throb, quiver

trēs, trēs, tria - three
triōnēs, -ōnum (m. pl.): oxen used for plowing
tristis, -e - unfriendly, dismal, sorrowful
triumphus, -ī (m.) - the procession held in Rome to honor a victorious general
trivium, -ī (n.) - crossroad, meeting point of three roads
Trōs, -ōis (m.) - Trojan
truncō, -āre, -āvī, -ātum - to strip off foliage
truncus, -ī (m.) - a trunk
~tū - you (sing.)
tueor, -ērī, tuitus - to observe, watch over, guard
~tum (adv.) - then, at that moment
tumescō, -ere - to become swollen or inflated, to swell
tumidus, -a, -um - swollen, swelling
tumulō, -āre, -āvī, -ātum - to entomb
tumulus, -ī (m.) - grave
tunc (adv.) - then, at that moment
turba, -ae (f.) - crowd of followers, attendants, troop
turbō, -inis (m.) - whirlwind
turpis, -e - loathsome, repulsive, shameful
tūs, tūris (n.) - incense
tūtēla, -ae (f.) - guardian, protection
tūtus, -a, -um - safe, secure
~tuus, -a, -um - your (sing.)

U
ūber, -eris - plentiful, abundant
~ubi (adv.) - where, when
ubīque (adv.) - everywhere, anywhere
ullus, -a, -um - any
ultimus, -a, -um - final, last
ultrā (adv.) - further, beyond that point
ulva, -ae (f.) - rush, marsh grass
~umbra, -ae (f.) - shade, darkness, shadow
umbrōsus, -a, -um - shady
umeō, -ēre - to be wet or moist
umerus, -ī (m.) - shoulder
ūmidus, -a, -um - wet, moist, watery
ūmor, -ōris (m.) - moisture
umquam (adv.) - never, ever (with nec)
ūnā (adv.) - at the same time
~unda, -ae (f.) - body of flowing water, river; water
undēnī, -ae, -a - eleven at a time
ūnicus, -a, -um - one, only one
~ūnus, -a, -um - one; alone
urbs, -is (f.) - city
urna, -ae (f.) - urn
ūrō, -ere, ussī, ustum - to burn, inflame with passion
usque (adv.) - all the way
usus, -ūs (m.) - use, purpose
~ut (conj.) - just as, like; when; in order that; since
~uterque, utraque, utrumque - each, each ... of the two
ūtilis, -e - useful
ūtor, ūtī, ūsus - (+ abl.) to make use of
ūva, -ae (f.) - a bunch of grapes, grape
uxor, -ōris (f.) - wife

V
vacō, -āre, -āvī, -ātum - to be empty, unfilled, vacant
~vacuus, -a, -um - empty, unattached, free, unoccupied

vadimōnium, -ī (n.) - a legal term referring to a guarantee that the parties in a suit will appear before the court at an agreed upon date and time
vagor, -ārī, -ātus - to wander, roam
vagus, -a, -um - shifting, moving about
~valē, valēte - farewell! good-bye!
vallēs, -is (f.) – valley
vānus, -a, -um - unreliable
vārus, -a, -um - bent outward
vastus, -a, -um - desolate, dreary, endless
~vātēs, -is (m.) - poet, prophet
-ve (conj.) - or
vehō, -ere, vexī, vectum - to carry
~vel (conj.) - either . . . or; at any rate
vēlāmen, -minis (n.) - garment, veil
vellō, -ere, vulsī, -sum - to pull up
vēlō, -āre, -āvī, -ātum - to cover
vēlox, -ōcis - swift, speedy
velut (adv.) - just as, just like, in the same way that
vēna, -ae (f.) - blood vessel, vein
venēnum, -ī (n.) - poison
venia, -ae (f.) - justification, excuse, indulgence
~veniō, -īre, vēnī, ventum - to come
venter, -tris (m.) - belly
ventilō, -āre, -āvī, -ātum - to fan, brandish
ventus, -ī (m.) - wind
~Venus, -eris (f.) - Venus, goddess sacred to love and lovers
vēr, -ris (n.) - the season of spring, the springtime of life, youth
~verbum, -ī (n.) - word
vērē (adv.) - truly, indeed
verēcundus, -a, -um - modest

vereor, -ērī, -itus - to be afraid
Vergilius, -ī (m.) - Vergil
vērō (adv.) - truly, really
Vērōna, -ae (f.) - the city Verona in the north of Italy
verrō, -ere, versum - to pass over, skim, sweep; to row
versō, -āre, -āvī, -ātum - to turn
versus, -ūs (m.) - a line of verse or writing
vertex, -icis (m.) - the top of the head
vertō, -ere, -tī, -sum - to turn into, change
verum (conj.) - but
vērus, -a, -um - real, genuine
vesper (irreg.) (m.) - the evening, the west
vester, -tra, -trum - your (pl.)
vestīgium, -ī (n.) - footprint, sole of a foot, track
~vestis, -is (f.) - clothing; cloth
vetō, -āre, -uī, -itum - to forbid, prohibit
~vetus, -eris - old, of a former time, ancient
via, -ae (f.) - journey, march, way
viātor, -ōris (m.) - traveller
vibrō, -āre, -āvī, -ātum - to wave, flutter
vīcīnia, -ae (f.) - proximity
vīcīnus, -a, -um - neighboring, close by
vicis (f.) (gen.) - exchange, interaction; **in vices** - by turns, alternately
victrix, -īcis - victorious
victrix, -īcis (f.) - victorious female
~videō, -ēre, vīsī, vīsum - to see, observe, gaze upon; to consider
vigil, -ilis (m.) - sentry, guard
vīlis, -e - worthless, common, ordinary

villa, -ae (f.) - rural dwelling
villōsus, -a, -um - hairy, shaggy
vinciō, -īre, vīcī, victum - to fasten, bind, tie up
vincō, -ere, vīcī, victum - to defeat, conquer
vinculum, -ī (n.) - chain, bond
vīnum, -ī (n.) - wine
violentus, -a, -um - violent, aggressive
vipera, -ae (f.) - a viper or poisonous snake
vir, -ī (m.) - man, husband
vireō, -ēre, -uī - to sprout, show green growth
virgineus, -a, -um - of or relating to a maiden, virgin
virginitās, -tātis (f.) - maidenhood
~virgō, -inis (f.) - maiden
vīs, vīs (f.) - (pl.) strength
viscus, -eris (n.) - innermost parts of the body
vīsō, -ere, -ī - to view
vīta, -ae (f.) - life
vitiō, -āre, -āvī, -ātum - to impair, cause defects in
vītis, -is (f.) - grapevine
vitium, -ī (n.) - defect, fault; vice, moral failing
vītō, -āre, -āvī, -ātum - to avoid
vitta, -ae (f.) - headband
vīvō, -ere, vīxī, vīctum - to live
~vix (adv.) - hardly, scarcely
~vocō, -āre, -āvī, -ātum - to call
volātus, -ūs (m.) - flying, flight
volō, -āre, -āvī, -ātum - to fly
~volō, velle, voluī - to wish for; to wish
volucris, -cris (f.) - bird
voluntās, -tātis (f.) - willingness, intention
~vōs - you (pl.)
vōtum, -ī (n.) - vow, oath, prayer
vox, vōcis (f.) - voice
vulgō, -āre, -āvī, -ātum - to prostitute
vulgus, -ī (n.) - general public, crowd, masses
~vulnus, -eris (n.) - wound, injury
vultur, -uris (m.) - vulture
~vultus, -ūs (m.) - facial expression; face

Z

Zephyrus, -ī (m.) - a west wind
zona, -ae (f.) - zone, encircling band

The Latin Literature Workbook Series reinforces practical approaches to reading classical authors in the original. Sets of exercises enable the student to quickly reach a higher degree of comprehension and appreciation of sight or prepared passages. Five to six exercises for each passage help students develop good translation habits.

An Ovid Workbook

Charbra Adams Jestin and Phyllis B. Katz

Student Text: x + 166 pp. (2006) 8½" x 11" Paperback, ISBN 978-0-86516-625-7 • $27.00
Teacher's Manual: xii + 172 pp. (2007) 6" x 9" Paperback, ISBN 978-0-86516-626-4 • $27.00

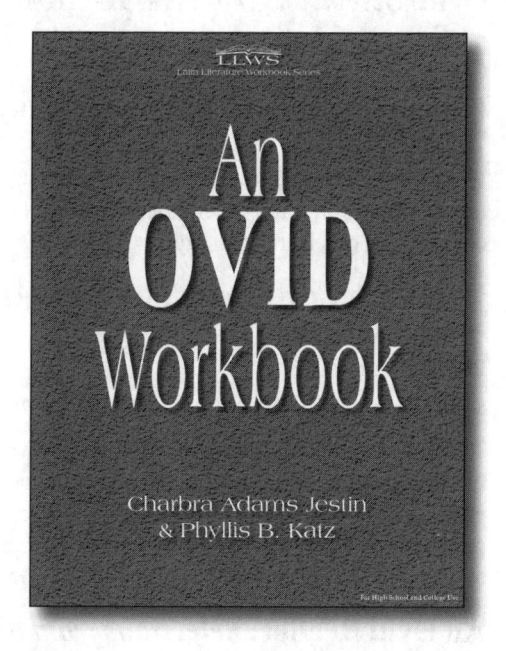

An Ovid Workbook contains selections from *Amores* and *Metamorphoses*; the selections from *Metamorphoses* tell the stories of Apollo and Daphne, Pyramus and Thisbe, Daedalus and Icarus, Philemon and Baucis, and Pygmalion. *Metamorphoses* I.452–567; IV. 55–166; VIII.183–235, 616–724; X.238–297; *Amores* I.1, 3, 9, 11, 12; III.15.

This aid correlates to 630 of the 907 lines of *Ovid: Amores, Metamorphoses*, 3rd Edition.

BOLCHAZY-CARDUCCI PUBLISHERS, INC.
www.BOLCHAZY.com

More Ovid Readers from B-C

Ovid: *A LEGAMUS Transitional Reader*
Caroline Perkins and Denise Davis-Henry

Student Text: xxvi + 132 pp. (2008) 8½" x 11" Paperback, ISBN 978-0-86516-604-2
Teacher's Guide: viii + 76 pp. (2010) 6" x 9" Paperback, ISBN 978-0-86516-734-6

This reader contains 202 lines of Latin selections from Ovid's Metamorphoses: Apollo and Daphne, 1.463–473, 490–502, 548–567; Pyramus and Thisbe, 4.65–77, 93–104, 137–153; Daedalus and Icarus, 8.195–208, 220–235; Baucis and Philemon, 8.626–640, 705–720; Pygmalion, 10.243–269, 270–297.

Ovid: *Selections from Ars Amatoria and Remedia Amoris*
Graves Haydon Thompson

Student Text: 168 pp. + fold-out (1952, corrected 1958, sixteenth reprint 1997) Paperback, ISBN 978-0-86516-395-9

Well-chosen selections (**2,414 lines**) and pithy summaries make this text an entertaining and effective learning tool. See our website for a complete list of selected passages.

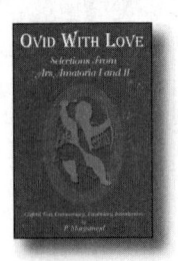

Ovid with Love: *Selections from Ars Amatoria, Books I and II*
Paul Murgatroyd

Student Text: x + 228 pp. (1990) 6" x 9" Paperback, ISBN 978-0-86516-015-6

This book contains 770 lines from *Ars Amatoria*, Books I and II, a full introduction on Ovid's life, 148 pages of vocabulary, and commentary that offers insights on Ovid's stylistic choices. The notes provide a wealth of information on Roman customs, mythology, history, and literary tradition.

An Ovid Reader: *Selections from Six Works*
Carole E. Newlands

Student Text: (forthcoming) Paperback, ISBN 978-0-86516-722-3

This reader introduces advanced students of Latin to the wide range of Ovid's poetry composed during the Augustan age in ancient Rome and in exile on the Black Sea. It offers selections (556 lines total) from six of Ovid's works: *Amores, Heroides, Ars Amatoria, Metamorphoses, Fasti,* and *Tristia*.

BOLCHAZY-CARDUCCI PUBLISHERS, INC.
WWW.BOLCHAZY.COM

Collections: Catullus, Horace, Ovid, Propertius, and Tibullus

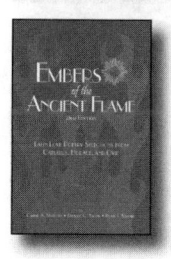

Embers of the Ancient Flame
Latin Love Poetry Selections from Catullus, Horace, and Ovid
Carol A. Murphy, Ryan T. Moore, and Daniel G. Thiem

Student Text: ix + 114 pp. (2005) 6" x 9" Paperback, ISBN 978-0-86516-609-7
Teacher's Guide: vi + 96 pp. (2013) 6" x 9" Paperback, ISBN 978-0-86516-

Embers of the Ancient Flame offers a wide-ranging selection of Latin love poetry from three of its masters: Catullus, Horace, and Ovid. This edition includes an introduction on Catullus, Horace, and Ovid, as well as on each of the 32 poems.

Little Book of Latin Love Poetry
John Breuker and Mardah B. C. Weinfield

Student Text: x + 124 pp. (2006) 8½" x 11" Paperback, ISBN 978-0-86515-601-1

This text introduces the love poetry (183 lines) of Catullus, Horace, and Ovid while still reviewing their grammar and syntax. Selections include Catullus Poems 5, 8, 43, 51, 70, and 86; Horace *Odes* I.23, III.9, and III.26; and Ovid *Amores* 1.5 and 1.9.

> Teachers of the classics are often told that Latin is a "dead language." The implication is that the study of Latin is irrelevant to the needs and experiences of modern society. The use of this transitional reader can serve as a reminder that love as a poetic theme, and indeed, as a life experience, transcends language, spans cultures, relates generations, and traverses millennia.
>
> – Laura Higley
> *Classical Outlook* 86.3, Spring 2009

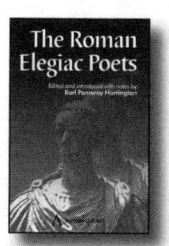

The Roman Elegiac Poets
Karl Pomeroy Harrington

Student Text: 424 pp. (1914, reprint 2002) 6⅛" x 9¼" Paperback
ISBN 978-1-89885-585-9

This classic college edition gathers together Latin text selections from elegy's four most celebrated practitioners: Catullus, Tibullus, Propertius, and Ovid (**3,684 lines**).

BOLCHAZY-CARDUCCI PUBLISHERS, INC.
WWW.BOLCHAZY.COM

ℬℂ LATIN Readers

Series Editor: RONNIE ANCONA, HUNTER COLLEGE AND CUNY GRADUATE CENTER

These readers, written by experts in the field, provide well-annotated Latin selections to be used as authoritative introductions to Latin authors, genres, or topics. Designed for intermediate/advanced college Latin students, they each contain approximately 600 lines of Latin, making them ideal to use in combination or as a "shake-it-up" addition to a time-tested syllabus.

See reviews of BC Latin Readers from *Bryn Mawr Classical Review, Classical Outlook*, and more at http://www.bolchazy.com/readers/

An Apuleius Reader
Selections from the METAMORPHOSES
Ellen Finkelpearl
xxxviii + 160 pp., 4 illustrations & 1 map (2012) Paperback, ISBN 978-0-86516-714-8

A Caesar Reader
Selections from BELLUM GALLICUM *and* BELLUM CIVILE, *and from Caesar's Letters, Speeches, and Poetry*
W. Jeffrey Tatum
xl + 206 pp., 3 illustrations & 3 maps (2012) Paperback, ISBN 978-0-86516-696-7

A Cicero Reader
Selections from Five Essays and Four Speeches, with Five Letters
James M. May
xxxviii + 136 pp., 1 illustration & 2 maps (2012) Paperback, ISBN 978-0-86516-713-1

A Latin Epic Reader
Selections from Ten Epics
Alison Keith
xxvii + 187 pp., 3 maps (2012) Paperback ISBN 978-0-86516-686-8

A Livy Reader
Selections from AB URBE CONDITA
Mary Jaeger
xxiii + 127 pp., 1 photo & 2 maps (2010) 5" x 7¾" Paperback, ISBN 978-0-86516-680-6

A Lucan Reader
Selections from CIVIL WAR
Susanna Braund
xxxiv + 134 pp., 1 map (2009) Paperback ISBN 978-0-86516-661-5

A Martial Reader
Selections from the Epigrams
Craig Williams
xxx + 185 pp., 5 illustrations & 2 maps (2011) Paperback, ISBN 978-0-86516-704-9

A Plautus Reader
Selections from Eleven Plays
John Henderson
xviii + 182 pp., 1 map & 5 illustrations (2009) Paperback, ISBN 978-0-86516-694-3

A Roman Verse Satire Reader
Selections from Lucilius, Horace, Persius, and Juvenal
Catherine C. Keane
xxvi + 142 pp., 1 map & 4 illustrations (2010) Paperback, ISBN 978-0-86516-685-1

A Sallust Reader
Selections from BELLUM CATILINAE, BELLUM IUGURTHINUM, and HISTORIAE
Victoria Pagán

xliv + 159 pp., 2 maps & 4 illustrations (2009)
Paperback, ISBN 978-0-86516-687-5

A Seneca Reader
Selections from Prose and Tragedy
James Ker

lvi + 166 pp., 6 illustrations & 1 map (2011)
Paperback, ISBN 978-0-86516-758-2

A Suetonius Reader
Selections from the LIVES OF THE CAESARS and the LIFE OF HORACE
Josiah Osgood

xxxix + 159 pp., 1 map & 7 illustrations (2010)
Paperback, ISBN 978-0-86516-716-2

A Terence Reader
Selections from Six Plays
William S. Anderson

xvii + 110 pp. (2009) Paperback
ISBN 978-0-86516-678-3

A Tibullus Reader
Seven Selected Elegies
Paul Allen Miller

(2013) Paperback, ISBN 978-0-86516-724-7

Visit **www.BOLCHAZY.com/readers** for a complete listing of the selections contained in each reader.

BC Latin Readers Coming in 2013 and Beyond

An Ovid Reader
Selections from Six Works
Carole E. Newlands

(forthcoming) Paperback, ISBN 978-0-86516-722-3

A Propertius Reader
Eleven Selected Elegies
P. Lowell Bowditch

(forthcoming) Paperback, ISBN 978-0-86516-723-0

A Roman Army Reader
Twenty-One Selections from Literary, Epigraphic, and Other Documents
Dexter Hoyos

(forthcoming) Paperback, ISBN 978-0-86516-715-5

A Roman Women Reader
Selections from the Second Century BCE to the Second Century CE
Sheila K. Dickison and Judith P. Hallett

(forthcoming) Paperback, ISBN 978-0-86516-662-2

A Tacitus Reader
Selections from ANNALES, HISTORIAE, GERMANIA, AGRICOLA, and DIALOGUS
Steven H. Rutledge

(forthcoming) Paperback, ISBN 978-0-86516-697-4

BOLCHAZY-CARDUCCI PUBLISHERS, INC.
WWW.BOLCHAZY.COM

Annotated Latin Collection

Read Catullus, Cicero, Horace, and Ovid with these well-annotated texts designed for intermediate to advanced students. With same-page notes and vocabulary, introductory essays on each author and work, full glossaries, and helpful appendices, reading unadapted Latin has never been more rewarding.

Writing Passion: *A Catullus Reader,* 2nd Edition
Ronnie Ancona

(2013) Paperback, ISBN 978-0-86516-784-1

This bestseller now features four additional poems (75, 83, 92, and 107), which expand the elegiac selections about Lesbia. The new edition also includes updated bibliography. For those who want a little more spice in their Catullus and love the style of this book, a supplement containing poems 6, 16, 31, and 57 will also be available both bundled with the main text or on its own.

Text includes the unadapted Latin text of 46 Catullus poems (827 lines): 1–5, 7, 8, 10–14a, 22, 30, 31, 35, 36, 40, 43–46, 49–51, 60, 64 (lines 50–253), 65, 68–70, 72, 75–76, 77, 83–87, 92, 96, 101, 107, 109, and 116

Ovid: *AMORES, METAMORPHOSES Selections,* 3rd Edition
Phyllis B. Katz and Charbra Adams Jestin

(2013) Paperback, ISBN 978-0-86516-784-1

— Forthcoming —

Horace: *Selected ODES and SATIRE 1.9,* 3rd Edition
Ronnie Ancona

Cicero: *PRO CAELIO,* 4th Edition
Stephen Ciraolo

Cicero: *PRO ARCHIA ORATIO,* 3rd Edition
Steven M. Cerutti

Cicero: *DE AMICITIA,* 2nd Edition
Patsy Rodden Ricks and Sheila K. Dickison

BOLCHAZY-CARDUCCI PUBLISHERS, INC.
WWW.BOLCHAZY.COM